Wrestling
Is My Gimmick

ALSO OF INTEREST
AND FROM MCFARLAND

American Women in Amateur Wrestling, 2000–2022
(Jason Norman, 2023)

New Jack: Memoir of a Pro Wrestling Extremist
(New Jack *and* Jason Norman, 2020)

*Welcome to Our Nightmares:
Behind the Scene with Today's Horror Actors*
(Jason Norman, 2015)

Wrestling Is My Gimmick

My Life on the Wrong Side of the Three-Count

BARRY DAVID HOROWITZ
with JASON NORMAN

Foreword by Joshua Horowitz

McFarland & Company, Inc., Publishers
Jefferson, North Carolina

ISBN (print) 978-1-4766-9610-2
ISBN (ebook) 978-1-4766-5493-5

LIBRARY OF CONGRESS AND BRITISH LIBRARY
CATALOGUING DATA ARE AVAILABLE

Library of Congress Control Number 2024042749

© 2024 Barry David Horowitz. All rights reserved

No part of this book may be reproduced or transmitted in any form or by any means, electronic or mechanical, including photocopying or recording, or by any information storage and retrieval system, without permission in writing from the publisher.

Front cover image: The author's meet-and-greet photo showing off his signature move—the self-pat on the back (author collection)

Printed in the United States of America

*McFarland & Company, Inc., Publishers
Box 611, Jefferson, North Carolina 28640
www.mcfarlandpub.com*

I'd like to dedicate this book
to my parents Robert and Doris,
my loving wife Diane,
my sons Joshua and Michael,
my daughter Melissa,
my immediate family,
and my close friends.
Thank you for all your love and support.
—Barry Horowitz

Acknowledgments

Here's a list of people who played a serious role in my career. I learned something from them all, and I hope they, those are still here, read this and know they affected my career on the mats: Lenny Greenburg, Boris Malenko family, Karl Gotch, Karl Vonstronheim, Mike and Eddie Graham, Jimmy Valiant, Rufus R. Jones, Sonny Fargo, Johnny Weaver, Jim Brunzell, Hillbilly Jim, Tony Garea, Rick Martel, Gorilla Monsoon, Joe Marella, Dave and Earl Hebner, Don Morocco, Rocky Johnson, Tim Horner, Scott Armstrong, Bret and Owen Hart, the Hart family, Jake Roberts, Jose Estrada, Johnny Rodz, Curt Hennig, Otto Wantz, Jerry Jarrett, Richie Sorrentino, Mike Chioda, Bob Backlund, Bobby Heenan, Capt. Lou Albano, Jose Rivera, Ron Simmons, Butch Reed, Terry Gibbs, Danny Davis, Tim White, Baron Mikel Scicluna, Nick Bockwinkel, Chief Jay Strongbow, Ronny Garvin, Adrian Street, Gordon Solie, Gordon Nelson, Reggie Parks, Ted Dibiase, Wahoo McDaniel, Keith Larson, Chris Candido, Afa and Sika, Cocoa Samoa, Jimmy Snuka, Barbarian, Fatu Jr., Haku, Mr. Fuji, Samu, Gene Anderson, Junkyard Dog, Lenny Lane, Bad News Brown. Tracy Smothers and his family deserve a shot-out of their own, as Tracy did more in his short life than most people who are around much longer.

And a special thanks to my son Josh, for helping me fine-tune my journey through this book.

Table of Contents

Acknowledgments vi
Foreword by Joshua Horowitz 1
Preface by Jason Norman 3

Welcome! 5
Wrestling Begins 10
Learning My Dream 13
My College "Career" 17
Time to Train 18
The Years 1981–1983 28
Jimmy Snuka 34
Making It to Starrcade 40
Losing Job, Matches. Finding Success, Love 44
Near Death, a Few Times 51
Taking the Florida Title 54
My "First" Goodbye 58
Up to Tennessee 61
Up to the World 65
"Piledriver" 70
Getting Broken by the Harts 75
My (Not at All) Ultimate Departure 81
First Trip to WCW 85
Going "Global" 89
Title Time 94
Another Near-Fatal Moment 96

Table of Contents

A New Addition!	98
My First Daughter	101
Almost Losing It All	105
Too Many Sad Endings	108
End of Global	113
Going Around and Around (and Around!)	117
Back in the WWF	118
I Get "Knighted"	121
A Part of Country Music History	126
In the Ring and Out of Trouble	131
Finally Moving Up a Bit	136
Hitting It Big with Skip	139
My Pay-Per-View "Debut"	146
A National Award!	158
Moving Down in the Ranks	161
Landing Back in WCW	168
Getting Struck by Gold	171
Working with the Flairs	175
The Night We Lost Owen	178
WCW Winds Down	180
Wrestling Loses WCW	185
Never to the Extreme	188
Making the Best of It All	190
Training: Past and Future	194
Finding a New Path	199
Living in a Dark Hole	203
The Bio That Wasn't	206
Conclusion	209
Index	217

Foreword
by Joshua Horowitz

My father went by many names in the world of pro wrestling. Jack Hart. Mr. Technical. For the most part, his real one—Barry Horowitz.

But for me, he was first and foremost my dad. I didn't really understand what he did until I got old enough to really grasp his career, but I do have vague memories of being in brightly lit hallways backstage, flashes of the rings he would wrestle in, and meeting other superstars. It didn't really click until I was able to see it and comprehend it.

The first time I saw him wrestle, I was about nine or ten. He was the heel, or in wrestling terms, the bad guy. But he had explained the basics and how everything worked, so of course I was still rooting for him. The moment I saw him dropkick his opponent, his body suspended at least six feet in the air, smashing his feet into their chest, I knew he could do something special. I've seen him perform many times since then and it's always a mix of anxiety that he'll get hurt, but also being in awe of the feats he performed. Even though he's my father, I can say, as a big fan of the sport, that he was an incredible professional wrestler.

He was often on the road early in my childhood, but it never damaged our relationship or put a damper on the time he would make for me and my mom. He made sure to make the best out of the time we had, and it was one hundred percent worth it so he could live his dream. As I got older and his career slowed down, we started to spend much more time together and bond over our mutual love for pro wrestling. He never pushed it on me, but his passion for it

Foreword by Joshua Horowitz

was very infectious and I've come to really appreciate it as almost a form of art. Some of my fondest memories with him don't have to do with wrestling. Once a week for a long time we would go get Icees together, and that meant as much to me as seeing him win in the squared circle.

My dad also has some incredible fans. They're all so genuine and kind. They have the utmost respect for what he represented to the wrestling world. To this very day, he still gets fan mail, people telling him how much he meant to them and asking for autographs. They make him art-like wooden plaques of his image, hand-drawn comic book hero versions of himself, homemade championship belts and much more. It's really something how much they truly appreciate his contribution to the spectacle that is professional wrestling.

I'm so proud of him for what he's accomplished and how he's balanced that with being a great role model and father. He puts so much thought and care into whatever he's doing. Whether it be in the ring or with his family and friends, he always gives it his all. My father was in the business for over 21 years straight and continues to entertain his fans to this day. In person at meet-and-greet events or over social media, it doesn't matter. He's always there for them, and he's always there for me. He's a technical wrestler who loves his craft and his family. I've gotten to see him in both worlds, and he never ceases to amaze me with his hard work and dedication. He really is a legend in my eyes, and I know he can't wait to tell his story.

Preface

by Jason Norman

Ever since my sportswriting days, I've always prided myself on focusing on those that form the backbone of their respective teams, even if it's others that get the credit. With this book, it's the same thing.

Barry Horowitz certainly has one of the worst win-loss records in wrestling history, but generations of squared circle fans know his name. Coworkers, promoters, everyone remembers him, despite him not being a full-time competitor for decades. People know him and respect the job he did, pardon the pun, and not all of his colleagues enjoy such respect. That's a hell of an accomplishment right there, and it deserves even more acknowledgment.

This piece focuses, of course, mostly on his wrestling career. But, as is always the case, there's more to Barry than what we as fans saw, in the ring and behind a microphone. And while every wrestler begins at the enhancement level, learning how to make others look good and losing all the time, few stay there for long. Some are lucky enough to move up; most just leave.

Not Barry. No matter where he went, as least as far as the big leagues of the WWF and WCW were concerned, his winning percentage stayed slightly above zero. But he managed to turn it into a career, staying there and doing as well as he could, and there isn't a more respected "jobber" in the history of wrestling.

That's one question that keeps getting answered throughout—why he stayed in a business that didn't treat him as well as he treated it, even as he faced almost all of wrestling's biggest names, from Ric Flair to "Stone Cold" Steve Austin. But there are also the years away

Preface by Jason Norman

from the WWF and WCW, such as starting off in Florida, winning titles in Global Wrestling, and even plying around the independents after WCW went down in 2001.

Along with that, there's a look at his life outside of the ring. His first marriage that didn't last and his second one that did. His brief foray into the country music world. And, yes, the death of his daughter that tossed Horowitz himself into a depression that seemed to last forever.

For far too long in wrestling fanship, viewers didn't acknowledge the importance, if not the difficulty, of those in the prelim matches, the ones whose job it was to take all the major moves and lose big, allowing those on the way up to use them as everything but a practice model. People cheered and booed the stars—those handed wrestling-based monikers, interviews, and entrance music—and didn't think much at all about those on the other side. Today, it's a bit different. Those same fans who grew up watching Barry and other show-openers, sometimes in hindsight, feel and show a little more respect to them.

Better late than never, right? But now let's learn all about the fellow who, by losing so often for our pleasure and the elevation of others, played an integral role in the betterment of the toughest of businesses.

Welcome!

> He was *the* jobber, if you want to call it that. People like to use the words "enhancement talent," and it's like, "Dude, that guy was perfect at enhancement." That was his role in the company, and when he went out there, to wasn't it make himself look great. It was, "How can I showcase this other person?" If you want to send somebody who can go out there and say, "OK, you have three minutes of TV time. Make this guy look good," you got to have somebody out there who can say, "OK, this is where I need to be at this point. This is where I need to be at that point. This is how I should be selling these moves. This is how I need to feed this person in such a way that it made their offense look good," and Barry always nailed this.
> —R.D. Reynolds, owner of *WrestleCrap.com*

A popular sports saying is that winning isn't everything. Well, for me, as far as pro wrestling fans go, it was an almost never thing.

I was a prelim man of the mat. I'd been called a jobber. Eventually, myself and others like me became labeled as "enhancement talent," in the same way that a garbage man is a "sanitation engineer," a cashier is a "customer service representative," and dead people "pass on," "go to eternal rest," or "become terminally inconvenienced."

In any case, if people knew the name of Barry Horowitz, they knew a guy who many had never seen win a single match. A jobber trademark in wrestling is to go by one's real name (the Ortons, Hardys, Harts, and Kurt Angle being obvious exceptions); those of us who show up and fall are rarely given the gift of a gimmick or character. Those things take time and effort, get pushes, and sell tickets, and that's not expected of us.

But we do have a job, pardon the expression, and it's a hell of a lot harder and more important than many in wrestling will ever know.

Wrestling Is My Gimmick

Since I'd shown back up in the then–World Wrestling Federation (WWF) in 1991, my second go-round with the group, I'd lost from one coast, country, and even continent to the others.

But I could tell the company still believed in me. The fans had always been behind me. I'd been around enough that people still recognized me, even if they knew why I was there and what was (probably) going to happen when I stepped into the ring.

Yeah, most guys get into the business just *knowing* that someday, they'll be the best in the game. Right off the bat, they'll just happen upon that gimmick that blasts them to the wrestling ionosphere! Headlining *Wrestlemania*, winning all the titles, selling out arenas around the world.

Sadly, that doesn't happen, and not just because wrestlers don't have as many big-time options as they used to. World Championship Wrestling and Extreme Championship Wrestling, who helped the WWF (eventually World Wrestling Entertainment) form one of the biggest booms in wrestling history in the 1990s, are long gone. It'll be interesting to see if Impact and All Elite Wrestling can ever threaten the WWE's position at the top.

But I digress. Wrestling's an unusual business, but it's similar to others in one way: starting from the bottom up. You begin by honing the most important thing a wrestler can learn in the ring: how to get whomped. You pay your dues by taking bumps and make them look like they hurt a hell of a lot more than they do (hopefully!).

You do that by losing, but getting bumped and thrown all over the ring. The more experienced wrestlers, or those that promoters hope to push, get in the ring and knock the stuffing out of you for a few minutes, long enough to show their new skills and strength. Then, hopefully, they go up in the company and you go on to the next put-over work. If you're facing a face, you show a little cowardice and conniving nature. If you're the good guy, you show some courage. You insert little things like that, even when you're getting squashed.

Along the way, you show up on time. You don't cause problems backstage. You work your tail off, regardless of your role, and you hope your profile, and your paycheck, rise along the way. If you know their names in wrestling, they probably started out enhancing and found a way up.

Welcome!

It's part of proving yourself to your bosses and co-workers. It's part of being a team player. And no one would ever have reason to doubt me there.

Those guys who go roaring into the business expecting to be at the top by the next week, don't last. They may just get frustrated at losing so much, or get impatient because that push they'd hoped for (or, to be fair, may have been unfairly promised) doesn't happen, or the money they expected to make doesn't appear, or whatever else. They show up, they lose, and they leave, forgetting that there will always be an arena-sized load of people ready to take their place at a nanosecond's notice.

Sometimes even those who expect to be enhancement get in there for the wrong reasons. You'd see guys show up for one or two shows, lose like crazy, and disappear forever. Clearly, these guys just wanted to brag to their friends, "Hey, I got in the ring with the Undertaker!" and then go back to stocking shelves at Wal-Mart or mopping up a gas station bathroom at 4 a.m.

But I'd always persevered. Other enhancement talent had come and gone about every month during my WWF tenure, but Barry Horowitz would be there as long as anyone needed him.

I was usually a heel, and I was pretty sharp. I'd hide in the ropes, yell at the audience, do all kinds of small things to get people upset. I'd even developed something of a trademark along the way. I'd jump into the ring, motion for the fans to hush up and watch, and then … reach over my shoulder and pat myself on the back! Inspiration and heat at the same time! Eventually, my ring jackets came with a handprint implanted on the back.

The fans knew what was coming. They booed, they laughed (sometimes at me, sometimes with me), but they kept caring. It's amazing the small things that wrestling fans will pick up on and carry right along with you.

And along the way, they'd been there. I'd proven to the WWF that I was there to stay, and the fans saw it as well. Devotion to a craft, whatever it may be, is something people respect.

Over the past few years, that exact respect had started to push me into a few beams of the spotlight. People backstage started to notice. I'd been given a spot at the *Royal Rumble* and *Summerslam*, albeit in dark matches. I'd gone to battle at *Survivor Series*, albeit under a mask.

And yes, I'd won a few matches along the way. I'd actually beaten some pretty big names there before, and would again, but no one was talking about that. But, about halfway through 1995, I was about to make some history for myself and the company.

"Barry! Barry! Barry!"

I'd been hearing the chants from the fans as I went to the ring, even when I didn't get much of an intro. Sometimes the chants would carry into the match. I'd seen more and more people back-patting themselves right along with me. And certain people were starting to notice.

Earlier that year, fans of *Monday Night Raw* had been pretty surprised. I'd gotten an interview, which people at my level hardly do. I'd scored a title shot, and for some time, it looked like I might come out on top there, but I hadn't.

Through the first months of 1995, WWF fans had been seeing vignettes of a blond, blue-eyed pair known as the Body Donnas. A man and a woman, full of pride in their looks and their physical prowess ... and all too anxious to look straight down on those who'd spent less time in the gym. They'd been telling WWF fans that they'd be there soon, and that audiences damn well better be ready to line up to show respect to a pair they'd never measure up to.

Of course, that wasn't them in real life. At least, the guy wasn't. I had worked with Chris Candido in the past, and he'd always been a great guy in and out of the ring. Great matches that were simple to have. Now he'd be arriving as Skip, ready and hoping to be booed out of arenas around the globe.

Yes, the pair's unofficial leader was his lady, Sunny. The talker, the main heat magnet of the squad, she had a gift of getting under people's skin in a way that few women in wrestling have or since.

But I'm not talking about her with this. Not because of any issues I ever had with her (I didn't) or because of anything she's done since. I never knew her all that well, and I don't know any more than anyone else about her. Skip is who I was battling.

I was the newcomer's first common opponent, and the company trusted me to make him look good. He'd pinned me all over Canada

Welcome!

in May and America in June. Then, while I'd gone off to take tombstones from the Undertaker, he was working with others.

Early on the afternoon of June 26, I walked into the Marts Center in Wilkes-Barre, Pennsylvania, for the next edition of *Wrestling Challenge*, the weekend precursor to *Raw*. If there's a show to be taped, you show up around noon, even if the show doesn't start until around seven. You might have interviews or vignettes to tape, booking meetings to attend, or maybe nothing at all to do but wait. It's one more example of how much more there is to a wrestling show than the general audience sees or knows.

Whether it would be Skip, Undertaker, Yokozuna, whoever, I sat around waiting for my next defeat assignment. Then someone pulled me aside.

It was Diesel. Born Kevin Nash, he'd been the company champ for about eight months.

Was he giving me a shot at his belt? Would I get the honor of being the next victim of his jackknife powerbomb, which had won him the title the November before and helped him hang onto it against Shawn Michaels at the next *Wrestlemania*?

Not quite.

"Keep this under your hat," he leaned down to stage-whisper (I'm a big guy myself, but Nash raised almost seven feet in the air). "But you're gonna win tonight!"

Huh? OK, so it wouldn't be my *first* win, but it would be the first in front of the cameras. It would be my first in a while. It was probably a joke, and Nash had always had a sense of humor that made him fun to be around.

I went along with it. I went about my day as I always did, stretching, getting ready, checking for the schedule. I didn't get my hopes up. Wrestling and its partakers have never fully been known for honesty, and while I certainly didn't think Nash was doing this out of malice, it wouldn't be beyond him to just try to find some humor in a long, tedious day. If I had been played, I wasn't going to whine about it.

But later on, the news came. The wrestlers grabbed a bite from catering, and people began to clear out.

Then Pat Patterson showed up. A longtime right-hand man to

WWF head Vince McMahon, he wasn't one to play around, not when business was involved.

He brought me into a room with some other officials and told me about the new direction my career would take over the next few hours, days, weeks. Maybe even months if it got over with the crowd. Many people would be surprised by what would happen. Hopefully, they'd like it.

Skip was OK with it. Everyone was OK with it. A meeting that lasted about as long as it's taken you to read this section would find a spot in history that still lives today.

That evening, I stepped out into the ring, my suspenders on (I didn't have my usual Star of David on my tights that night, for some reason). The Body Donnas got a long intro, ring music, and a promo from Sunny. I don't even remember if my name was announced. While Sunny explained to the crowd just how much better she and Skip were than the mere peon mortals in the stands, I rolled my eyes and warmed up a bit. Surely, I'd never be the one to reach up and knock this guy off his pedestal.

Or would I?

Wrestling Begins

"Abracadabra!"

Poof, and I made my wrestling career happen!

Well, not exactly. It's never even remotely close to that easy in the mat business. Nothing happens instantly.

If I had made it to the top of my first career goal, however, something else, something similar, might have occurred.

Checking out some TV shows as a kid, I happened upon the works of legendary Canadian magician Doug Henning, and, along with millions of others, I was, well, spellbound by the creator of the show *Spellbound*!

Wrestling Begins

That was it. I was following my new main man into the magic business. I was going to be pulling sleight of hand tricks, illusions, everything, on TV and everywhere. I was going to turn iron into gold, transport myself from one end of a theater to another at the snap of my fingers, escape from a welded-shut container a hundred feet in the air, and pull a life-size whale out of a beanie!

As Henning's shows started selling out across Canada and made their way to Broadway, I decided to bring a slightly miniaturized version to my St. Petersburg, Florida, homeland. Any allowances I could save, any time my parents could spare a dime or three, I'd be out of the house and off to the magic shop about fifteen minutes away. It got to the point where the clerks and I knew each other on a personal basis.

In school, I did well enough that I was accepted into the DECA Club, which gives students a chance to, quite literally, work on the job. You'd spend half the day in class, and then you could leave. But not to go home or party with your friends; you were heading to employment. I worked at a restaurant in the mall. Along with shoes, clothes, hair dye, and, in the very distant future, a car, I saved up for my career in illusions.

For years and years, I studied magic. I checked out every TV special I could find, Henning and others. I even started putting on little shows of my own. You couldn't find any Florida preteen who was better at turning three billiard balls into six, getting a pitcher of milk to suddenly vanish, or making a can float in the air, break apart, and—voila!—become a bouquet of flowers!

To this day, I still love magic. It's about doing something that leaves an audience in awe and wonder, and knowing all the secrets yourself. Yes, I know you could say some of the same things about wrestling, but magic doesn't require bouncing all over a mat to do so!

And, yes, I was into sports. Like just about every American boy, I dreamt of making it from the little to the biggest leagues. The Miami Marlins weren't around yet for me to root for, so I decided I'd settle for first base or the outfields of Yankee Stadium. Hell of a concession, isn't it?

I remember the glory days of the local Miami Dolphins, mainly for that legendary 1972 season in which they strolled all the way to the Super Bowl without losing, then marched straight through to a victory there. Everybody freaked out whenever a game got close—one win during the season came by a single point, and another by only three—but millions were proud when that 17–0 mark was finished.

But those two weren't actually my favorite sports. Funnily enough, I was huge fan of roller derby. I was really enthralled by how those skaters could look so agile, so graceful with wheels on their shoes, and the ways they could take a good whack, go flying into the railing or off the track, then get right back up and haul back into action, especially with a hell of lot less padding than protected football or hockey players. It was like wrestling on skates.

In my spare time, what little of it I had with school and work, I happened upon the Northwest Youth Center—and a future.

For free, kids got a chance to hang out and kick back. Away from the streets, away from the problems, away from everything else. Kids could step into the Center, shoot a little pool, play some ping-pong, go swimming, anything they wanted.

Again, all for free. Places like that can make a big difference in a kid's life, usually in a positive way. It sure did for me. I became something of an unofficial neighborhood champ in pool and ping-pong, and I was all too anxious to defend my titles. I was there almost every night, and if I didn't have school or work, I'd stay for hours.

One day, I was walking past the Center's stage, when I glanced up and saw a weight set. Nothing too huge, but it looked intriguing. A neighbor of mine had a set like it, and I'd seen him work out a few times. I decided to give it a shot.

With no one to show me how to do it right, when to do it, how often, I just plowed ahead. Not too fast that I burned out quickly, but enough that I could sort of see the benefits. It felt good. I started to look a bit better. I was into it.

And right around that time, fate tossed another asset my way. The Center was putting together a wrestling program. Not the sports entertainment type, but the amateur type, with mats, headguards, takedowns, and points. It's been a great starting point for many who have made it all the way to the squared circle.

Just like with the weights, I didn't have a real trainer. Some of the center administrators would come in and help us out, but this was more for supervisory reasons than coaching. We were in there as self-learners, teaching each other the fundamentals of the mat game.

However, I still didn't exactly see this sport as my future profession. That last push, though, would come along *very* soon.

Learning My Dream

I don't quite remember exactly when I found this out, but I actually wasn't the first member of my family to step between the ring ropes, albeit different than the ones I'd hoped for. When I was about eight or nine, someone informed me that my father had once been a prizefighter. That sounds like something most fathers would brag to their sons about a thousand times, but he never did.

His name was Robert Horowitz, but he'd shortened the last name to Howard during his ring time, which had actually landed him on the cover of *Ring Magazine*. First off, it was easier to pronounce. Secondly, during this time, being Jewish in any public context could lead to controversy. Jews had dominated the boxing world before World War II (almost a third of the sport was Jewish in the 1920s and '30s), but by his time, Jewish athletes, especially the outspoken types, weren't in very high demand or regard.

I thought it was pretty cool to find out that my father had been so into sports, especially the most physical type. When he found out I was hoping to get into the ring, he showed me some footwork moves, how to get around the ring effectively. He ran me through some jabs and hooks, and I'd use them later on. A major part of wrestling is making things look as real as possible, and this certainly helped me there.

So I guess you could say that those outings might have been the seeds for my wrestling career. When I was about thirteen, though, that's when things really got going.

Wrestling Is My Gimmick

My family and I had just moved into a new house, and not everything was in place. There were lawn chairs in the living room, and a TV stacked on some boxes. The moving truck, as it seems to so often for everyone, had gotten lost or was running late, and we had to make do with what we had.

Channel flipping, I landed on pro wrestling. More specifically, *Championship Wrestling from Florida*. I watched Thunderbolt Patterson, still in the first half of a career that would become legendary, up against Mr. Clean, who'd soon cover up his head and face with glasses and a turban, move over to the WWF, and become the Grand Wizard, one of the first and greatest heel managers in wrestling history.

Yes, back then it was still the World Wrestling Federation, hence the initials. Not until 2002 would it switch to World Wrestling Entertainment (WWE), and both Wizard and Patterson would eventually snare spots in the company Hall of Fame.

I don't remember anything that happened for the next few minutes. I was enthralled in a way I'd rarely been in my short life. When the moving truck finally arrived, my parents had to almost drag me out of the chair to get them to come help bring everything in.

For the next week, I counted down to the show's next episode, almost to the minute. And that Saturday night, I was right back in front of the TV, although from an easy chair this time.

Just as he had in Texas for so long, Dusty Rhodes was now wowing the crowds a few states east. Jack Brisco was a favorite of mine, as was Don Muraco. Superstar Billy Graham was tearing it up even before he'd win the WWF title. I was knocked all over by Eddie Graham and his son Mike.

Ironically, when I broke into the game myself, one of the first major programs I'd work was with Mike Graham. So great when things like that come full circle.

Other guys would come in and out. People like Terry Funk and his brother Dory would appear and disappear, as would Paul Orndorff.

Oh, and there was someone else in that category as well. Only a fellow named Hulk Hogan. By the time I'd actually meet him, we were in the WWF, and he'd reached the top.

Learning My Dream

I couldn't believe how effortlessly Gordon Solie made things sound on color commentary, tying everything together with his wonderful wordsmanship. Obviously, I couldn't know this then, but I was watching some of wrestling's biggest trendsetters, in and out of the ring.

I couldn't stop watching. I couldn't believe how athletic these guys were. It was amazing to me that a guy could have the tar beaten out of him for minutes at a time, then suddenly jump up, toss his tormentor back around, and walk out with a win, all his suffering washing away. It broke my heart that a guy could try so hard and do so well, only to have his opponents, or their manager, cheat at the last second to steal away something he'd worked so hard for. How great it must have felt to have so many of the audience roaring for you? How could someone enjoy it so much when the audience despised them?

Clearly, I hadn't quite distinguished the combination of sports and entertainment in these programs. To me, it was as legitimate as the two Super Bowls my Dolphins had won earlier that decade.

But it was more than that. I was checking out the promos, the interviews, everything. These guys would tear it up on the microphones, letting everyone know exactly what was going to happen soon, and what would occur to anyone stupid enough to get in their way in the bargain. The creative threats, the violent descriptions, the charisma they showed was just off the charts.

They certainly made me want to come back the next week, if only from my living room, to see what would happen. It must have worked on the millions of others that kept the show going for so long.

I could do that. It could be me on that show. The name of Horowitz could someday be on the minds and voices of pro wrestling fans. Not just in Florida, but everywhere. Someday, I could be the one doing those moves. Taking a beating and coming out on top. Giving a beating and coming out on the wrong end. Either way, it would be worth it. It could be me with a microphone, getting people behind or against me with those words. Wouldn't my classmates, and even my teachers, be surprised if they turned on the TV and saw Barry, who they'd just seen struggling his way through a chemistry test, holding up his newfound belt as a wrestling champion?

That's when my career, and my athletic life in general, really

Wrestling Is My Gimmick

kicked into high gear. There weren't many steps I could take, not at this age, but I could get started. I wasn't sure how much training these guys had had, or where they'd obtained it, but I could take a step here and a step there.

I had basically outgrown the youth center, but my parents had bought me a larger weight set, and I was still using it. Now I started beating the living hell out of it. I was lifting day and evening, though not too late at night; I still had that "B" average to maintain in school.

No wrestling school at that time and place was going to train a ninth-grader, and I'm not sure that any should today, as those kids might not have the mental or physical know-how to get into wrestling. But I'd already seen a few chances that I could grab hold of a little tighter.

The first was my weights. They'd always be there for me. I needed help with something else.

I'd learned as much as I could from the amateur program of the center, but now I had a new and stronger direction there as well. It was my new school, Dixie M. Hollins High, and the wrestling program it offered. Now I had a coach, teammates, opponents, experienced folk that could help me find much more direction than before.

All the while, I was still training with those weights. I was self-taught there, but I researched like crazy in every muscle magazine and book I could get my hands and eyes on. I'd mainly been about 140 pounds until high school came about. Through my four years of wrestling, the weights buffed me up to the 171 class, then to 185. I wasn't the top star, but I made it to state competition once. I was pretty satisfied with how my high school career turned out. There's no pro wrestling league for that sort of mat action, but this had prepped me for the squared circle like I hoped it would.

Right there on the team with me was a guy who carried the same dream as myself. His name was Bruce Woyan, but wrestling fans would soon know him as Buzz Sawyer.

Buzz and I never wrestled in each in school, as we weren't in the same weight class, but we worked out together. He'd end up as a state champion, making it to the top five in the country. Then he'd head to the pro ranks, battling Mike, Dusty, and others all over Florida and elsewhere.

And just as with Mike, he and I would form our own full circle, as we had some great matches for the NWA in Charlotte and South Carolina. Sadly, Buzz's career and life would end far too soon, his wild lifestyle and drug use finishing him at 32. Those of us who knew him, or even knew of him, weren't very surprised when he passed away so soon.

Today, when kids who'd like to take their first steps into the wrestling business come to me for advice, amateur wrestling is at the top of my recommendation list. So is college. After four years at Dixie, I was ready to combine the two, moving up to new levels in both wrestling and education.

As they hardly ever do, things didn't go as I'd expected or hoped. However, as it usually is not, that wouldn't be such a horrible thing for me, as a person or a wrestler.

My College "Career"

In my first days at Florida State University, I had a few things on my mind. The first was to keep wrestling. I was sure that I could continue the improvements I'd seen in high school to become a solid part of the Seminole wrestling team. Four years of honing my skills there would turn me into a mat machine, making my journey into pro wrestling that much simpler.

I also wanted to study sports nutrition. I could help people learn to eat right, or at least eat better. If they needed help finding a strong diet, I'd be there for counseling. If their weight got out of control, too high or low, as it can do so quickly, I wanted them to trust me enough to turn to.

Pro wrestling was still my goal, but I also had a Plan B there too. Actually, considering all my targets, it was more like a Plan G or H.

If college and wrestling weren't to work out, I was heading into the Marines. That was a branch of the military I'd always had a tremendous amount of respect for, and I'd be both following and creating a Horowitz tradition. My dad had been in the Army, and my older brother had served in the Air Force. I'm sure I could have done a pretty good job. The Vietnam War was already over, so I wouldn't have to worry about getting sent to Hanoi.

But I knew that wrestling would be there for me, now and in the future.

It wasn't. Neither was college itself.

I stepped onto the FSU mats, and I got my ass whooped. Then again. Then another time.

No longer was I the big man on campus, or as close as I had been back at Dixie Hollins. I was the new guy, and I'd have to pay my dues all over again. There's one hell of a difference between high school and NCAA, just as there's another between NCAA and higher competition than that, like the Olympics, and I wasn't anywhere near ready to bridge that gap.

Not that I was ready to give up. I hoped to keep going. I did pretty well with my studies there too.

But there was one obstacle that I couldn't overcome.

Money. Finances. I didn't get any grants or scholarships, and my family didn't have enough to keep up my tuition bill. I certainly didn't have it on my own.

Before I was anywhere near a sophomore, I had to call it quits in college. No degree, no money. But I still had my targets. I still had my goal. I still had a dream.

Now that had to be enough.

Time to Train

I met Barry in the late '70s or so. We probably put a couple hundred guys through the school. Automatically, you would

> get a sense of whether or not people would ever get it. Just being in the ring and being able to make your way through a match is one thing, but to make it through a match and be convincing and what you do look solid, and he was one of those guys. You get a bunch of guys who get to a certain point and then just go through the paces. It's a convincing way of doing things. We had a good handful of guys like that, and he was one of them.
> —Joe Malenko

It's never been a question of if it's going to be hard to get started in the wrestling business, but how much so. And I'm not talking about your debut on the mat, complete with a ring announcer to roar your name and audiences to cheer and boo and music to play—that's *way* in the future.

From the moment you even think about training to be a wrestler, there's already a couple of strikes against you, objects in your way. You could always get taken by a trainer (or a "trainer") who not only lacks connections and ability, but might just take your money and skip right out of town. That's happened to many people I know.

And even if you can find the greatest, most ethical trainers, they might be cities or even states away. Unless you're pretty lucky with the family nest egg, there's a good chance that moving expenses might reach too high.

And even *then*, you've got to make sure you come across the right way with your teachers and classmates. You might think you're walking in and just showing off the self-confidence, but they might see it as an attitude and/or an ego, and they'll be all too happy to beat it right out of you and tell you never to come back. Even if you're with people that are ready, willing, and qualified to help you out, you say the wrong thing to them, and they'll put you in the ring, run you solid ragged, and finish up by breaking one of your limbs for you. Come across like that, and you're down and quite possibly out before you even started. There's probably a lot of guys who could have made it in wrestling, but killed their chances before they started just by coming in with such an attitude.

Out of college, I was driving around Florida, pondering all of this, when I happened to run into a friend of a friend. A buddy of mine was the daughter of a fellow named Lenny Greenburg, and the salvage yards he owned had made him millions.

She introduced me to him, and we hit it off pretty well. First off, we were both Jewish (didn't his name give that one away?). He liked pretty much everybody, but if you were Jewish, he was even more intrigued. Second of all, he could tell that I wanted some big things to happen, but knew that it would take some serious work to make them real.

One day out at lunch, he handed me an address. Lenny wasn't into wrestling himself, but he knew some people who might be able to help. That connection led to a Tampa fellow named Ed Maley.

By the time I met him, Maley had gone unbeaten for seven straight years in Florida judo competition, won national championships in the Air Force and elsewhere, been inducted into the World Martial Arts Hall of Fame, and been training others for decades.

Now he had rented a room in his school to one of the most renowned families in wrestling history: the Malenkos. Yes, the same one that helped Dean turn into one of WCW's top (but still horribly underused) stars in the 1990s.

Remember what I just said about not wanting to look too assertive on one's first few days at a school? Well, you don't want to go too far in the other direction, either. Walk in there tripping over your feet, stuttering, your head apparently glued to your chest, you're not going to be taken seriously. Your trainers will see early on that your heart's not in it, that you're probably not the kind of guy who's going to stick around for one of the toughest businesses.

I was probably closer to the terrified persona when I started. But not so much so that Professor Boris Malenko noticed or minded. He handed me a contract, with the costs listed. Several costs. High costs. It takes far too long to make much money in the wrestling business, and after winning world and Florida titles, he wasn't going to stop with the green now that his career was over.

But I signed. I signed fast. Wrestling was going to be my new career, one way or another or someway else. I'd make it happen on my own.

Remember, this was not an official wrestling school. Therefore, there weren't any "official" wrestling materials, still tough to find in

Time to Train

training locations today. I was getting body-slammed and suplexed on inch-thick judo mats with concrete underneath.

Three times a week, I'd work during the day, then hop in the car, drive almost an hour, then spend three hours lifting weights—what little there were of those!—and training. It took me a while, a pretty long while, to translate my amateur skills into squared circle acumen, but I progressed.

My day jobs were more ways to kill time between wrestling and make just a little money in the bargain. I worked construction, built lawn ornaments out of plaster, worked at 7-11, everything that I could do, just to keep from going broke. When I took these jobs, I'd never tell my bosses about my long-range goals, because they probably wouldn't hire me if they knew I was going to run, usually without a two-week notice, if I got a mat gig. That, and if people find out that pro wrestling is your end goal, they tend to look at you and treat you with some pretty strong disdain. Why would anyone see something so unrealistic as worth putting all this time and effort into?

Still, I never had a problem leaving one of these jobs if wrestling called, because I never saw any of them as my future. Wrestling was where I was, and where I was going to be for a while.

Back at the school, the crowds started to lighten. We'd started off with about twenty people, and fewer and fewer came back. The only guys who really stuck through it were me and a fellow named Al Perez. When he'd debut in the WWF in 1989, I'd be one of the first people he'd work with.

I trained with Dean for a while, and his brother Joe, who also became a pretty strong star on his own, albeit more in Japan than around here. Once in a while, the Malenkos would bring in local legends like Karl Gotch, whose three-decade long career was coming to an end after becoming one of the most famous wrestlers, nationality notwithstanding, in the land of the Rising Sun for decades. Karl von Stroheim, who'd also won titles all over the world, came along sometimes as well.

After about six months at the school, however, it was me who was leading the class. Boris, or whoever else was teaching on a particular night, would suddenly have to head out or go make a long phone call, hopefully from nearby promoters looking to fill their next show. They'd ask me to the do the training. I'd help my fellow students learn the bumps, the running, all the technicals that were already becoming part of my trademark repertoire.

Soon Boris found a new place to train, a run-down mattress factory right next to the site of Raymond James Stadium, which would one day host three Super Bowls (one of which the home Tampa Bay Buccaneers would win) and 2021's edition of *Wrestlemania*. There was a 20-foot ring, a 16-foot ring, and no heating or air conditioning, just huge fans to cool us off in a building where the temperature reached 140 degrees in the summer. Still much better than the judo mats, though.

I kept working, and everyone could see that. Even Boris and Gotch, both of whom had been wrestling since before I was born, never made me feel bad when I made one of my many, many mistakes. They knew I was there to learn. They taught me the moves, how to tie up, even how to get into the ring. That's not always as easy as it looks, and takes serious practice. You fall into or out of the ring at the start of the match, and it's going to be tough to get fans to forget it.

> **Joe Malenko:** In *Rocky II*, Rocky is working at Mickey's gym, and there's a guy working the heavy bag. Mickey is trying to tell this guy how to have a look, have a snarl. Then Mickey says, "Hey Rock, come here. Hit the bag. I want you to show this guy how to snarl," and Rocky slams it. You can hit a bag, but to really make it look convincing, you have to have a face. You want to come across like you want to tear that bag off the fucking chain.
>
> When I throw a punch, I want people to look at me and say, "Holy crap, he wanted to take that guy's head off." I don't want them to just be like, "Hey, that was a pretty good punch." Some guys have that look on their face, that legitimacy that carries from them, and it translates on out to the crowd. If this is even a word, there's a convince-ability piece of the business that not a lot of guys have, and Barry had that.

Everything but promos. The Malenkos felt that that should be one of the finishing touches of a wrestling persona. They considered that to be the attic of learning the game. Learning the moves are the foundation, polishing one's skills are the rooms, and promos are the last thing.

I needed more polishing. That's what you get from traveling with the wrestlers every night. That would be arriving for me soon.

Time to Train

When I was twenty-one, I made my ring debut. Boris lined up battles for me, occasionally against Dean, at flea markets, car lots, bars, little civic centers. These matches would be some of the most fun I'd ever have.

In my little remaining time, away from the school, the matches, the occasional job, I was self-teaching. I was always in front of a TV, watching matches from all over Florida, Georgia, and the Von Erichs doing World Class. But not so I could cheer for my favorite or boo the heels, or at least not just that. I was watching the moves they did, the techniques they used, how they sold. I was focused on the whole match, not the promos or what drew a big pop just for a big move.

I still love this today, once in a while. One of my personal favorite TV matches was against Dean in 1997 in WCW, and I love watching that match.

Joe Malenko: When guys would come to the school, I would say to them, "The chances of your getting into this business and having a legitimate career in this business is slim to none, and slim just left town. But if you do, you will probably consider it to be the greatest thing you've ever done." The business is a pretty fun career. So when a guy would working here and there, and you could tell he was good, but he wasn't going to hit it, you'd still be happy for him. I would tell those guys all the time, "For you, it may not be a career, but do your thing, get out in front of a crowd, have a fun time, make a few bucks, and leave it at that." But for the guys who really wanted it, who would put the time and effort in, and they would achieve that, that would end up with an actual career, we stood on that. Our school was only as good as our ability to put guys into a room and create careers for them. Not create a place where they could work a couple times a month and make $25 a pop. It was to get them to a place where they're on the national stage, and as a school, we did that dozens of times.

First and foremost, you have to have a love for the business. You have to enjoy putting the match together in a way in which everybody in that audience gets pulled into a reality that doesn't even really exist. If you enjoy that, that's your first piece. You have to willing to learn at all times. You never have it down pat; you're always gonna learn. Barry had all that going for him.

What an amazing thing it is to be able to get in front of a crowd or hundred or thousands and literally control them. The psychology of a match, if you do it well, you are in control of everybody in that audience. It's the guy who's the ring psychologist, who's the ring general, who dictates to the audience what the audience is gonna do and how they're gonna react. Barry was one of those guys. He's dictating to an audience how the audience is going to react at any point in time during the match, and he brings them along as

Wrestling Is My Gimmick

he sees fit, as he wants them to experience his match. That's a gift. It's a gift that comes with a lot of time and hard work, but it's a gift.

Along with everything else, there was one more thing I learned at the school that I would carry through my career. Well, they didn't really *teach* me, because this is something you can't exactly teach. It's not like taking you into a room and showing you a move or bump over and over again until you get it right. It's more about getting into the mind. It's about, in ways much more subtle than a dropkick, lessons on how to conduct oneself out of the ring. Something that helps you get in good behind the scenes, and stay just that way. Going in the other direction can get you tossed from any promotion faster than working sloppy between the ropes.

It was about ribbing. Not "Here's How to Steal Someone's Shoe and Get Away with It," but how to deal with this sort of thing when it happens to you. Because it's not about if, but when and how often.

Ribbing's something people do in the locker room and on the road to keep themselves entertained in ways other than watching their colleagues in the ring. When you're on the road for so long, without an off-season, you have to find some way to have fun, and, while there's really no easy way to say this, sometimes you do it at other people's expense. You learn to deal with it, or you don't last. Guys aren't going to leave you alone just because you ask them to, and firing off a few punches or even a tantrum over it makes you look like a crybaby, just as big a distraction as any other locker room cancer.

Stories about ribs and those that pull them have been passed down from wrestling generation to generation. I can't really say that one has been worse than the other, because, for the most part, that's all I've done—heard these stories. Listened to tales about guys spiking each other's drinks, slipping drugs into food, destroying someone's car if they pissed you off, even chopping up someone's personal items or expensive clothing.

They never did anything like that to me. Not because I was special or anything, but because I didn't really react like they hoped I would. I said I never had anything huge or harmful happen, but that doesn't mean I was immune to a wrestler's impromptu initiation into not just the business, but probably every federation he or she enters into.

Basically, there's two kinds of ribs. The first type is where you start, and where they (as in, your tormentors) decide where you're going to end up. These things usually happen in the locker room, or elsewhere out of the ring.

These are irritating, but not really harmful. Someone might hide your bag in a closet or locker, or go into that same bag and take something out to hide elsewhere. They might cancel your hotel reservation. And if you did get to that hotel, you'd get woken up at 3 a.m. for a phone call that your car was stolen or that someone wanted to fight you in the parking lot. All pranks, of course.

You'd roll over, go back to sleep, and go on about your business.

Of course, there's also the second part. Actually, you really hope you don't get to the second part, because that's when things get bad. That's when they do the horrible stuff to you. That's when you get physically hurt, when you lose your items forever, when you have to legitimately worry about something serious happening. That's when the ones that I mentioned earlier happen, and probably much worse than them.

Fortunately, I never made it that far. Because they'd do silly shit to me, and I'd laugh it off. And before you think I'm climbing a pedestal here, yes, I did my share of pranking. On Level One, of course.

If you look over his wrestling career, at least in the WWF, you'd have an easier time finding people that Dynamite Kid *didn't* rib. Some of the things he did were more bratty and childish. Other times it was worse, but I'm not going into detail there, because he didn't bother me much in that regard.

He did some stuff to me, and it fell by the wayside. In fifth grade, I might have gone into fisticuff battle over someone hiding my bag. That day, I just didn't care much. Dynamite respected me for that, as did the other people back there. He came up to me one time.

"Barry, you know why we like you?" he asked. "You're not a stooge. You don't tell on us." I never did.

In the ring, however, that was another story.

Once, I was working a battle royal in Wheeling, West Virginia.

Wrestling Is My Gimmick

Battle royals are usually pretty easy to work, as long as you're careful. Per usual, I got thrown out relatively quickly.

I pulled myself to my feet and started walking back to the locker room, glaring at the audience like it was their fault I didn't win. This was going to be *my* moment at last!

Then some idiot, who at that point was considered by many to be a company superstar, decided to step in. He thought it would be cool to pull my trunks down in front of the crowd.

That pissed me off. It's unprofessional, and Barry Horowitz doesn't put over that bullshit. I have a sense of humor as good as anyone (and, I'd like to think, better than most) but I draw the line at rudely embarrassing someone, let alone hurting anybody, for one's personal enjoyment.

The dumbass didn't know I'd been around for so much longer than him. I'd spent more time showering after matches than he'd spent in the ring in his career. This wasn't my first rodeo. I'd seen half-wits like him pull this stuff on others before, and I always took the time to double-knot my trunks and wear something underneath. I didn't put it over there, nor did I bitch about it in the locker room. Even though I was a generation ahead of him in the business, he was on the upswing in the company, and I wasn't. Seniority doesn't always buy you much weight in wrestling. If I'd whaled this guy, and I could have, it would have embarrassed him. It would also have gotten me fired. I'm not mentioning this guy's name, but he's dead now.

If you go backstage and start a fight over something that happened in the ring, or the locker room itself, everybody's going to laugh at you. Even if you kick someone's ass, and you're either the newbie or very low on the drawing totem pole, you're not going to last. If the guy you beat up has more friends and power than you, he and they are going to spread it around that you're some kind of immature hair-trigger who can't take a joke, and that's going to hurt your rep. You're not a team player. You don't know how to have fun.

It's not about being a coward. It's about being smart. Anyone who has been in the business for any length of time knows that ribbing is a part of it. It always will be. Maybe it always should be, to a point.

Time to Train

People in our positions have to find some way to amuse themselves out on the road, and as long as it's done in harmless fun, that's fine.

But this wasn't. That was one of the few times that things got real for me in the ring. Once, I was working in Japan, and my opponent kept "happening" to blast me with fists and shoes. I lit him up one good time, and that came to a halt.

I'm sure I did some pranking of my own, but I don't think a complete list of the stuff I pulled would fill a paragraph in this book. I never thought along the lines of, "He pissed me off for something personal, so I'm going to stick it to him real soon!" about my co-workers. I was about getting to the gym, making and saving my money, making my booking and my next flight, and being accountable. As soon as I got on the plane to a wrestling show, I was Mr. Technical, and I kept building up until I got the show. I didn't make it a common habit of being the spoon that stirred the pot in the locker room, and I didn't become the target of those that did.

Overeager pupil that I was, I was always asking for help. First to sharpen my skills, and then to share them elsewhere. I always made sure to let my trainers know how appreciative I was, and always would be. Still am. But I wanted to go and work for the major promotions. Head out to do my thing alongside the very stars that had pushed me into the business to begin with.

Shockingly, Boris didn't feel that way. Just another wrestler who put his own idea of readiness above, or at least alongside of people who knew a hell of a lot better.

The first time I asked Boris if I'd learned enough to leave, he turned me down in a second. The second time, he did so again, although with a little hesitation.

But the third time would truly be a charm for me. I'd impressed him enough to broaden my horizons.

Boris reached into his pocket. Clearly, he'd seen this moment coming.

He handed me a list. This was the unofficial school diploma.

The first entry was for a company in Arkansas that could make me some custom trunks and boots. The second was a list of wrestling gatekeepers. Portland wrestling powerhouse Don Owen's name and number was there. I saw the moniker of Carlos Colon, who controlled the overwhelming majority of Puerto Rico. I could get in touch with Stu Hart, head over a certain other wrestling family up north. There was Gorilla Monsoon, one of the big names in the WWF.

Slowly and surely, I packed everything I learned, however little it may have been, and packed it into my '74 Malibu Classic. Then I headed north—to where, however, was still unclear.

The Years 1981–1983

Looking to land in or near the midst of the wrestling business on the East Coast, I ended up right around the boardwalk on the Jersey Shore. Not exactly next door to the promotions of the time, but not *too* far away.

As I walked up to a pay phone, I suddenly felt like I was having another first day on the job in wrestling. This was like stepping through the curtain on the way to the ring, hearing my music play and hoping the crowds would respond, and my opponent would do some enhancing, which I'd need. It was like graduating high school and then starting college the next day.

It wasn't hundreds of audience members I had to impress. I might have preferred it that way.

Just one. A guy who could identify talent, or lack thereof, in about a quarter second, and had decades of experience in seeing a ton of guys a hell of a lot more talented, or at least experienced, than I was.

I was going to try to work a worker.

I dialed some numbers. A voice answered. Years later, generations of WWF fans would hear this same voice on years of TV shows and pay per views, but back then, he was fresh out of his own wrestling career, and now working behind the scenes for the then–World Wide Wrestling Federation.

The Years 1981–1983

I told Gorilla Monsoon that I had been working for, oh, about two years (OK, just a *few* months' worth of over-exaggeration!), that Eddie Graham had broken me in down in Florida (well, maybe as a fan!), and that my name was Barry Hart (the Malenkos had told me to use that last name, which wasn't as prominent as the real-life family would make it a few years later).

Fortunately, he wasn't big on fact-checking. With this many "applicants" to pick from, it was easier to just tell me to show up for a tryout. If I could actually work, maybe my truth fudging wouldn't be such a problem. If I didn't arrive, he'd have plenty of people to pick from, and wouldn't remember me in about five minutes.

Long before the WWF made Barry Horowitz a stereotypical nerd in character, I personified the real thing home in Florida.

But I was there. Believe you and me and everyone else, I was. The WWWF was holding TV tapings in Allentown, Pennsylvania, and it would be both the longest and shortest two-hour drive of my life.

One night in Allentown in October 1981, I stepped into a WWWF ring for the first time. On a temporary break from shots at current champ Bob Backlund, Angelo Mosca was warming up on me.

I was a little nervous, but not as bad as I'd been at other matches beforehand. I just wanted to do my job, literally and figuratively.

He worked a little stiff. Why not? He'd been in the business since

I was a baby, and he didn't have to pay any dues. If I lasted in the company or didn't, it wouldn't make much a difference to him. But I didn't get hurt, and I did OK. I thought so. I hoped so. Nobody complained, at least to my face, so I thought my first impressions were good enough.

They were. Every three weeks for the next year, I'd work a Tuesday in Allentown and a Wednesday in Hamburg.

That is, after my Hamburg debut almost traumatized me for good, and not just as a wrestler.

Bob Bradley and I hit the ring for a TV taping at the Hamburg Field House. Not to battle each other just yet, though we'd do our fair share of warring. No, this early on, we were teamed up.

And on the other side of the ring? The epitome of a guy who never asked for one ounce of help for his entire career.

It was André the Giant. In this handicap match, I was worried that we'd be the ones who ended up crippled.

As agile as he'd ever be, he moved around the ring like a guy half his size, and moved us about anywhere he wanted us to go. You could tell he really enjoyed being the big man on campus.

André gunned Bob out of the ring like a Ken doll. Sprawled on the mat, I was terrified that he was about to make me a permanent part of the ring, or maybe the floor below.

As his hundred-gallon ass barreled down at me, I was trying to remember if I'd put my affairs in order before the match. He landed, three count, it was over.

And I never felt a thing. The fans sure thought I'd just become a pancake, and I sold like the local funeral home was about to get some sudden business. But André'd taken care of me. Clearly, he'd been through this enough to know just how to make this sort of thing only look like it hurt.

André was one of the nicest guys in the business, and I made for damn sure to stay on his good side during the brief time I was in the locker room. It's still to this day terrifying that one mistake or wrong move, or if he'd been as sick or hurt as he was during his last few years in the ring, that he could have killed me. I'm sure thousands of other guys felt the same way throughout his career. My career, and more, could have ended in those seconds, and he probably wouldn't have gotten in trouble for it. Not because he was so well liked around the business, or not just that. But accidents and mistakes happen, and you become a wrestler knowing this.

Fortunately, I'd live to fight a few more decades. I'd kill time between wrestling shows working at a car wash, then go rushing back through the Keystone State, roaring into battle. With a hell of a lot of help from the veterans of the time, my techniques improved greatly.

Don Muraco was another guy who helped me out. One of the company's strongest heels at this point, he did a hell of a job working me over and making me look good while doing so, drawing not just strong heat for himself, but even some babyface cheers for me. Then I'd go over to the bad guy side myself, battling the British Bulldogs individually or as a team. Davey Boy Smith and I used to spend forever laying out our matches beforehand.

Little things, little polishings of my work would make a great difference in my work, in a good way. Even working as an enhancer, I'd occasionally make it through to the last match of the night. They'd even send me out to a few house shows.

You know, it's funny—for that brief period, I might have been the most well-known worker named Hart in America! Clearly, that wouldn't last.

And neither would I, not there, not yet. Just as had been the case back south, I got restless. I knew there was more to being a complete wrestler. I just wasn't sure what, or where to get it.

But I knew someone who might.

I was surprised at how quickly and easily I nabbed a meeting with the man in charge—none other than Vince McMahon. That's Vince McMahon, Sr., not Junior. The one who was a driving force behind the formulation of the World Wide Wrestling Federation (which had by now dropped the first word), and probably would have been content with it not expanding past a regional operation.

But we had a quick and easy chat, and he arranged to send me over to Portland. With Jimmy Snuka as a messenger, Vince sent word to Don Owen, the man and mind behind Pacific Northwest Wrestling. Surely, there had to be a place for me there.

He was next to me in the enhancement ranks in the WWF, but

Buddy Rose had been a smash in that area for years, selling out buildings all over Oregon and Washington. Maybe I could follow him over and have that same success. Perhaps I could even work with one of Rose's main foes at the time, a fellow named Roddy Piper. How about Jimmy? Maybe Curt Hennig, on his way up in the ranks there as well.

But none of that ended up happening. Owen responded that he just had too much talent to allow for an unproved newbie like me. Poor fellow!

Instead, Vince sent me back down to the Carolinas and Virginia, working for Jim Crockett and his National Wrestling Alliance's Mid-Atlantic shows, down alongside the Iron Sheik, Ricky Steamboat, and, ironically, Piper.

Now I was working five or six nights a week, and hardly ever with the same guy twice in a row. Once a month, we'd be up in Canada, working at Toronto's Maple Leaf Gardens. I got some new polishing in the form of road trips with the fellows I just mentioned, as well as Mike Rotundo, Jimmy Valiant, and so many others. Where did you expect to draw, or fall flat? What did fans in *this* territory truly want, as opposed to *that* one? Would I have to go full-blown heelish in our next tour, or was this crowd sophisticated enough to pick up on some subtlety?

My enhancing skills kept enhancing from within. A fellow on the booking committee kept letting me know how pleased he was, and putting me in high-end matches for my tenure.

Oh, his name? Ric Flair.

Eventually, I found my way back to the WWF, albeit in Charlotte, long an NWA power center. I started hanging out with a fellow named Bob Bradley, who was even newer to the business than I was.

Like most of us in the business, Bob was a huge fans of the Samoans. It's always seemed like there's an unwritten code amongst their entire genealogy in the wrestling family sense. If they're not related by blood, as many are, they're still brothers in a way. They don't like weird gimmicks. Certainly not stereotypes. Nothing like that, but you could always count on them to work as hard in the business as anyone.

It was right around that time that I met one of the most well-known figures in the history of wrestling, and for reasons far past his ethnicity. A guy who many felt for a time—right around that very time, actually—might have been the biggest name in the wrestling business, and would soon wind up with the WWF title.

By then, Jimmy Snuka, who'd helped train Bob, had been in the business for over a decade, and was already getting title shots against then–company lead Bob Backlund. He'd started in the WWF as one of its most hated, but fans loved the guy so much that he went good, and would stay there for almost all of the rest of his career.

Point is, as a veteran and a star, he may not have been expected to even acknowledge, let alone interact with, the newcomers. But he did. Not just with me, but for about everyone there who hoped to get anywhere near his level.

He was always friendly to me. He gave me some pointers in the ring, as we did a couple of TV matches together. He kept me safe, even when he was flying halfway across the ring to splash me for the pin. Once in Long Island, he was wearing this green shirt. I mentioned how cool it looked.

He ripped it right off and insisted I keep it. I did, for a very long time. That whole, "give you the shirt off his back," saying wasn't just a cliché for him.

Once or twice, I even met his girlfriend, Nancy Argentino. She wasn't around as much, but she was always very friendly to everyone there.

I loved Jimmy Snuka's work in the ring, as most people did throughout his career. But my next interaction with him, as it were, wouldn't be especially upbeat.

Bob and I showed up for TV one day, and went to meet with Dory Funk, Jr., and Michael Hayes, who were running the show. They told me it was time to change my name.

One of the first great heel managers in the business, Gary Hart and his booking had helped turned World Class Championship Wrestling into a basic monopoly of the south, as successful a regional promotion as any before or since. Now Hart was occasionally plying his trade in the WWF, and the bookers didn't want anyone to think that Gary and Barry were related or even the same, although it's difficult to imagine anyone mistaking us as family.

"What do you want to call me?" I asked. "How about Bret Hart?"

Yes, that was a legitimate question. I didn't know there was another wrestling youngster named Bret Hart tearing things apart in Canada, and don't think I would have minded if I did. They told me they'd think of something. Soon, they let me keep the name.

Bob and I kept working together, and he usually beat me. Right near the arena, there was a Best Western that had been converted into an impromptu wrestling frat house. There were ten rooms that were made up like suites, breakfast every morning, even a pool. I think I lived there for a year.

But Bob was gone in a week. Maybe.

"Barry, I'm homesick," he confessed to me one day. "I'm leaving."

"What do you mean?" I almost sputtered. "Bob, you wanted this. This is your dream."

"Just tell Dory I left," he said.

Whatever. I went to TV, and he went to work in Washington, D.C., and Massachusetts. I never saw him again, but he did a lot of wrestling in Samoan garb, tributes to his trainers, and fine-tuned the Snuka splash almost as well as Jimmy had.

Oh, yeah, about that again. That issue with Jimmy Snuka I mentioned earlier. Let's chat about that.

Jimmy Snuka

As the new round of TV tapings in Hamburg kicked off on the second weekend of May 1983, I did what I always did to make my presence known at these things.

As in, dressed, ate, and sat down to watch promos and interviews.

Per usual, I was one of the first there, so not much was going on. Just a few guys there to step behind a microphone and in front of a camera and let audiences who weren't there know exactly what was going to happen to their next opponent. That could mean the next week, later that summer, or even further along. Guys chattered and threatened as if they were five seconds away from going head-to-head in the ring; some of these programs were weeks or months away from even beginning. It was easier to keep secrets hidden from audiences of then.

As I sat and watched, more and more colleagues trickled in. I always made it a point to *not* listen to conversations that didn't involve me—and as the newest of newbies, I was involved about as often as a solar eclipse!—I kept hearing Jimmy's name.

People noticed that he hadn't shown up, and he wasn't one to randomly miss shows. Was he sick or injured? He'd seemed fine the day before at the tapings in Allentown. Maybe he'd been in a car accident in the drive over to Hamburg. Perhaps some crazed fan had jumped him, although that wouldn't have been a good idea for them.

Whoever did the scheduling worked him out of the day. I went on with my match, watched everyone else do theirs, and went home. I liked Jimmy very much, everyone did, but I just figured something had happened and would be straightened out soon, and that I'd see him at the next event.

I'm not sure when I got the full story. The real story. I may have heard bits and pieces of it there in the locker room, and if I did, I might have brushed it off as sensationalism, someone just trying to make things up for attention. Back home detailing cars, I stumbled onto a newspaper and found out just how true and terrifying his absence truly was.

The night before that taping, I'd been staying at a Days Inn in Allentown. Traveling alone, I'd picked a small place with a nice gym instead of a larger place with a nice bar. Like, say, the George Washington Motor Lodge just down the road a few minutes.

That's where Jimmy and Nancy had been. It was the last night they'd ever spend together. It was the last night Nancy would spend anywhere.

Sometime that night, Nancy had been rushed to a hospital. Soon after, she'd passed away of a terrible head injury.

That's about all anyone agrees on from that horrible night. Jimmy talked to the police, and Vince McMahon got involved, and no one was ever arrested. How she died, accidentally or because of someone else, will probably never be known. Decades later, there are still believers either way.

This probably wouldn't be the case today, but public interest in the matter faded very fast. It was as if fans, as well as fellow wrestlers, were telling themselves, "Hey, if the law's not convinced that Jimmy did this, we should give him the benefit of the doubt as well." Others just figured it wasn't their business.

Just a month after Nancy died, Jimmy was back, now as a good guy working against Don Muraco. That October at Madison Square Garden, he flew off the top of a steel cage onto Muraco, a moment that legends like Mick Foley, and others, credit as pushing them into the business. In March 1985, Jimmy was in Hulk Hogan and Mr. T's corner for the first-ever *Wrestlemania* main event.

I was long gone by then, back in Florida, and I didn't see him for years afterward. But when he came back to the WWF in 1989, I was there too, and I was one of his last steppingstones as he moved through a program with Ted Dibiase on the way to *Summerslam*.

Jimmy remembered me when we met again, and he was as friendly as he'd ever been. I certainly never knew enough, never wanted to know enough, about his past issues to chat about them. Even if I had, it wasn't my place to mention anything from his past. Some guys might have discussed it with him, maybe even gotten in his face about them, but I never saw any of that.

He'd keep wrestling until he couldn't do it anymore, and even then came back every once in a while. But the whisperings about Nancy's death never went all the way away, and in September 2015, he was arrested in the matter. But nothing would come of it; the next year, he was deemed unfit for trial, both from cancer and dementia, the second of which undoubtedly stemming in part from years of head-based ring action.

Just over two weeks into 2017, Jimmy died. I'm really glad I got to know him, limited as that was, and work with him, and I'll remember him fondly as both a fan and an in-ring foe.

Someone else, though, I can't say the same about, in any capacity. A guy whose actions a quarter-century later would nearly destroy the sport and blemish it in ways that will never fully heal. Horribly ironic that someone known as one of the hardest workers wrestling had ever seen almost fed it a fatal poison.

I'm not going to insult anyone's intelligence here. Yes, I'm talking about Chris Benoit, the personification of wrestling infamy.

I think I met Chris Benoit for the first time around 1988 in his Canadian homeland. I don't think it was the WWF, but a federation based out of Vancouver or Winnipeg was holding tryouts for the locals. I don't recall anything special about him then, assuming it was him to begin with.

I ran into him again a few years later, this time in Japan. Me and my Global colleague Del Wilkes were doing some freelance work for All Japan, and we happened to run into Chris, along with his long-time pals Dean Malenko and Eddie Guerrero, whose own tragic November 2005 passing would be, in my opinion, one of the knock-out punches for Benoit's murderous rampage against his family a year and a half later.

But his wife, Nancy? Amazing woman. One of the friendliest, down-to-earth ladies I've ever run into in this business. I'd actually spent time with her before she ever got with Chris, working down in Florida with her ex, Kevin Sullivan, and she fit in everywhere in the wrestling business.

That's always been my criteria for hanging out around with women in wrestling. I basically talked to them the same way I'd talk to the male colleagues. Maybe it came from growing up in a family of wrestlers, but Rockin' Robin morphed into the locker room real fast, and I always got along fine with her, although I wish she'd been there for longer.

Some women appreciated being treated like some of the wrestlers. Most didn't. I never chatted with Sable or Sunny. I couldn't have talked much to Miss Elizabeth, since Randy Savage guarded her with everything but a machine gun, not that he couldn't have kicked most of the guys' asses anyway.

After reading that, this next part might be a bit surprising to wrestling fans, mainly because, when it came to character, she certainly was a diva to the extreme, so much so that many fans might have feared it bled over into her personality. But behind the scenes, Debra McMichael was one of my closest lady pals. She and I would

Wrestling Is My Gimmick

chat at conventions. Always friendly to everyone. I haven't seen too many colleagues that were better to their fans.

But back to Chris. In June 1998, before he had any inclination to head to the WWF, he and I worked out our match for a TV taping. That was how WCW did it back then, taping a month or two's worth of matches in a weekend.

We'd both been in the company for a while, but hadn't interacted much. I don't really see myself as a full-blown extrovert, but this guy was everything but a locker room agoraphobic, going long periods of time without even interacting with his closest friends or the people he was working programs with, let alone a one-shot deal like me.

Still, I knew he could work, and I knew I'd get a good match out of him. Of course, he'd be winning, but we both knew a squash wouldn't help anyone.

"Hey, Chris," I explained, "I'd like to get in this suplex, if you don't mind."

He looked at me like my face had just turned green.

"Yeah," he sneered, "as long as you don't drop me on my fucking head."

That ticked me off. He knew who I was, and he, along with everyone else, knew I could work. I don't know if he didn't trust me, if he thought I was overrated, if he thought that he was in for a tough night.

Or maybe I just took it wrong. Either way, it was time for action.

I fired one cheap shot, hands and feet involved, after another to get him on the mat and keep him there. I was working pretty stiff with him, but not so much that he'd think there was anything personal. I tossed him across the mat, then hit that suplex I'd told him about. It was one of the best I'd pulled off in a while.

He kicked out of a couple of pins, then kicked and chopped me. But I slipped him into an abdominal stretch and rolled him over.

Here's where things really could have gone in a few directions. If I'd been unprofessional or even more pissed off, I could have held him down for the three. The way I had him tied up, he couldn't have kicked out if I hadn't wanted him to.

But I didn't do that. Mainly because I would have gotten fired, his push would have continued, and the match probably would have gotten edited off the telecast anyway. It's about looking past the issues you have with an individual for the greater good, for both yourself and the company.

He got away (rather, I let him get away), and managed to get me down long enough for the umpteenth diving headbutt of his career, one of the reasons his brain would get beaten into oatmeal. He pinned me, but I'd run the show for most of the match, and he knew, at least by then, that I could wrestle.

Aside from a post-match handshake and quick conversation, I don't think I ever saw Chris again after that, and if I did, I didn't spend time with him.

And then came that sad weekend in June 2007 in Fayetteville, Georgia.

You never want to believe that anyone could do something like that. Especially someone you knew. Even if you barely knew him, even if you hardly cared for him, no one, including me, wanted to believe that Chris had been behind the deaths of Nancy and their son Daniel.

Certainly no one in the wrestling business, from the performers to the fans. That's why the first stories told about that nightmarish day had to do with robbers and intruders. Of course someone had broken into Chris and Nancy's home. Chris was a tough guy, but maybe he was outnumbered. Just in the wrong place at the wrong time. Maybe it had been a huge bunch of scumbags, disgusting creatures, probably with weapons. Who else could take Chris out, then slaughter a woman and child?

No one knew how to react. No one could have ever prepared for that. Everyone wanted very much to believe that the three had been victims, and should be remembered as such. When *WWE Raw* held a tribute to Chris the next day, we just waited for the law to go out and find the cretins that did this. Maybe the cops would be decent enough to forgo jail and throw them to a locker room full of the Benoit family's friends.

But then the evidence started to trickle in. More and more, a heartbreaking reality took form. We learned a truth that made a tragedy that much worse. One by one, we all started to accept that, as strange as Chris was, the depth of his depraved nature had gone farther down than anyone could have guessed.

It's not even remotely possible to rationalize something like that. Killing your own son? Your seven-year-old son? No one can even conceive of it. I'm sure that the thousands of bashes in his unprotected head smashed Chris' brain well past the point of coherence, but there's never going to be any kind of excuse for what he did to Daniel. Imagine slowly choking your own son to death, him screaming, "Stop, Daddy, stop!" until his voice and struggles slow and disappear. It's obscene.

And after murdering Nancy and Daniel, Chris finally killed himself. If he had just done that to begin with, people might have felt a little sympathetic towards him. When someone commits suicide, people may respond with anger, certainly sadness, but with a little understanding. Many wrestlers, far too many, have committed suicide for all kinds of reasons, and while I won't name names here, I think the wrestling fanhood has been pretty good about remembering those people for what they did in the ring, rather than the final choice they made. With Chris, we can't do that.

Not long after Chris died, his idol Dynamite Kid, in a rare interview, said that he was glad Chris was dead. Somehow, I think that would have hurt Chris even more than the damage his crime inflicted on the business as a whole.

Making It to Starrcade

Dear Jack (Hart):
I enjoyed seeing you at the Miami Airport on July 13. I hope your matches in Nassau were victorious and financially successful. Wrestling had come on very strongly in the United States in the last few years, and I am glad that our state has

> been such a significant part of its success.
> —Bob Graham (1985), Florida governor, 1979–1987

If there are a few memories that really drive home my time with Crockett, some are little more personal than professional. One, though was a part of history.

Two of them had to do with *only* working with a couple of legends in the business. One was just starting out; the other was supposedly around the end of a career that had already gone farther than about 99.9 percent of other workers.

Like I said, supposedly. Even he said so. But how mistaken everyone would be.

My first battle with Roddy Piper would be probably the worst outing of my career to that point, and since then, I haven't had too many that I'd rate lower.

Not because he couldn't work; he certainly could. Or because he was a jerk out of the ring; far from it, as he was very nice. And not because we didn't click between the ropes; we did.

At least, considering the circumstances.

Up against him in Florence, South Carolina, early in 1983, I was trying to get the fans on my side. He was looking to get them against him, although that would come as much from his mic mugging than in-ring work.

Unfortunately, Mother Nature had decided to take us on in her own personal handicap match. By drenching us in a torrential downpour, she was winning. He and I slipped all over the place, too awkward to hardly move, let alone leave our feet. Some things you just can't prepare for at all.

But we'd make up for it a few years later. In the midst of a long-overdue comeback and babyface push, and a feud against Rick Rude in the WWF, he made short work of me at a 1989 TV taping.

Not long after my Piper debacle, there was a special show that we taped one day in Savannah. It was more of an exhibition for our Japanese population, as we had several visitors from that area, and the show was being broadcast to another continent.

Ric Flair was on the show. Chavo Guerrero was there.

And so was I. Not only on the program, but the opener. The one to get everybody in the mood to carry all the way through to the main event.

And my opponent? Terry Funk. Ironically enough, even then in 1983, people were sadly accepting that the Funker was just about finished. After almost two decades in the business and enough titles to cover an arena floor, it was time for him to move on from the business.

Yes, he destroyed me that night. A few months later, his spectacular "Forever!" retirement speech was a legendary end to a legendary career.

It lasted a year, maybe. Three decades and even more retirements later, he was still stepping in and out of the ring. Even when Terry died in August 2023, many people still probably couldn't accept the fact that his career would be over.

Now for the larger memory.

This was going to be a moment that no one would forget. Not just because we knew it would be a huge success, but because it had never really been tried before. If it worked, it could create a whole new market for the business.

Moving from house shows to TV tapings was a monumental moment in wrestling. People had disbelieved in it when I had begun, but now it was commonplace. Not a big deal anymore.

This, however, would be something else.

Would people be willing to get up and leave home just to see a wrestling show, and not even a live, in-person one? Would they be willing to sit in a crowded bar or some other such place for a show?

Maybe. Maybe, if they knew they were getting more than their money's worth. If fans could believe that this show would be something special, that it would be different, hopefully beyond what they were used to seeing on weekly television, and then have their hopes realized, they might come back again. They might spend a few extra bucks if we could make it worth it.

A show that would not be available on regular TV, but on the closed circuits. I'm not talking about pay-per-view, which would soon allow fans to bring these special shows into their homes. This was about broadcasting the show to special places. A bar, a theater, all sorts of public spots.

Making It to Starrcade

By the early 1980s, the name Ric Flair was already becoming household in the wrestling world. This guy had talent, he had charisma, he was willing to work every single night. This guy might just emerge far enough to be the face of a company for a long time.

He'd gotten a trial title run in late 1981, and it had worked. Well, eventually—fans hadn't quickly taken to the new guy with the belt, and hesitated about handing him their time and his bosses their money. But the company had enough foresight to give him some time with the championship, and he and it had gotten over.

People were coming to see him at shows, hoping that they'd be lucky enough to see *the* show where the bad guy finally lost. It wasn't that Flair was particularly physically intimidating—certainly not like the comic book-type supermen that would soon inhabit the WWF—it was that he would do anything to win. Lie, cheat, steal, even backstab his own friends, as long as he walked out with the title.

Could someone, anyone, knock him off? Ironically, Flair actually lost the title three separate times before his first reign officially ended. Dusty Rhodes, whom Flair had beaten for the belt, put on a mask as the Midnight Rider and won in February 1982, only to find out that the facially hidden were ineligible to hold the belt (one of those rules that promotions sometimes invent to move a storyline forward). On worldwide tours, Flair dropped the belt to both Jack Verano and Carlos Colon, but, as the changes occurred outside of America, no one needed to admit it.

Harley Race finally grabbed the belt for a then-record seventh time in June 1983, but everyone knew it was coming back to Flair very soon. The NWA had to make this something special.

And they were going to call it *Starrcade*. Two years before *Wrestlemania*, the NWA took the first steps toward putting wrestling on pay TV.

I was there. In front of a sellout Greensboro Coliseum, I was there. I don't even remember if I worked a dark match or who I worked against. But I can remember occasionally glancing out from behind the curtain and knowing that this night was something special. Whether it was the Briscos battling the Youngbloods with my old WWWF foe Angelo Mosca reffing things, or Greg Valentine and Roddy Piper beating the hell out of one another in a dog collar match, I knew this night was going to be a supercard, even if that word hadn't become part of wrestling jargon just yet.

At the end of the evening, Flair managed to slip past Race for the title (the show being sub-named "A Flair for the Gold" might have given things away early) in a steel cage. He was far from a full-blown face, but had proven that he could get over with the fans either way, and the Coliseum almost blew apart.

And I was there again. Me and a few other babyfaces had been sent to the ring to parade Flair around, the belt above his head and the fans' cheers in all our ears. Clearly, we were as excited as he was.

Maybe, obviously, I wasn't actually main-eventing one of the most notable moments in wrestling history. But to be right in the ring, and the spotlight, at its conclusion was the next best thing.

And it would have to be—because my NWA time was about to end as well.

Losing Job, Matches. Finding Success, Love

I'd always been a huge fan of Dusty Rhodes. As a fan in Florida, I'd seen him reach iconic levels in the company. He'd been a cornerstone of Florida Championship Wrestling. By the time of *Starrcade*, he'd already won the NWA title twice, and would do so again a few years later. Now he had the chance to book out the territory.

When a new booker takes over at a wrestling promotion, there's always some major changes. Everyone has, to a degree, a different idea of what makes an effective drawing card. Almost every booker changes the focus of the shows. More or fewer interviews. An increase in high flying, or in amateur-style mat action. More faces go over. More heels win. Higher paychecks. Slashed remuneration.

Losing Job, Matches. Finding Success, Love

You do what you can to adapt to new leadership. It's part of the "team player" mindset that wrestlers carry, the ones that stick around. Unless you carry some serious backstage weight, you'll be following orders for most of your career. That's OK—the people that give the orders are probably from a place of previous success. What they are doing has worked for them elsewhere in the past, and they believe that it'll work here. Sometimes they're right, sometimes not. You just hope you don't have to change too much for the new style.

Mainly, though, it's about who gets pushed and who doesn't. Not just who can carry the load, but who can carry the type of load the new booker sees.

Dusty's booking had long been pretty effective in the past, and I figured that, with the track record I'd established here and elsewhere, he'd find a place for me.

That didn't happen. Not long after *Starrcade*, I walked into his office, and he had everything but a notarized pink slip right there waiting for me. It was obvious that Barry Horowitz had never really been a part of Dusty Rhodes' future.

Well, of course I hadn't wanted that. But I still thought that he could help me out. With his legendary status down in Florida, one quick phone call, recommendation included, could have gotten me some quick work back down near Disney World.

Let's just say, he didn't accommodate me. Now I was out of the big leagues.

I was sitting at home, pondering my future in the business, when a few things dawned on me.

First off, I needed a place to work. Fortunately, I got lucky there too.

During my past in Florida, I'd traveled a *lot* with Jay Youngblood. He knew he could count on me to do my job to the best of my abilities. He, along with fellow common companion Ricky Steamboat, would help me get hired back there.

I called Jay and stated my case, and he put some wheels in motion. Quickly, work got back to Eddie and Mike Graham, who were running the joint, that I was a free agent, and they signed me. I'd been out of a job for less than a month.

But something about my character needed to change as well.

Wrestling Is My Gimmick

I'd long been the plucky good guy, the one who tries and tries and tries and usually ends up falling just short. Just when fans thought I'd actually come out on top, my opponent would get, and occasionally steal, the final break, and I'd go down again.

Maybe I could try the other route, a little farther. After years and years of working and traveling with heels, maybe I could actually step all the way into that role. I'd been sort of heel-ish at times in my career, mainly when I was acting as an enhancer to the babyface community. Now I could do a little bit more. The deeper I could show of the character, the more likely the fans would be to get behind, or heavily against, me in the ring. Rather than the superficiality of a guy who gets to do one match at a time for a few minutes, no interviews or anything to back it up, maybe Barry Horowitz could find a little substance.

Following the tradition of every villain from Satan to General Zod, I added one of the oldest physical signs of evil: a beard! Now people could look and see who I was out for.

Now there was the matter of my name. Michael Hayes was still doing the booking, and he decided my new moniker should be *Jack Hart*. I loved the change, as Jack Brisco had long been one of my favorites, and now I was giving him a special tribute.

I started out in Florida just as I had before. I was working with Mike Davis, Hector Guerrero (Chavo Sr. and Eddie's brother) and Mike Golden. Per usual, I was always losing.

But I wasn't displaying that self-confidence and courage I always had. Now I was cowering at times from the tough good guy. Loudly letting the fans know that I deserved more respect than they were giving me. Hitting from behind, poking in the eye, letting the rules fall by the wayside.

And tossing sportsmanship out the door after the match. Where I'd sometimes shaken my opponent's hand or even hugged him before leaving in the past, now I'd kick and yell and smack the mat and turnbuckles.

Fans started to notice. They weren't sure how to react at first, and, per usual in the wrestling business, they responded with anger. Booing like crazy. What were they going to say? "Wow, Barry's suddenly turned into a jerk, so let's bring him back with kindness and apologies"? Yeah, wrestling fans aren't like that.

Losing Job, Matches. Finding Success, Love

Before long, I was getting booed as much as my opponents were getting cheered. People didn't just want to see the faces win; they actually hoped to see me lose, and probably take a good beating in the bargain, one they hoped I wouldn't come back from.

The bookers saw and heard this, and ran with it. They were starting to see me for more than just my work ethic. Fans kept coming to see me go down. Before long, graphics were being shown on the wall and screens nearby to let everyone know just how low my winning percentage was. Fans could count up one loss after another after another. This went on for about a year, and I don't think a person's ever gotten as over with such a negative record than myself.

And I got some more exposure. Gordon Solie would be doing an interview or some commentary after my matches, and I'd sudden roar onto the set and crash hell out of his conversation. I'd be boisterous as hell, roaring at him that my breaks always happened to be a centimeter out of reach, and demanding why everyone else got so much that they wanted, while I just never did!

One day, in the midst of one of my rants, someone came out from backstage and handed me a card.

"I can make you a winner," he snidely promised.

Why not? I'd gone as far as I could go by myself. Other people had managers. Maybe this guy could help me out.

His real name was William Moody. His managerial name was Percy Pringle. Another future Hall of Famer just starting out.

Giving a performer a manager is one of the biggest signs that a promotion has faith in you. Managers don't work free, and can't be used for every single wrestler, and giving a manager too many charges can water down his impact. He's there to expand your personality with his own.

And Pringle did that. Not just for me, but for the rest of the people in his personal Pringle Dynasty. I'm talking Rick Rude. I'm discussing the Grappler and Rip Oliver, who I'd just missed getting to work with when my trip to Portland hadn't worked out.

He could talk, and we could talk. Sometimes the entire Dynasty would be standing together while one of us did an interview, and all I'd have to do is flex a little and look intimidating to get the fans upset at me. I was getting somewhere, and it was like driving a dirty Studebaker into the show and coming out in a squeaky-clean Ferrari.

Soon, I was put in a program with Pez Whatley, whose wrestling career at the University of Tennessee at Chattanooga had been significantly more successful than my own collegiate jaunt.

Now, in one of my first interviews directed at an individual, I didn't get any scripting or advice. They just told me a few words they wanted me to include.

"I'm going to outwrestle you!" I promised Whatley. "I'm going to destroy you! I'm going to stretch him until he's taller than Blackjack Mulligan!" Considering Mulligan was almost seven feet tall (even above his son, Barry Windham), that would be, quite literally, a tall order.

Typical for a heel, I lost the match. Eventually, though, the promoters realized that Jack Hart would never get all the way over with the fans if he didn't win somewhere.

At the next TV taping, I managed to slip past Leo Von Stroheim with a simple inside cradle. But then I really started firing up the heat. I had started to wear a black glove during my matches, and telling everyone it was a good luck charm, or maybe just made me look more intimidating.

I'd be in a match, and usually getting a beating. Then the ref would get hit or distracted, and Percy would slip me something to hide in my glove. Something small, but exceedingly dense and heavy. The babyface would turn around or stand up, only to feel my glove smashing into his head or face. He'd be out for the count. I'd pull out the object, toss it back to Percy, and lay across my opponent for the pin. The fans would yell and scream, and I'd act like I had no idea what they were upset about. Sure, the ref could check my glove. There was nothing in it and never had been! How dare anyone suggest otherwise?

But, as I was looking for a way to set a local irritation record in character, something else was going on for Barry Horowitz right around then.

I'd first gotten married right out of college. I was just old enough to vote, and hardly mature enough for this sort of thing, but nobody was going to tell me that. Not my friends, my father, everyone else who could find a diplomatic way to say, "What are you, crazy?" I knew this was love, and I knew it was going to last forever.

It didn't. Thank God. In about two years, I was back to being single. I wasn't sure if I'd ever try that again, but I vowed I'd think a hell of a lot more about it beforehand if I did.

As I did almost every weekend, I was relaxing at the beach, resting up for my match that very night at the Eddie Graham Sports Complex. I decided to step off the sand and take a dip in a nearby pool. But I hadn't counted on a bunch of kids following me over, taking a special chance to harass the guy they'd seen in the ring and on TV lately.

Yes, to them, I was still Jack Hart, and I was a bad guy. Real bad. They were going to let me know.

One of the leaders, I remember, had a *real* mouth. I'd been around dozens of adult fans that didn't spew out the blue streak he did.

Basically, I told him, as I did all of them, to buzz off. That's about as much as you can say to kids and still maintain a heelish persona.

The kids went running over to a few women sitting near the pool, tattling on the mean wrestler that had just scared them. The loudest one's mom called me over.

"Hey," she reprimanded. "That's my son."

OK. What now? Could I try to chat with her after that kind of impression? Should I try to make a move and still try to balance Jack the bad guy with Barry the real guy?

I did. We got to talking.

"I'm wrestling tonight," I finally told the lady I'd just known as Diane. "I gotta go." I asked to take her out sometime.

"You have to call me," she said, handing me her number, written on one of the tiniest pieces of paper I'd ever seen.

And wouldn't you know? I lost it. Couldn't find it anywhere. Looks like I was missing out on a new chance in my love life.

Fortunately, my mother happened upon it in the condo we were staying at. I counted my blessings. Diane and I got to talking more. Hanging out more.

After rushing into my first marriage like a train with its brakes cut, I went very slowly here. She didn't even know that my name

Wrestling Is My Gimmick

wasn't Jack Hart for about four or five months (even at appearances today, people still recognize me as him). I wanted to make sure this was going to end right.

On Valentine's Day of 1986, we decided we'd waited long enough, and exchanged vows at an altar. Nearly four decades later, we're still going pretty strong.

Oh, that kid who couldn't wait to badmouth me back at the pool? Michael's turned into one hell of a stepson.

By the way, like every wrestler, I'm always getting asked about the worst injury of my wrestling career. Well, I've got an answer—and it's not what you're going to expect. See, it happened right around that time and far from the ring.

Once a month, myself, along with the rest of Florida's top stars, would fly down to the Bahamas. Not because the promotion had a big enough heart to give us a weekend to lie around in the sun and chill at a luxurious hotel, but to wrestle. Usually, the guys from down there would be the faces, and we'd be the ones putting them over.

A few days before such a trip, I'd been out swimming. Not long after, my ear had started to ache. Hoping there was just a bit of extra water in my ear, I'd ignored it, hoping it would just go away. But then it got worse. And worse. And worse. Whatever bacteria had found its way inside my eardrum; it was hanging out, multiplying, and waging all-out war on its surroundings.

I was afraid of even doing anything about it, because any sort of physical contact caused me to almost scream in pain. Flying from Florida to the Bahamas is only about an hour, but when your ear is already roaring from the inside out, it's going to seem like a day.

I explained to Héctor Guerrero, my opponent for the trip, what had happened. Or at least, I tried to; my ear had swollen so far shut that I don't think I could have heard a heavy metal band with a front row seat.

And it got worse in the ring. Even a headlock caused as much pain as I'd ever felt in my life. The fans might have thought I was doing one hell of job selling his strength and moves. For one of the only times in my career, I wasn't selling. I actually did hurt like hell, and I just wanted to finish this and get the hell out.

Finally, I had to get it lanced and drained. My hearing came back, I felt like someone had dumped some kind of healing potion down the side of my head, and that I'd just lost a few dozen pounds out of my skull.

If I had to name anything even remotely close to that sort of pain from throughout my career, I'd say maybe the headaches I've gotten from a concussion or three. But that's as bad as I've ever felt that I can pinpoint.

Near Death, a Few Times

Of course, there was the time that my life was basically saved on a plane.

On a WCW trip, I was sitting in coach, and I remember being starved out of my mind. As in, not worrying too much about the rules of kosher gobbling!

I was wolfing down something or other. It might have been a bun, a bagel, something that was thick and grainy. I tossed it down the hatch and didn't waste time chewing.

And almost paid for it with everything.

Whatever it was, it must have enjoyed the feeling of my throat, because it was staying there. The wind trying to get up the pipes was disrupted.

I tried to swallow. Then again. It didn't work. I tried smashing myself in the stomach, sort of a self–Heimlich from the front. Nope. It wasn't moving.

As anxiety and panic became the only things I could feel, I lunged forward and smashed right into Bobby Eaton's seat. He hardly noticed at first, but then I tried to grab his soda.

That got his attention, first because I don't partake in that kind of cuisine. Then he saw what was happening, and almost dumped the drink down my throat for me.

Wrestling Is My Gimmick

It worked. I thanked him almost every time I saw him before his too-soon death in 2021. Sometimes I wonder what would have happened if he hadn't been there, or if he didn't happen to have a soda nearby.

Another trip down to the Bahamas gave me one of the most memorable moments of my career, but sure as hell not in a good way.

Wrestling fans in that area took their sport, shall we say, much more seriously than Americans. As rowdy as Old Glory's audiences can be, they pretty much yell, scream, cheer, boo, cuss, wave their signs, and that's about it. They know that there's a difference between Barry Horowitz the person and Barry Horowitz the wrestler, although they put that aside for the hours it takes to watch a wrestling show. At least, they do that if we've done our job.

Elsewhere, that's not always the case. Sometimes the line between wrestling and reality gets forgotten. Sometimes it gets erased, and willfully so. Not just with the audiences, but backstage as well. Any fan of wrestling history is familiar with the watershed example of this: the Bruiser Brody tragedy in Puerto Rico in July 1988, when Brody was killed backstage at a wrestling show over an in-ring matter.

I've wrestled down there too, and I've never seen or been around anything like that, but Puerto Rican fans have personally threatened me, rushed me, chased me and my colleagues in and out of the building. They've also blasted us with one identified flying object after another, mainly rocks and other shit that could seriously injure us or worse if the aim and velocity were right. The wrong match could turn them into stampeding savages.

That happened in the Bahamas as well. Probably more than once, but this is the one that sticks out, and you'll see the irony in those words momentarily.

I was battling Tyree Pride, and I knew I would lose. I was a champion in Florida, but I could come down here, do a job for him, and still go back with my belt. No one would mind, and the fans at the islands would be thrilled.

Pride was a Florida native, and he'd even win a few titles there eventually, but he was called the Pride of the Caribbean for a reason. They loved him down there, and to have some interloper show up and beat their boy would be taken personally. Too personally. Maybe dangerously personally.

The only question would be if he'd pin me or win by disqualification. But we could certainly have one hell of a match beforehand.

And we did, just like we always did. Tyree was always fun to work with.

He'd knocked me around for a while at the start of the match, but I, in typical heel style, had used a slew of foul tactics to take down the hero. I had him on the mat, and I was on fire. Yes, Bahamaniacs—your guy was going down tonight, and I was going to laugh in your faces and then hop on a plane and get the hell out of there before you'd have a chance to get revenge—any kind of revenge.

As he attempted to raise himself off the mat, I raised my arms in true winner style, and stepped forward for some more major moves.

Then I felt it. A huge pain in my back. I'm not talking about a pulled muscle, or even a torn one. I'd felt those, or something like them, before. This was something else, and I thought for a moment that I'd actually been shot or stabbed. Should I jump out of the ring and get to an ambulance? Maybe kick the living shit out of the SOB that did it, as long as I could stay conscious? Was it about to happen again, seconds later, and would the next wound be even more, shall we say, accurate? Was this going to be it for my wrestling career, or even my life?

I reached behind me, and found the object in my back. It was an umbrella. I had an umbrella stuck in my lower left shoulder.

Yes, someone had managed to finagle an umbrella into the building, then get close enough to the ring to hurl it at me—and it had stuck.

As I turned all the way around, it fell out and landed on the mat. As I stared at it, I wasn't sure what to think. I guess I was glad it wasn't a machete or a bullet. But if that thing could hit me—and it could have done a hell of a lot more damage if it had hit somewhere other than my back—something else could at any moment. I'd never felt totally safe wrestling in the Bahamas, as no one from the Florida promotion did, but this was too much.

And it was enough for me that night. I dove to the ground, yanked Tyree atop me, and almost shouted at the ref to count me down. He did, and we hastened straight back to the dressing room.

Tyree thought it was pretty cool. He'd actually been through this sort of thing in the past, the fans contributing a little more than cheers. It was just one more example of how much people loved him. After a while, I could laugh about it myself.

But it would be a while before I'd be back down there. Would someone be bringing a Magnum next time? If they could get an umbrella in there, let alone throw it at me, and, as far as I knew, get away with doing so, a gun would hardly be an issue. I'd been down to Puerto Rico, and fans had stampeded there too. Every American wrestler who'd wrestled there was familiar with Bruiser Brody's tragic murder—and subsequent denial of justice to his family when his killer was acquitted—and people still worry about that stuff today. You just can't help it.

Taking the Florida Title

From the Disney World area and back again, I was battling everyone from my old friend Adrian Street to Barry Windham for Championship Wrestling in Florida. Barry had recently held the company title, as had Superstar Billy Graham.

Early in June 1985, Hercules Hernandez, on his way to the WWF a few months later, worked one hell of a program with Wahoo McDaniel, late in a career that had taken him through the WWWF, NWA, AWA, and back and forth to Florida a few times.

Just after Hercules took the title from Hector Guerrero on the last day of June, he and McDaniel's feud spilled out of the ring. Switching the squared circle for the dressing room, the veteran and the newbie went fist to fist, battling it out with just their co-workers as an audience.

It didn't last long—and, because of it, neither did Hercules' time with the company. This newbie had just slapped himself as a troublemaker with an attitude, and that's not how anyone ever wants to begin in this business. No way was a fellow with McDaniel's pedigree going to get shipped out in favor of the unproven.

Taking the Florida Title

Now it was time for wrestling to do what it always does with titles suddenly become vacant: put together a round-robin tournament. Who would be next in line?

Not long after the company became champion-less, I walked into the University of Tampa's Spartan Sports Center. That was familiar stomping ground (literally!) for me, and I glanced over the board for the evening's show.

The tournament was set. I had a feeling I might make it somewhere that night, but not all the way. Hector might be getting the title back. Maybe Mike Graham; we were, after all, in his hometown.

Either way, I was amazed at the size of the card. Almost twenty matches in one night! And this was on a Tuesday! Even in the summertime, that's a long time to ask an audience to sit through on a weeknight. *Wrestlemania IV*'s tournament a few years later was about that long, but those guys were working all day on a Sunday, on pay-per-view! We'd be here a while.

Nobody told me too much as the night started, only that I'd get rolling with a win over Coco Samoa, who the company had tried to recreate as the next version of Jimmy Snuka. I liked Coco well enough, but that wasn't going to happen. Some guys just can't be copied.

As fellow competitors like Rick Rude, Billy Jack Haynes, and even Wahoo himself went into tournament battle and were eliminated, I soon came out ahead of Hector.

Now it was down to me and Mike. This was already a very special moment for me. It's great when you get to work with those who helped you get started in front of the public.

Very few people thought I would win. Hercules had been a villain, and now it was time for a good guy to run the show. Mike had held the title once before, but it had been years ago, and not for very long.

He and I went at it for a while, me taking every opportunity to cheat my way to victory and Percy there to help me out. I got booed, he got cheered, everything was going fine.

I launched him into the turnbuckle, and went charging in to squash him. It's a move that works about .00001 percent of the time in wrestling, and it sure as hell didn't here.

He lurched out of the way, and I splattered into the corner. Then he rolled me up, and things looked to be over.

After spending my first years in wrestling bouncing from one federation to another, I finally got my first stronghold in Championship Wrestling from Florida in 1984.

But then I reversed back, and suddenly he was on his back. The ref counted one, then two, and it looked like he was going to kick out.

Wrong. As the official raised his hand to strike the mat the third time, I grabbed hold of Mike's tights. He felt it, the fans saw it, everybody but the ref knew what was going on.

Before anyone knew it, he smacked the mat the third time. I was the champ.

No one could believe it, least of all me. Dusty Rhodes had held this title a whopping twelve times, along with Windham, Brian Blair, Jack Brisco, and so many other top-tier guys, and now Barry Horowitz's name (or at least Jack Hart's) was right there along with them. Up until that very afternoon, I had no idea my first major singles title was coming along.

Still, it wasn't a feel-good moment for anyone. Well, except for me and Percy. The hard worker finally coming out on top is a heartwarming tale that wrestling had told before that moment, and has many times since.

But not now. I was, after all, a hardcore heel.

I charged out of the ring and into Percy's arms, as a stunned Mike tried to comprehend what had just happened. Rather than celebrating with the fans, we laughed in their faces.

And they went insane. They were screaming and cussing at us, throwing things, spitting on us. But Percy and I had come out ahead of all these mean, mean naysayers, and now we were on top.

Man, if only I had grown that beard a few years before! What a difference a few facial hairs made!

> **Joe Malenko:** Barry's title was the ultimate compliment to me, my dad, my brother. The ultimate outcome that's desired by everybody for your school is that you create an opportunity for someone to get into the business and earn a living.

As I stumbled back to the dressing room, I did want to celebrate. Almost got emotional. It was tough to be a heel in a moment like that. It meant a tremendous amount to me, and I would have liked to share it with the fans and everyone else. But because Jack Hart was a villainous backstabber, I couldn't be a nice guy.

My co-workers did their best, even Mike. In the dressing room, I got congratulations from everyone there. The other wrestlers, the promoters, everyone took the time to say way to go.

And then tragedy struck.

My "First" Goodbye

He'd only been in the business a few years longer than me, but Jay Youngblood had already helped me as much as anyone, and about as much as one person ever has since.

I'd first met him in Charlotte, freelancing for Mid–Atlantic Championship Wrestling under Jim Crockett, and Jay'd gone out of his way to keep me booked around there, even when he and future Hall of Famer Rick Steamboat were winning a multitude of tag titles. I used to travel with him, alongside Rufus R. Jones, Jimmy Valiant, and so many other veterans, and I got a Harvard-level education about the business during those trips. Coaching techniques, interview tips, enough road stories to fill a library. I was in my early 20s with very little in my life aside from wrestling, and these guys were more than enough to fill those voids as we made our way from show to show.

During the 1970s, Jay's dad Ricky had been one of the top draws in the South, along with stints in every major federation. Jay gave me a jacket his dad had worn to rings all over Texas and Mexico, and I'd carry it down aisles for years.

Then he'd helped me get booked in Florida, where those road trips continued. Ironically enough, as much time as I spent with Jay behind steering wheels, I don't think I ever shared a ring with him.

Hey, maybe we would have someday. But that would get stolen from us.

Not surprisingly, my reign as the champ down in Florida wouldn't last too long.

The WWF had used its first *Wrestlemania* to break through on pay-per-view just a few months before, but I, along with so many others that September night in Tampa's Sun Dome, felt that Championship Wrestling of Florida's *Battle of the Belts* show might have been of a bit better quality, at least wrestling-wise. Nick Bockwinkel? Harley Race? Stan Hansen? The Road Warriors? Ric Flair in the main event? That would be anyone's supercard for anywhere in the 1980s.

And then there was my title defense against Kendall Windham. Ironically, we ended up getting more time than every *Wrestlemania* match except for the main event.

With Percy outside cheering me on, I dominated for much of the match, and, when that didn't work, I resorted to the same begging techniques that Flair himself would make legendary, along with the old reliable foreign object. But Kendall did the typical babyface comeback in the end, pinning me with a bodypress to take the belt.

Not long after, I was gearing up for a rematch. I had come out of the dressing room with the finish down pat, and was literally standing there behind the curtain, within a few moments of hitting the ring.

Then Percy stepped up to me—and the next few seconds would burn the bridge between us forever.

He informed me that Jay had just died. Yes, right then and there, he chose to break this to me.

OK, so there's never a *right* time to let someone know that his old friend is gone forever. But Percy had decided to give me this news mere seconds before I was to go perform. He could have told me later that night. Hell, he could have waited the fifteen or so minutes it would take to do the match and let me know as we were re-entering the dressing room. Even that would have been ever so slightly easier for me to handle. At least that way I'd get to go off and mourn, or flip out in emotion, or anything at all in a situation that no one can ever prep for.

No, Percy did none of that. As I was literally about to morph into Jack Hart, the hated heel, I'd just learned of one of the biggest tragedies of my life, and I'd have no time at all to grieve or even react, at least not right away.

I should have clocked him right then and there. I should have refused to go out. But I didn't. Don't ask me how, as I don't have a clue, but I still managed to go out there and have my match. But I'd despise that fucking moron for a very long time.

Less than two months after his thirtieth birthday, Jay had been wrestling in the South Pacific when explosive stomach pains sent him to the hospital. Too late, doctors found that his pancreas was bleeding, and, of course, many today are sure that this occurred during a match.

Maybe. Doesn't really matter anymore. His stomach and kidneys slowly went down. Then came the heart attacks. Then the coma. When he died, he'd been under for weeks. Obviously not something that would stay secret today.

Soon after that, Percy left. Not quite to become Paul Bearer, but to Texas and eventually the USWA, where'd he ironically manage Mark Calaway years before the two became one of the most infamous duos in WWF history. After the incident following Jay's death, I wasn't exactly sorry to see Percy go. Even when we'd both be part of the WWF and he was on the outside as I battled the Undertaker, I kept my distance from him.

But I ended up OK in Florida. I'd been watching Oliver Humperdink manage Buddy Roberts and Jerry Brown as the first Hollywood Blondes back in the 1970s. He and Mike had had a few run-ins in Florida in the past, and Oliver was coming back to re-light the fire. Now I'd have him in my corner, and he and I would be just as successful as I had been with Percy.

After dropping the title to Kendall, I got an extra gift by the end of the year. Frustrated about not being able to win the Florida title himself, Jessie Barr (whom WWF fans would soon see as Jimmy Jack Funk, a fake relative of Terry) stepped into a managerial role for one night as a close friend of his showed up to put on another special show for the fans.

His name? Ric Flair. His opponent? Me.

The winner? Take a guess. But Flair didn't squash me that night. It wasn't a long match, but he gave me enough token offense that I came across as a threat at times. Either way, while he headed back to the Carolinas or wherever to defend his title, I'd be able to show back up the next week in Florida and have the fans still believe I could make it back to the gold level.

I'd get close a few more times, but never all the way back. Windham, Rotundo, and others would pass it back and forth until the title ended in the summer of 1987.

That was about the time I got back to the WWF myself. But there was one stop to make beforehand.

Up to Tennessee

As my time in Florida started to wind down, someone I knew recommended I head a few states north and to the west.

Not too far. Just to Tennessee.

And my friend had a special assist for me: the phone number of none other than Jerry Jarrett. I'd heard of him, and I knew he'd been very successful with the Continental Wrestling Association, one of the hottest territories of the time.

But maybe *too* successful. Maybe this would end up like the time I'd looked to go to Portland. Jarrett's company had been *the* place to be in the Mid–South area for years, so he certainly wasn't low on "applicants." His son Jeff was just getting started, but he had Bill Dundee, Rocky Johnson (yeah, the Rock's daddy!), and, of course, Jerry Lawler. There might not be a place for a guy who had been out of the local area for a while.

I was a little leery. This might be too good to be true.

It wasn't. One quick phone call that consisted of him inviting me to come and compete and me saying yes without trying to sound desperate was about the extent of it. Now Jack Hart was heading up there.

Again, it wasn't for long. I was only there for about seven months. But just listen to the memories I took away.

First off, I got a new taste of gold. This time it was in the tag team sense. Alongside Chick Donovan, we scored the Southern Tag Team Title right in the middle of the legendary Memphis Coliseum. We did it by overtaking not just Johnson, but Soul Train Jones, who WWF fans would quickly meet as Virgil.

Wrestling Is My Gimmick

We had to give up the belts pretty soon when Chick got hurt, but our names were already in history's annals.

The next one was a personal change in me.

I'd taken to riding with Tojo Yamamoto, one of wrestling's hardest core heels since using his Japanese heritage to mock American audiences in the 1950s and '60s—as in, old enough to remember what his Axis homeland had done to Pearl Harbor (ironically, not only had Yamamoto been born in Hawaii, but had served in the Marines just after World War II). After holding dozens of tag team titles. Yamamoto was starting to move into managing and training.

But that's not the point of his inclusion here.

Up to that point for me, just over a quarter century on the earth, country music just drove me nuts. It came on the radio, I changed the station. Someone was listening to it in the dressing room, I walked outside. Someone used it for his entrance music, I worked *very* stiff with them that night (OK, maybe I just dreamt about that last one, but I sure as hell wanted to!).

But in Tojo's car, we listened to what he wanted to listen to. He was the veteran with the nice car; I was the greenhorn lucky to get a ride. You don't make demands in a situation like that.

And he loved country. Don't know why, don't think he ever really told me, except he just enjoyed it.

And eventually, I started to do so as well. Within about five months, I was hooked.

Now it's all I'm about. I don't hardly listen to anything else, even today. I might pump some Van Halen or something more adrenalin-inducing into my ears when I'm at the gym, but country is my thing. I'm all about the small-town country life, to the point that I'd like to move back to Nashville someday.

I'd even go roaring over the pop culture line from wrestling to country music right before the height of my WWF career. But we'll talk about that when we reach it.

Before that, though, one of the earliest rough moments of my career revolved around that very lyrical genre.

Flying from back to my then-home to Nashville from a WWF show in St. Louis in 1989, I was trying to take a nap in the air, never an easy thing for me. Just before my eyes started to close, I noticed a fellow a few seats down, flirting all over with one of the stewardesses.

He glanced at me. Then he double- and triple-took.

"My dad's a huge pro wrestling fan," he gushed, rushing up to me for a high-speed handshake. "Can you send him an 8 × 10?"

I couldn't believe he recognized me. I'd sure as hell identified him pretty fast. It was Joe Bonsall, one of the Oak Ridge Boys, who'd moved from gospel music to country and torn it up in the 1970s and '80s.

Aside from being one of millions to grab up their double-platinum album *Fancy Free* a few years ago (ironically enough, the group's next and last number-one hit, "No Matter How High," would arrive later that year), I was a huge fan of the country music talk show *Nashville Now*, which filmed at Opryland, close enough to Nashville that I'd been to a few tapings. Bonsall wasn't the regular host (that was late great Ralph Emery, who'd help twang country music into the national spotlight with the series *Pop! Goes the Country* in the 1970s before taking over *Nashville*), but he'd subbed in from time to time.

"I'll tell you what," Bonsall informed me after hearing this. "You get this picture out to my dad, and the next time I host, I *will* get you on. Not in the audience—I'll get you on for an interview."

Who knew where that could lead? As lucrative as wrestling was becoming, mainstream media was still iffy about giving the business too much coverage. Major stars like Hulk Hogan and André the Giant had shown up on David Letterman's set, itself the very site of the legendary 1982 Jerry Lawler–Andy Kaufman pseudo-brawl, but this could be huge for the WWF. And, maybe a little selfishly, for me as an individual performer. Lord knows I'd have some great stories to tell about my experiences between the ropes, as well as with Bonsall's type of music.

Yes, this could be a landmark. Needless to say, I got that picture out to his dad a few nanoseconds after that plane hit the ground. As much as I thought of Emery on that show, I couldn't wait for him to be absent.

Bonsall would go on to host that show at least two more times that I know of. And each time, I heard the same thing.

Wrestling Is My Gimmick

Nothing.

No phone calls, no other contact, nothing whatsoever. Not a call to come on the show. Not an apology to say he couldn't hold up his end, even for reasons out of his control. Not a thing.

Just a broken word from a guy whose music I'd enjoyed for so long. Even today, if I hear one of his band's songs on the radio, I turn it off. If he's on TV, I can hardly resist the urge to put my foot through it.

That's always been a serious pet peeve of mine. I've always tried to fulfill my end of the bargains I set, which is part of the reason why I still get calls for signings and appearances decades later. But on the few, hopefully *very* few instances when life drops an obstacle in front of me and I can't back up my promise, I call. I apologize. I try to make up for it in the future. I don't think that's anything special, but sometimes I wish it was more common.

In Tennessee, I even scored a new manager. Ironically, he'd just come from Florida himself, although I hadn't been around him. He was backing up a giant masked muscular mastodon named Lord Humongous at that point, although it wouldn't be long before the Lord ripped off his mask and headed to the NWA in the persona of Sid Vicious.

And the manager in question would follow him, although in a different context.

That was the first time I ever met Paul Heyman, who would go on to wrestling worldwide infamy as Paul E. Dangerously, first as a hardcore NWA/WCW motormouth manager, then the creator of Extreme Championship Wrestling, and finally to the WWE.

But for now, and for the rest of my Tennessee tenure, the youngster adorned with glasses and tresses of long hair, but without his soon-to-be-trademark cell phone, was leading me.

What a jokester he was. Great sense of humor. Not the most self-confident type, but, hell, there he was surrounded by a bunch of fellows who'd been around the business and didn't like punks who ran their mouth. That's a rank that only comes when you earn it. I could tell he wanted to be a booker someday, and he had some good storyline ideas, but, again, you keep those to yourself when you're that new to the business. An idea like that can seem 300 IQ brilliance when it comes from a seasoned, respected pro is often written off as nosy and overstepping for the unproven.

But as green as he was, Paul was a good manager. He didn't have the heel presence that Percy or Oliver had, but, again, they'd gotten it mainly from experience. Before long, he'd have that in abundance.

And he could sure as hell talk for me. Not as much as he would be doing in the coming years, but both before and behind the camera. That was always a strong benefit for me.

Then there's another memory that's gone forever. As my time there wound down, I was in a tag match in Evansville against Bill Dundee, who'd been wrestling since I was in elementary school, and his Australian friend George Barnes. With me on the mat and just about out, and not just in the selling sense, Barnes launched off the top rope.

I'm not sure if he intended to land on my chest or where, but he went slightly higher, and smashed me right in the head. Now I didn't have to sell being knocked out. As far as I would know, the next few minutes just didn't exist.

I was OK. I didn't have a concussion. George is a great guy. He was apologizing up and down after the match, and he called me all the time to check on me while I was at home recuperating.

Along with that, a new call name, and it snapped me out of my fog *very* quickly. A few years before, he and Lawler had been engaged in one of the biggest feuds in CWA history. He'd managed Chick, the Iron Sheik, Kevin Sullivan, Ken Patera, and others (including a fellow named Hogan) against Lawler before heading to the WWF in 1985. Now he was extending a similar invitation to me.

It was Jimmy Hart.

Up to the World

"They want to bring you back," Jimmy told me of the WWF. "Bret Hart's there."

Wrestling Is My Gimmick

I was excited. Maybe I'd be the next member of the Hart Foundation! Bret and his brother-in-law Jim Neidhart had just won the titles from the British Bulldogs, and I knew I could fit right in, just as I had with the Pringle Dynasty. Ricky Steamboat had taken the Intercontinental strap from Randy Savage, and, with Hogan on top, the WWF never liked to have both champions on the babyface side. What a splash it would be to have Steamboat tear me apart, only to have Bret and Jim run in and coldcock him behind the ref's back, leading me to get the pin! One stable holding two of the top titles would have gotten us over fast, and Steamboat and I could have made magic doing a long program together. After getting to know me like he had back in Florida, I think he would have been OK with it.

Well, that wasn't up to Jimmy. But he didn't get my hopes up either.

"I don't know what they're going to do with you," he admitted. "Just call Pat Patterson."

I did, and got some good news and bad news. Bad news, I wasn't going to be working with the Hart family. The title picture wasn't within reach for me, and didn't appear to be a priority for those that make the decisions.

"It's like this," Patterson spelled out to me. "You're not going to be a main-eventer. But you'll be working every night ... and making triple what you are now. Vince is going to want you to go back to your real name, too."

I couldn't pass that up. Five years before, I might have chosen high rankings and title reigns over a heavy paycheck, but with a family to worry about, it wasn't even a question. I had to do what was right for more than just me.

Oh, and I didn't just make triple what I'd been pulling in down in Tennessee. It was much more.

I arrived in Glens Falls, New York, fully expecting to rush right into a program with local alumnus Jim Duggan, one of Glens Falls' claims to fame. That didn't happen, but I got one hell of a compensatory gift instead.

Jake "The Snake" Roberts. What an experience.

What about him has not been said or written or thought or

anything else, good or bad? For me, as with most people I've met in my career, it's much more good, both in the ring and (mostly) in the locker room.

Jake helped me learn some new stuff, like how to do a leglock better, or protecting myself when I got slammed. When a huge muscular guy picks you up and fires you onto your back, even onto a soft surface from a few feet up, you're pretty vulnerable. Your hips, arms, shoulders, and especially spine take a hell of a hit, and that's just from the outside.

You're usually coming down on your lower back, so your kidneys can get hit pretty hard too. Almost crying while you're peeing blood isn't a really fun pastime. Jake taught me a few things about how to lessen the blows to an area that's hard to protect.

OK, to walk away from this without mentioning the personal issues that have dogged him for decades would be unprofessional. Many people like to focus on the mistakes he's made, usually to climb up on a pedestal and get a few extra people to read their web sites and books, but that's not me. I don't have hardly any of that information, and if I did, I wouldn't share it anyway. Jake was a great guy to me, and I don't have a reason to badmouth him, like way too many others have done.

Once in a while (a *very* great while, and not for very long), he and maybe a few others would invite me out for a drink here and there. Nobody even talked to me about doing drugs, because they knew it would be a waste of time and breath. But hitting the bar once in a while, most guys did that. Nobody saw much wrong with rewarding a hard day's work with a few cold ones.

And I don't either and didn't then. I'd never fault the friends of mine, the colleagues in the business who toss one, or more than one, back now and then. A beer here and there doesn't make one a drunk by any means, and I'd be right up there on that pedestal if I expressed an issue with it. Giving other people grief about a habit like that will turn you into a self-righteous locker room pariah real fast, and that's the last thing I am or would ever want to be. I've known some guys who did that, and I found them just as irritating as those who bothered others to drink.

I just didn't indulge myself. I'd get asked quite a bit, at least at

Wrestling Is My Gimmick

first, and I'd always beg off. I was too tired. I had a big match the next day. Something was hurting.

Sometimes I'd just say no. Other times, I *might* have said I'd be there, and then just not shown up. Not proud of that.

And the women were there too. I'm not talking about the valets, like Miss Elizabeth, who made Randy Savage the envy of millions of jealous guys for years. I mean the fans, the ones that wanted to get an autograph, or maybe something more. It would be a while before the term "ring rats" would come into common jargon, but they were there.

But I was busy. Busy trying to find a new AT&T calling card to call my wife every night. Busy trying to find a pay phone that worked to ask how her day had gone. Busy trying to get back to my room to call before she went to bed. That was the way I always was. I was hanging out with guys who also found a reason not to indulge in the heavy life, like my close friends, the team of Demolition (Bob Backlund had been that way too, and he had made my first go-round in the WWF a heck of a lot easier sometimes).

Jake was one of the guys I worked with for my first year back in the WWF. The other was Koko B. Ware. That was, shall we say, a bit different.

Look, in the personal sense, he's an OK guy. But one of the biggest aspects of great workers is that they are not limited. They can work around their opponents' injuries and other limitations. Even when they're working with an enhancement talent and are on offense for ninety-eight percent of the match, they don't have to do the same thing every day. A guy who does the identical things every time he's working might be lazy or unmotivated, or he might just be untalented. The best workers don't make it all about themselves, and say, "You do what you have to do to make me look good, and tough shit if you get hurt." Guys like Lex Luger, the Ultimate Warrior, and a few others just had a punch, a kick, a clothesline, and that's about it. It's hard to work with and around people like that.

Unfortunately, that's sort of what it was like to work with Koko. He had plenty of talent and ability, but when it came time to end a match, things got problematic. His brainbuster finisher involved him picking you up like he was going to suplex you, then instead dropping you straight down on your head.

Up to the World

Those types of moves are tough and scary for anyone, giving or receiving, which is why you don't see the piledriver or its variants too often anymore. But a guy like the Undertaker, whose tombstone was legendary, is a bit more trustworthy with it, mainly because he was tall and strong enough to keep you from the mat.

With Koko, that wasn't the case. In the wrestling community, he wasn't one of the biggest or strongest. He'd often be picking up guys taller and heavier than him. Letting a guy that's significantly shorter and lighter than you pick you up is nerve-wracking to begin with. Trusting that he'll be able to protect you when dropping you straight down is almost impossible.

Yes, he usually did. For the most part, I'd come out of the matches OK. But not always. Sometimes he wouldn't catch me, at least not all the way. My head and neck would take a smash, and sometimes that pain wouldn't go away for a while. Sometimes it would still be there the next time I climbed into the ring, which didn't make my next outing any easier.

In situations like this, most guys would come up with something new for the time being. Koko could have done a ton of other things if my neck was temporarily bad. As quick and agile as he was, he could have gotten in some high-flying moves, or do something subtle to outsmart my chicanery, anything for the short time it would take me to get all the way back.

But, no. It was the brainbuster almost every time. It was the damage, over and over again, that eventually would lead to me going under the knife. *Way* under.

Guys like Bret and Owen Hart, the Armstrong family, so many others could work around these issues. If you couldn't do something, just for one night, they could make a quick substitute. I've tried to be like that. If someone couldn't do a suplex, I'd switch to working over his arm or leg. If his back was in sad shape, I'd try to have a great match without slamming him, tossing him into the turnbuckle, anything. You focus on changing things up, not getting into a rut if obstacles pop up in a business as unpredictable as wrestling.

A few years before WCW went under, I was working with Eddie Guerrero there. One night, he told me he wanted to beat me with a brainbuster.

Then I showed him the scar on my neck. I explained that I didn't do that sort of thing, by force instead of choice.

The bad workers would have stormed away and demanded someone else to work with. Not a guy like Eddie, who saw it as a challenge. He was fine with it. He even asked me what I'd prefer instead.

I trusted him. I knew we could work something out. I didn't want him to think that I was limited myself, that I'd just do anything else he wanted. Like the great worker he was, he came up with a new finisher in about two seconds.

"I'll just do the frog splash," he assured me, making it seem like that move was a piece of cake. No way, but he made it look so, and the crowd always loved it. Like millions of other wrestling fans, I really miss seeing him in the ring.

"Piledriver"

Ironically, my most-seen "match" with Koko wasn't even a match.

We'd worked at house shows and TV tapings here and there, but we were, obviously, never the focal point of a card. In late 1987, that changed.

The WWF had tried to break into the music world a few years before, with the whole "Rock N' Wrestling" connection atmosphere that dominated much of the wrestling world in the 1980s. Cyndi Lauper had been nice enough to not just bring a few WWF stars into her "Girls Just Wanna Have Fun" music video, but show up not only at the first *Wrestlemania*, but the weeks of promotion leading up to it.

Later that year, she'd done backup on "Real American," still recognizable to millions of fans today as Hulk Hogan's theme. That same year, it would become a part of the WWF's *The Wrestling Album*, on which fans got the vocal "pleasure" of hearing Junkyard Dog, Nicolai Volkoff, Hillbilly Jim, Gene Okerlund, and others.

"Piledriver"

Two years later, it was time for another shot at music stardom for the company. Koko would be one of the leaders.

One day at TV, people were talking about the upcoming musical experiment. Eventually, someone pulled me aside. We were moving over to San Francisco's Cow Palace for one of the biggest shows of the year that August. It wasn't *Summerslam*, as that would make its debut exactly a year and two days later, but about everyone was going to show up for this show. Everyone was excited, as the Palace looked to be bringing in a sellout crowd as we churned out a month's worth of TV tapings.

But before any of that, in front of an empty audience, Koko and I would put on an exhibition that less than two hands' worth of people would see live, but (the WWF hoped!) millions would desperately want to check out under different circumstances.

In keeping with trying to get fans to see the men in the ring as more than just their wrestling characters, the WWF handed some the chance to sing their own theme songs. "Piledriver" would be the title track to the WWF's next album, and Koko's solo sung work.

And a video would back up his lyrics. The film storyline had multiple wrestlers working on a construction site, in between pranking each other and ogling lovely female passersby. Even Vince McMahon himself cameoed to check out the gals.

Along the way, Koko would be singing, explaining to the audience that while, "Sometimes love just feels great ... sometimes love sounds like a fight, it sounds like an argument, it sounds just like a piledriver!"

Yes, the song compared love, the loveliest of all things, to getting one's head smashed straight into the ground!

And during the song's music video, fans got a look at Koko in the ring. That's where I was involved.

Leading up to the Cow Palace event, people had been running up to me, letting me know what was going to happen.

"We're gonna film this thing with a plexiglass ring," I was told. "You're gonna take Koko's finish." They knew I was experienced at taking bumps, especially that one in particular. I was also getting paid a few extra dollars for it, which was always nice.

Wrestling Is My Gimmick

The show was absolutely one hell of a success. It did sell out, nearly 15,000 people sitting there to watch. Hogan defended his title, as did the tag champs Hart Foundation and the new Intercontinental champ, the Honky Tonk Man. Demolition, just starting to make an impact, was there, as was Randy Savage, whom fans were already calling for as the next world champ. Superstar Billy Graham and André the Giant showed up. People backstage were going crazy with the success we were having.

But I could take some secret pride. My match would have the largest audience of all. Maybe not then, but soon, and still today.

Earlier that day, some workers had cut a hole four feet wide out of the ring and placed the plexiglass under it. A camera under there, they started shooting my pseudo cameo.

Viewers saw Koko picking me up in slow motion, a fake audience behind us. He hoisted me up for his finisher (why he didn't do a piledriver for a song *named* "Piledriver" was a mystery).

Then, somehow from below, he was shown dropping me straight down for the finisher and the win. He dropped me onto the plexiglass, which was softer than some rings in which I'd taken the move.

I think we did it in two takes. Multi-million Hollywood movies might take days to film such a scene. I put my jacket on and headed back to get ready for the show (he'd ultimately beat me again later that day), while Koko stayed behind to lip-sync some lyrics, again for an audience that only appeared to exist.

The video showed up on *Saturday Night's Main Event*, then on the album's video release. It's still all over the Internet today. I personally have seen it maybe twice, but I'm proud of it.

And while no one saw my face in the "Piledriver" video, I'd get to make another quick appearance as nearly the entire roster joined up to do "If You Only Knew," wrestling's answer to "We Are the World." Standing with a group of my fellow heels, we gleefully reminded those dastardly faces that, "Your destiny ... belongs to me!" One might not think of a group chorus line of being intimidating, but Koko, Tito Santana, Don Muraco, and the rest of those good guys showed up to do their own singing.

To me, this was one of the first signs of kayfabe disappearing. If these guys hated each other in real life, as many traditionalists of the wrestling world still clung to, how could they all be brought together to cooperate in a song? Fans outside the ring were starting to see this as just as much entertainment as sports.

By that point, I'd started working with some other people. Brady Boone was there, and I even beat him a few times. He always struck me as a guy who could have done some great stuff in the business under the right circumstances. He and I had traveled and trained together, but things never really took off for him on the mat, as a wrestler or referee, until his story turned tragic.

I lost to Sam Houston, whom, no one but the inside track knew at this time, was actually Jake's real-life brother. I beat Lanny Poffo, whom, no one but the inside track knew at the time, was actually Randy Savage's real-life brother.

I scored a few more wins, one over David Sammartino, who was put in the impossible shoes of trying to live up to his dad Bruno's accomplishments. He and I were supposed to do a longer program, but something happened, and he was removed. Instead, I got tossed into a tag team with Steve Lombardi, another underrated worker who busted his tail to get other people over, back then as the Brooklyn Brawler and eventually as one of the Doink clowns.

In the summer of 1987, he and I managed to escape the Civic Center in Springfield, just around the corner to the Basketball Hall of Fame, with a win over two fellows trying out for the WWF.

One of them was Scott Hall. He didn't get picked up that day, or for a while. But five years and a name and *Scarface*-inspired gimmick change later, he'd become Razor Ramon.

I think Steve and I could have made a pretty good babyface team, that fans could and would have gotten behind us as the plucky underdogs who never gave up. If they saw us supporting each other as we battled the larger, stronger heels, they might have supported us just as much. But he'd eventually get more over as a heel when he joined up with Bobby Heenan's family, and I'd keep putting over the bad guys.

Another guy started off in the WWF in July 1987, and I was one of his first common opponents. The guy certainly had the look for the business; his physique showed his past as a bodybuilding champ. He'd been in Oklahoma and Texas for a few years and done pretty well with the fans, if not so much with his opponents or backstage population.

Wrestling Is My Gimmick

He was called the Dingo Warrior. That obviously didn't last long. Did people think he was out battling those Australian dogs in his spare time? Maybe he was their human form or representative or something.

Before the end of the year, his name had changed. And working with him would be a little short of Ultimate, then and later.

Unfortunately, right around this time, my career nearly crashed right into a brick wall.

In Knoxville for a show, I woke up in my hotel room, feeling like someone had stabbed me in the left arm with a thousand-degree sword. Hoping it was just an extreme pull or strain, I managed to get clean and dressed. But before I ever stepped through the arena doors that day, I knew this was something serious.

I always prided myself on my reliability, to make all my dates ahead of time. You don't have to mess up too many times in this business to get a reputation for unreliability, and these words spread fast in the wrestling community, though much faster today than back then. If I give my word, it's going to be good, and there have been many times when I didn't need a signed contract to fulfill my credibility.

So when I showed up that day, I'm sure everybody could tell I was hurting. Wrestlers always are. But when I walked up to the company officials and told them I needed the night off—some of the hardest words I'd ever had to utter at that point—I could see bulging eyes all over the room.

Barry Horowitz didn't just randomly take time, even single nights, off. This was something serious.

I was sent to a chiropractor. Then I saw an orthopedic surgeon.

Three days later, I was under the knife for a ruptured disc in my neck.

You expect to pay a price for a job this physical, but it's still hard to accept when probability becomes reality. This sort of injury had ended careers. I wasn't even thirty years old, and everything that I'd worked for could have just disappeared if things had gotten worse or gone a little bit more wrong. Working heavily since the start of my career had taken its toll, although I'm sure that all of Koko's brainbusters had been, pardon the pun, the knockout punch.

I was laid up for a while, and it took even longer to get back on my feet. Actually, it probably was about one-fifth as long as it seemed, but that's what happens when you make a living at (seemingly) Mach 3 speed movement. At times, it was tough to tell which hurt more, between the pain from the injury and the frustration and depression of me losing a huge chunk of my wrestling prime.

But I knew I could come back. I didn't spend a lot of time comparing my injury to others', and that was fortunate. Paul Orndorff had gone from headlining shows across North America with Hulk Hogan in 1986 to retiring (not for good) from an arm injury just over a year later. Dynamite Kid, long one of the biggest risk-takers in the business, had destroyed his back in a tag match in December 1986 in Canada only to come back the very next month. It was far too soon, and he'd never be the same again, even close to it. Thinking about that kind of stuff can bring you down fast.

My rehabilitation began, and it moved pretty quickly. I could walk, then run, then, very slowly, get back to a wrestler's life.

When I climbed into the ring for a workout with Tracy Smothers almost a year later, I might (*might!*) have still had the slightest doubts of myself. But it took all of about two minutes of bumping and bouncing to show Tracy, the onlooker, and especially myself that I was back and as good as I'd ever been. I was giving and taking armdrags. Tracy was always a safe worker, but falls still hurt unless you take them right, and I did. I even launched myself into the air for a couple of dropkicks.

Yes, Barry Horowitz was back. For now.

Getting Broken by the Harts

> "Horowitz could win about 90 percent of his matches if they were all verbal! Unfortunately, they're not!"
> —Gorilla Monsoon, 1989

I'd worked with Bret Hart and Jim Neidhart both in singles matches and with random partners against the Hart Foundation for some time before. Just after coming back from my neck injury, I started working with a younger, smaller, though many would argue more talented member of the Hart family.

Milling around the Viking Hall in Bristol, Tennessee, getting ready for a show with the rest of the WWF crew, Chief Jay Strongbow yanked me aside and told me we were heading to the airport to pick up my next opponent.

Next, in this instance, meaning we'd be working together that very night, and just maybe at the start of a new program.

We picked up Owen Hart, and he and I spent the trip back to the arena working out our match.

He'd actually been in the company for a while, but this was the first time I'd met him. Also, he was under a mask and a full-length cape, working as the Blue Blazer. I guess the Federation's creative minds were *really* trying to personify the cartoonish nature of wrestling in the 1980s and '90s with this.

Or maybe they were just going to whatever lengths necessary to hide his relationship to Bret. Who really knew? Either way, it was the start of something big for me.

Owen was still pretty young and inexperienced at that point, not surprisingly. He'd worked for his dad and with his brothers up in Canada in Stampede Wrestling for a few years, then in Japan for a while, but he was just starting to branch off from his homeland, and I don't think he was quite used to having a boss he wasn't related to. Starting off in a place where you're at or near the bottom after you've been the promoter's kid can be tough.

But Owen always made the best of every tough situation, and that's something I'd already gotten pretty good at gauging myself. He didn't know who I was, and he worked a bit stiff. Not because he had an issue with me, but just because he hadn't learned any better. It's one of the many wrestling lessons that you can't get anywhere but between the ropes.

Once he found out that I wasn't going to try to shun him or out-wrestle him, make him look bad because he was the newbie or, probably falsely, been accused of carrying the label of nepotism, he and I warmed up and loosened up very quickly.

He didn't last long in the Federation that time, but when he came back to team with Jim for the New Foundation and Koko B. Ware with High Energy, he and I kept working together, and we always put on one hell of a show. He had loosened up big time, especially after his son was born in March 1992, and we tore things up and down.

One of the main keys to working a long program with somebody is to keep the matches fresh, and we never had an issue with that. One night, I'd work on Owen's leg like crazy, and you could tell he was in serious pain when he powered me into the Sharpshooter for the early finish. Or I'd mess up his back so much that he could barely roll me up for the pin.

No fans want to see the same show every match, and no one wants to get a reputation for being too predictable. But after a while, we'd earned the respect of the fans and the trust of the people backstage. Some of the time, ultimately most of the time, Owen and I didn't have time to even talk to each other before the match. Someone like longtime referee Dave Hebner would walk up to us separately and say something like, "You've got twelve minutes, and Owen's going over with the Sharpshooter. You figure the rest of it out."

And we could, believe me. Some of the best matches of our program came when we walked in having no idea what we were going to do. I've been able to do that with many of my opponents, and Owen learned to do it very well himself.

That's how I was taught, and how he'd been instructed back at the legendary Hart Dungeon up in his family's legendary Alberta home. Not many guys learned that way, not nearly enough. Some guys, even today, need a huge script written down, each move worked out word for word for word.

There's so many problems with that. First off, if one or two things go wrong, the entire flow of the match can get disrupted, and the unprepared can turn into deer in the headlights. Mistakes happen in wrestling, and people need to know how to improvise. Secondly, focusing every single thing on the ring ignores something else important during a match—the crowd's reaction. You never know when you might try something new, and the place might just come apart when you do something that might not have seemed explosive on paper. You have to be ready for that. You have to change things around sometimes and listen for what the crowd wants. Doing a move here and there, selling for a while, and then switching from offense to defense won't bring you a good match from that stance, if you're not giving the crowd what they want to see.

Like I said, you might get to the high point of your script, and they might not think it's worth reacting to. You might do something you feel is minor, and they might go completely insane. That's why you need to be ready to call it in the ring, because things can change from one bump to the next.

Some guys were in the back writing out five or six pages' worth of a script. If me or one of the trainees back at the Malenkos' school had tried something like that, three things would happen in the next match. First, you'd be paired with someone with a hell of a lot more experience than you. Secondly, he'd ignore literally every single thing you'd scripted out.

Third, he'd stretch the ever-loving hell out of you, then kick your ass from one side of the ring to the other. You wouldn't be trying that again. I'm guessing that that happened to a lot of young wrestlers who were coming up at the same time I was.

As it turned out, after so many years, and quite a few departures and returns from the WWF, I'd finally make it back to the pay-per-view level in the summer of 1993, with Owen standing right across the ring from me.

Before *Summerslam*, the portion that fans at home would actually see, kicked off at the Palace of Auburn Hills near Detroit, Owen and I started things off with one hell of a dark match. As would be the case for much of my career, we got more time than some of the "main" eventers. As his brother Bret got ready to battle both Doink the Clown and Jerry Lawler later on, Owen beat me in the event's non-aired battle.

Hey, Owen must have liked me quite a bit; I was one of the few people that he never crank-called, put Icy Hot in my underwear, sewed my pant legs together, or anything else that so aptly earned him the title of king of backstage ribbing. This was ironic, consider that there wasn't a more formal, straitlaced guy in business history than his brother Bret.

At least, that I know of. The backstage jokers always do their thing when you're out in the ring, so even if word gets to you there, you can't do anything about it. What are you going to do? Call a quick time-out, get your opponent to feign unconsciousness while you charge to the dressing room and knock the hell out of the prankster, then haul back in and pick up where you left off? Not exactly.

Also, any ribber worth his salt knows enough to cover his ass while in action. Not even enough that the victim can't figure out that it was him, but even fooling somebody into believing that someone else did it. Curt Hennig was great at this—stealing something and hiding it, telling its owner, "Hey, so-and-so just stole your stuff and hid it over there!" then running out of the room—or maybe staying to watch a misinformed victim go to impromptu battle with someone innocently accused!

Yeah, with those two, Mr. Fuji, and other such clowns around, I may very well have been a victim. But it wasn't going to bother me.

Something else around the time, however, certainly did. It showed me that sometimes you have to draw a line. That, "I'll do anything for the company," should only go so far. That being a team player isn't the same as letting yourself get used, and there's a way to stand up for oneself without being an asshole in the process.

Right around the time of *Wrestlemania VI*, the WWF had found a new monster, someone who might just be able to infuriate and/or terrify fans into buying tickets and pay-per-views. Hulk Hogan had been one of the biggest draws in the history of the business, but his star was starting to dim, and the company needed someone to take his place.

This wouldn't be actually accomplished for a while, but the Ultimate Warrior would be the company's first shot. Meanwhile, Hulk needed something to stay strong.

Maybe the Earthquake would be the answer. Unlike most of Hulk's opponents, this guy was ahead in size and strength, and he damn sure knew how to use it. He could pull off ring evil and intimidation like few ever could. After less than a year in the company, he was already heading for main events against Hogan, and even winning by countout on some house shows.

He just needed a little polishing. John Tenta had been a college wrestler and champion sumo wrestler over in Japan, but this was different. He was just starting to learn some great interview skills, and his ring work was coming along, but he needed a finisher.

Like most guys of his size, it was going to be something weight related. But just jumping on top of his opponent would be nothing new. What could be added?

I don't know who exactly came up with the Earthquake Splash, but no one's going to forget it. He would jump all over the ring, and you could almost feel the arena shake as he did, then run back and forth, finally landing ass-first on his opponent's chest. Don't think too many people kicked out of that one.

There weren't many more painful-looking moves than the Quake Splash, but it needed fine-tuning so it only *looked* crippling. One day backstage at a house show in Tennessee, I was strapping on my gear. Word started getting around that they were looking for someone to be the Quake's training partner. It would be a while before the crowds arrived, and now would be a chance for him to work on the implied devastation for rehearsal purposes.

Some idiot manager rolled through the door.

"Horowitz will do it!" he blared. "Yeah, he'll go!"

Excuse me?

"Tell me," I inquired to this buffoon, "would you have done that to somebody else, or would they have cleaned your clock?"

"Job security, brother!" he smirked. I was about to be the one to do his clock-cleaning for him.

"Really?" I roared right back. "My job security is that I know how to wrestle and show up on time, not fail drug tests or go, 'Me, me, practice on me!' like a dumbass."

He got the message and slinked away. I made my own appointments. No one was going to tell everyone else what I was going to do until I knew myself.

And after all that, guess what I did? I went right out there and helped Earthquake practice his move. He did it once or twice, did a heck of a job, never hurt me at all. And then, as he always did for everyone, Earthquake switched back to John Tenta, one of the quietest, most respectful people in the business. He said thanks, sounding almost sheepish, like he felt he was inconveniencing me by getting me to come help him. Then he turned into the Earthquake, destroyed his opponent with the splash (probably a few extra ones to show how heartless this character was), and took another large step toward the top of the company.

I've never minded doing that, and I still don't. If he had come and asked me himself, or even if that loudmouth manager had just *asked*, rather than tell everyone else, I'd never have had a problem. I didn't mind at all helping the Quake learn. And I'm not taking credit for it at all, but his splash ended up being one of the heelish moves of the decade, including putting Hogan out of action for most of 1990 (OK, so he actually needed some time off to film *Suburban Commando*, but this was back when people believed that everything between the ropes was real!).

And, hey, I'd get to work with a champion too! But unlike the Quake, who'd battle Hogan and off for years and then remain a top Federation star after that, my program, along with my WWF tenure, was about to close.

My (Not at All) Ultimate Departure

For most wrestlers, a pay-per-view might be a monumental career moment, something that really made a mark in one's career. But it wasn't really the case with me. I had to go back and watch it to remember writing about it for this piece, and it was only reading back over my own career history that I recalled it at all. It was just one more good match I had with Owen, who I'd worked with so many times before.

A few months later, though, we'd do something a bit more special on a special show. But I'm saving that for a few pages.

As I showed up at the Greensboro Coliseum in late July 1989,

Wrestling Is My Gimmick

I probably came out on the losing end of this battle against Paul Roma, but, as always during my enhancing career, I had some great moments.

Blackjack Lanza walked up to me. There was another new guy looking for full-time Federation work, and I was going to introduce him. Trained by Buzz Sawyer, his name was Vince Torelli, and he certainly looked right for the wrestling business.

"Throw him around a bit," Lanza instructed me. "Let him throw you around a little bit. Let's see how it goes." I did, they saw it, and I thought we did a pretty good job. I came out with the win.

Like Scott Hall before him, Vince didn't get into the company just yet. I didn't see him again for about a decade. But the next time he made it to the WWF, he got all the way to the Intercontinental title and the 1998 *King of the Ring*. That is, after winning everything in the Ultimate Fighting Championships.

Recognizing something yet? Yeah—unlike Mankind, Chris Jericho, and the Rock, I can say that I stepped into the ring with Ken Shamrock and never lost!

Against someone else, though, it was the same story.

I'd worked with Jim Hellwig in the past, and he'd been pretty humble for the most part. He told me about his family, his marriage, we shared things. Now, however, it was different. Not in a great way.

He'd just won the WWF title, beating Hogan in the main event

My (Not at All) Ultimate Departure

of *Wrestlemania* in 1990, no less. After just about two years in the Federation, and only a few other years in the business itself, he had reached the top—well, the Ultimate Warrior had.

And far, far too soon. Honestly, I think Jim just underestimated what being the WWF champ actually meant. He'd been a champion bodybuilder, and I feel he saw the title as just like another mesomorph tournament. You work hard, you diet, you put yourself through all kinds of training, in and out of the gym, and then you get on stage and compete you heart out.

And then it's over. It's far from easy, even for those who don't win, but you get into a tournament, it ends, and then you go home and recover, no matter your finish. If you want to, you come back and do another very soon, but it's up to you.

No, that's not the case in wrestling. You win the title, and it just kicks things up a notch. You're the face of the federation, and you're on someone else's time. You're on the go 24–7, doing appearances, doing interviews, your mug in the press all the time. Not only are you headlining virtually every single card you're on, but you're expected to put on the best match of the night, be it house show or TV or pay-per-view. You're supposed to be there at the end of the night, standing there as the fans say a satisfied goodbye, the last thing they see.

First off, Jim didn't have that kind of wrestling ability. It took a lot of wrestlers with a hell of a lot of talent at the game to make him look good. He was over because of his image, his look, and those things only take you so far.

Not that the Federation didn't try with him. Just after he took the title, they wanted him to look like an unstoppable monster, something more than human. Something ultimate.

And they turned to me. I was out there with him, and it just didn't work. Even when you're there to overpower everybody, you still have to bump around every once in a while, just to keep your opponent safe as well.

With him, it was like wrestling a brick statue. He'd hit you with clotheslines that nearly caved in your chest, stiff the hell out of you otherwise. He press-slammed me in Missouri, splitting my arm open to the point that I almost had to go to the hospital. Of course, you'd hit him with everything but a baseball bat, and he'd hardly blink.

I can live with that for a while, but night after night, no one's going to put up with it for long. I was getting hurt worse in three minutes with him than I had in hour-long matches elsewhere. Lots of other guys felt that way after stepping out of the ring with him as well. There's a reason why Jim was the champion for less than a year. The pressure just got to him all at once.

I don't think it was all his fault. There's probably no real way to be fully ready to be at the top, but he seemed miserable from the time he got there. He was listless, nervous, and just didn't have the passion for the business. I was surprised that he kept coming back to the WWF, and later WCW, but not shocked that none of those returns lasted for very long.

It's not that I have a problem working with huge, muscular guys who have more look than ability. Want to know who gave me the safest press slams of my career? None other than Lex Luger! He always took care of me in the ring.

And so did a bunch of other guys. I think I only worked with Sid Vicious a couple of times, but he was a pleasure. He was safe in the ring, even if he didn't always look it. Sometimes he'd get a little crazy, but never to the point that he was dangerous. We worked together and then go work out and eat together. If he hurt you, he'd apologize in two seconds. Sadly, Sid died just before this book came out. Lots of people, including me, will miss him.

Kevin Nash was another guy I had a great relationship with, both when he was Diesel in the WWF and as himself in WCW. He always told me he respected my ability and showed it. Just like with Sid, his Jackknife powerbomb didn't hurt much at all, because he didn't just pick you up and drop you like certain other people would.

As hard as I had worked in and out of the ring since coming back to the WWF, I felt that I'd really earned my keep. I'd kept putting people over, and making the few I defeated look good before winning. I'd wowed them by coming back fast and as strong from something as potentially dangerous as neck surgery. Certainly, I'd impressed enough of the higher-ups as an asset to the company. I was sure I would be there for a while.

First Trip to WCW

I was wrong. Later in the spring of 1990, I kept getting told that the roster was full, as though the WWF, unlike a pro sports team, can't employ as many people as it wants. A company that gave contracts to Black Bart, Pez Whatley, and so many others that were hardly used, and then only as enhancement talent, much lesser-known than myself, couldn't find room for me.

Fortunately, someone else, somewhere else, quickly could.

First Trip to WCW

Once in a while, a wrestler gets a chance to make things very personal—in a good way. Sometimes, there's more to a program, or even just one match, than fans, even promoters or co-workers, can see or know.

I'd started off in World Championship Wrestling in May 1990, less than a month after finishing up in the WWF. A couple of phone calls to a couple of promoters had been all it took. Not even in the prime of his own career yet, Brian Pillman had welcomed me with a show-opener in Georgia, and I was in dozens of matches over the next few months. I even got a world title shot at Sting, but, even with the mysterious Black Scorpion (building towards *Starrcade* later that here) there to help me out, he *just* managed to escape.

Then came something special, if only for less than a handful of people at first.

Most fans probably bought tickets and pay-per-view buys to 1990's edition *Halloween Havoc* to see if Sid Vicious could actually wrest the title from Sting, as he'd promised so many times leading up to it. Or maybe they wanted to see Doom and Ric Flair and Arn Anderson try to pull off a great match between two heel teams.

But they probably didn't think too much about my battle with Tim Horner, mainly because only those in Chicago's UIC Pavilion would see it.

Still, it was important to us, and we were going to make it special, no matter the audience. There was a hell of a lot more history to this than anyone but the two of us would know.

I'd known Tim since 1983, and we'd even lived together for a while, working hard for Crockett Promotions, both of us trying to put together our own futures in the wrestling business. He'd helped me out a whole lot in the ring—he'd started in the business a few years before I did—with tune-up things, small movements, selling things, facial expressions, little touches to make the matches a little stronger and more realistic. Like me, he'd always known how to avoid the destructive side of wrestling.

Tim Horner: When I met Barry, we were both at a crossroads. He was a natural heel. He could just look at you and piss you off. A lot of guys would flip fans off and say something. Barry could just look at them and pat himself on the back, and they'd just go berserk. We were living together while we were working against each other. That was the time of kayfabe, so they'd have probably fired us if they knew we were doing that, but nobody ever knew about it.

When we got into the business, the business liked big guys, and we weren't big guys. I knew that if I was gonna stay in the business, I needed to learn my craft and learn how to work, and the mentality was the same with Barry. We were like the utility guys on a baseball team. We could work the first match or last match. That's good in some ways, and in some ways, it's a curse. You were so good, you made everybody else look good, and more valuable as a utility guy than to help you move up the card.

Once we were working in the WWF in 1989, and we were the second match. Sometimes those northern towns were hard, because they'd just boo you out cause they wanted to see the main event. Barry and I had the people in our hands. Everything we did, they yelled, they screamed. We tore the house down. Grizzly Smith, Jake the Snake's dad, was working as an agent at the time, and Rick Rude came up to him and said, "What the hell are we gonna do now?" Grizz said to him, "Maybe we need to change the order of the matches."

Barry and I were working in New York, and the top rope broke during the match. He was like, "What are we gonna do?" I said,

"We're gonna wrestle." He'd get up, and I'd do something, and he'd do something, and we had the people behind us. We got to the back, and the boys said, "Y'all should have just quit." I said, "Why? Cause it wasn't in the script? Heck no."

So if he and I got a chance to steal the show at *Havoc*, we certainly would.

And I think we did. The fans there got a good special show. The promotion showed some pretty strong faith in us that day—not only were we the opener, albeit before the show itself, but we got more time than some of the "shown" matches. Tim and I bounced all over the ring, showing off our stuff, and got some pretty great reactions from the crowd before he went over.

That match would be a highlight of my career. It would certainly be the top point of my first WCW tenure—but considering that I was only there until that December, that's not saying too much.

Right around then, up in Canada, I had one of the lowlights.

Years before that, Jesse Barr had been one of my first common opponents down in Florida, as he'd been one of the most hated men in the territory. Unfortunately, his success hadn't carried up to the WWF, where passing him off as Terry Funk's fake brother Jimmy Jack (man, what is it with guys from Florida always having to wrestle, at least for a time, under names that start with J?) had fallen flat.

Now I'd been assigned to work around the loop with his younger brother Art, whose character development had been a bit more extreme. Less experienced than his brother, he'd begun wrestling as Beetlejuice, clad in face paint and jeans—yes, a bit different from his namesake movie character!

Copyright issues had turned Art into the Juicer by the time he'd start with me, WCW trying to break into the cartoonish market that the WWF had commandeered for so long. But by then, and unbeknownst to me, there was already a huge dark spot on his career.

Around that time, bringing the crowd into the matches themselves was a newer thing. Of course, you expected, or at least hoped, that they'd cheer or boo you before or after the match, and when you pulled off a big move. But other specifics were rare. Them counting along with you, one punch at a time, when you climbed up the ropes and whaled your hapless opponent. Chanting your catchphrases during a match. Staying quiet when you asked them to help you play possum and prank your opponent.

That would grow in popularity, and you didn't mind it much. But when Art and I fought it out up north, we heard something else.

We'd had some pretty good matches. I was pretty sure they'd continue. Fans seemed to like the guy who'd been spawned by a hit film.

But one night, they started making the wrong kind of noise. Booing him, the babyface, would be bad enough, but that's not what this was.

Honestly, at this point, I wasn't even sure what they were saying. Not my name, not his, nothing like that. But I could tell it was bothering Art. His timing was slowly slipping away, and the louder the noise, the more he lost focus. You can't do that in the midst of a match. Fans might cheer, boo, chant, or whatever else, but you just keep working. If fans are trying to piss you off, and you let them see that it's working, they're going to kick it up a few levels.

And they did with Art. Like I said, I wasn't sure what I was hearing. But as we finished up, and I left the ring, I kept hearing the chants. Then I saw some signs in the crowd.

"Rapist." That's what they'd been calling Art. This was far too close to reality.

Like I said, I hadn't heard about it yet. But before he'd even made it to WCW, Art had pled guilty to a sex crime. Even without the high-speed news coverage of today, fans had found out, and would be all too happy to serve as his judge, jury, and—I'm sure many would have enjoyed—executioner.

You can't blame the fans for running their mouths about that stuff. It's just human nature, and not the bright side. But when it throws off your timing and totally screws up the match, you don't get to blame your opponent. That's what he did, pissing and moaning about and ultimately to me back in the dressing room, blaming me for everything he'd gotten wrong.

I'll take my lumps if I deserve them, and this has been the case quite often. But not here. Whatever he'd done or not done had had nothing to do with me, and he wasn't going to make it so.

I told him that if he wanted to make things real right then and there to go right ahead and try it, and I'm confident I would have come out ahead, or at least convinced him not to try it again. But he didn't, and our program ended soon after. Because of his criminal issues, so did his career in WCW, and I never saw him again after that.

After the company let him go, Art had gone down to Mexico and became one of the most famous, or infamous, in the country. He's still known as so today, certainly at the top of the ranks of Mexican lucha libre mat battles, especially in the non–Hispanic community. Ironically, and not in good way, he worked as the Love Machine (whoever gave him that name either didn't know of his past or hoped that no one else did), teaming all up and down with Eddie Guerrero.

And, as longtime wrestling fans will always remember, both of them will forever be known for leaving us too soon. In November 1994, eleven years to the month before Eddie fell, Art died in bed alongside his son back in Oregon, just over a month after his twenty-eighth birthday. Like Eddie would, he'd been the victim of a heart ravaged by drink and drugs.

Just before the 1990 winter holiday season, I got a call from someone. I wish I could remember who to thank here, because this would be one of the biggest breaks of my career.

There was a new federation opening up down south. Not in my native Florida, but half a country over.

The minds behind Global Championship Wrestling had heard about me. They knew I'd work my ass off for them, and they were ready to give back as much as I'd give them.

As 1991 kicked off, Texas beckoned, and Barry Horowitz was about to become a Winner.

Going "Global"

At the time, if you were traveling with a group of guys, one would get called up, and he'd say to everyone, "Hey, you

Wrestling Is My Gimmick

> wanna go?" Everybody would say, "Yeah, I wanna go!" A lot of the guys from Tennessee were going down. Barry got called, and the Global guys said, "Anymore guys you got up there?" Guys from Tennessee knew how to work, and when Global came along, they got a bunch of Tennessee guys. They knew we would work for them.
> —Ben Jordan

I hadn't known Eddie Gilbert all that well on a personal level, but I learned pretty early on that he had one hell of a mind for the business. Booking a card, making a great match, building characters. The man could do that as well as anyone.

And he'd heard enough words on me to make me a focal point of his new foray.

Well, maybe the Global Wrestling Federation wasn't quite Gilbert's, not as the owner or anything, but he'd quickly become one of the major faces of it shortly after it kicked off way down in Dallas in the summer of 1991. But as loyal as Texas wrestling fans had always been, they wouldn't be the only ones who would see us in action. Not long after the legendary American Wrestling Association closed its doors, Global reached right out and grabbed its spot on ESPN. Not even just once a week, as had long been the case for the NWA/WCW and WWF; wrestling fans could run through the door after a tough day at school and see us every weekday.

And, just as the "World" Wrestling Federation rarely stepped even outside of North America, let along across the planet, Global's Earth-circling title was a bit misleading as well; the shows were held in Dallas and Fort Worth, and that was it.

We also managed to get in a much shorter workload than the TV audience would ever know. We'd drive down on Thursday, sometimes early Friday, tape the full week on Friday and Saturday, then head back. I'd be working in Global one day, then back to enhancing more WWF talent on Monday, even if *Raw* wasn't quite around yet! One time I finished a taping on Saturday, stopped off and did an indy show on the way home, then went straight back to the WWF.

I wouldn't be the top seed in Global. At first, that went to the Patriot. Actually a great guy named Del Wilkes, he was a mask-wearing, red, white, and blue blood who couldn't wait to demonstrate his name (without the mask, he'd actually been tearing up the AWA for years as the Trooper. It's amazing how many people still thought he was brand-new to the business). Clearly, Global wanted the same sort of real American that had been gold (actually red and yellow) for the WWF.

And Gilbert thought enough of me to hand me some serious mic and ring time, and even gave me a nickname.

The Winner. That's right. A guy who hardly ever came out on top would now be labeled The Winner.

This showed that I'd made one hell of a mark in the business. Bringing in a new guy and just giving him that moniker would have been cheap heat. He'd have come across as just an arrogant jerk with little to get himself over. Fans probably wouldn't have taken to him, or maybe they would. But this turned into a great inside joke. Fans had long since known me as the guy who made a living coming out the wrong way in every match (at least, that most of them had seen). Now Barry Horowitz was here, turning his career around, and letting everyone know that, despite his past, he considered himself to be a true winner in the business—and everyone else had damn sure get ready to respect it.

And I actually would win more. Just a little.

While GWF'ers like me, Bad News Brown, One Man Gang, and Gilbert himself were known mid-carders trying to break up to the upper level, Global also became a jumping-off point for some talent. Scott Levy would end up as Raven. The company would be one of Harlem Heat's last stops before jumping toward eight WCW tag titles. Rod Price, who had one hell of a look for the business and a multiple Global titlist, had been one of the first tag-team partners of a fellow named Steve Austin.

I didn't dislike Eddie Gilbert, but I quickly learned that he wasn't someone I was going to spend much time with by choice. He was one of the guys who lived on the edge, someone whose idea of fun was a few extra cases of booze and a trip to the strip club. Never my area. Probably a reason why he became one of many in this business to leave us far too soon.

Ben Jordan: Eddie Gilbert turned Barry loose and let him do some things, and Barry didn't let him down. Barry always had his mind on what we're doing next. We eat at *this* time, we work out at *that* time, we get to bed, and we get to the building this far in advance. I was used to riding with guys that were just willy-nilly, who would do anything. They wanted to go out to a club after a show or eat at the gas station, Barry was going to eat Subway, then carry protein bars and other healthy food around. He's gonna get you a deal. We'd go into Denny's and get the $2.99 meal, and he'd get them to add everything and still get the $2.99 deal. He said, "Ben, you gotta get road smart. Hang sweaty clothes over a lamp to dry, get the hotel's continental breakfast, take the bananas and the yogurt with you."

One of the first guys I went to ring battle with was, quite accurately, known as the Handsome Stranger. Clad in a Zorro mask that he'd somehow usually manage to keep on for the entire match, he'd step to the ring hugging and kissing women, handing them roses. Not entirely unlike a male stripper.

Later on, in a different time and place, he'd start going by his real name—Marcus Bagwell. As in, several years later, Buff.

Buff Bagwell: Bill Eadie (Demolition Ax) was in charge of Global, and the story that was told to me was that his wife thought of the Handsome Stranger. In those days, they didn't ask you if you wanted to do it. They told you. I came up with being a male stripper and all that. I came up with the bow tie and the jacket. I used to look on it as a little embarrassing. Today, I'm very proud of that gimmick. During the matches, you think of a stupid little mask that can slip right off, and me handing out roses, it's kind of stupid, but once I got out of that character, and a couple years in the business, guys would say to me, "You know, I liked that whole Handsome Stranger gimmick," and I'd be like, "What?" I thought they were joking me, but later on, I realized that was a really good gimmick.

He and I got along great out of the ring. Gym-wise, he was definitely one of the company's hardest workers. Once, right in the middle of a taping, I tripped him to the ground, then put him in a crossbow.

Bagwell almost submitted for real.

Going "Global"

"Don't do that!" he grunted at me as I held him in pain. "I worked my legs today!"

Too bad. I rolled backwards and yanked even harder. We were mainstream on live TV, and we weren't going to switch up. I'm not sure how many of his selling tactics were just a performance.

He was cool, and he didn't stick around long. By the end of the year, he was in WCW, going by his real name, moving up to the top level fast. Years later, after I was back there myself and he'd become Buff in both look and name, we had a fun match together.

Just before he went over to the big leagues, I asked if he'd sell me his jacket.

He refused my money. Soon after, I received it in the mail. Then I had a seamstress remove the sleeve and sew a huge hand on the back. Over the next few years, long after Global ended, thousands of fans would see me wearing it on my way into the ring.

Buff Bagwell: That was great when he bought my jacket. It was a lot of fun to talk about, seeing the Handsome Stranger jacket with the big hand on the back of it.

The whole Global thing was only about three months for me, so I think Barry was one of my first matches. He was so great at what he did, such a great wrestler, that it made me look better than I'd ever looked. That match was the first match that I came back from the match not embarrassed. The match was one of, if not the best match I had in Global. When I wrestled Barry Horowitz, it was the first time in my short career that I felt like I could do this for a profession.

Vividly, I remember being proud to show my friends and family that match. I was friends with (longtime WCW diva/manager/commentator) Missy Hyatt, and I showed her that match, and she said, "Mark, you're actually pretty good at this, your timing and your charisma." I remember ending that match and being like, "You know, I think I can do this."

Barry was the first guy that explained it to me and brought what little talent I had in me at that time, he was able to see and bring it out to me. Me being honest about throwing punches, and I'm not good at this, and I'd good at that, he just taught, really the best anybody'd ever talked with me before. He helped me understand what was going on in the match.

I kept winning, more so in that year and the next few than I'd had in several years in the past combined, not that that was saying much. Sometimes Eddie would beat me. Sometimes I'd beat him. Sometimes we'd team together. Then I'd go off and face Tim Horner or the Patriot or the Lightning (soon to be 1-2-3) Kid or whoever.

Then there was Jerry Lynn. In a short time in the business, he'd gotten quite a bit around, from the AWA to the USWA to international battles. Of course, he'd done some WWF enhancing beside me. Now he had the Global Light Heavyweight title ... for now. He'd knocked me back a few times, but I kept coming.

Yes, I'd won a few matches ... but would an actual title be realistic?

Title Time

> I was gonna quit going (to Global), cause they had cut my pay. They were gonna put the strap on me, but I told them, if I don't get my money, they can keep the strap. Then everybody called me. The Gilberts were calling me, saying, "This is a good opportunity for you." To get any kind of belt, it's a great honor. It puts your name in the books. Anywhere I would get booked, they would use that.
> —Ben Jordan

I'll always consider the belt I wore in Florida to my proudest titular accomplishment. Never before or since have I felt more on top of the wrestling world than when hundreds of my statemen (and women) booed me out of the University of Tampa after slipping away with the Florida Heavyweight championship.

Title Time

Global Wrestling allowed me to personify my "Winner" trademark in 1992, twice scoring the company Light Heavyweight title.

But I've got to give the Global Light Heavyweight title its due; winning it would garner a *slightly* larger audience.

Technically, the weight limit for the belt was 225 pounds, but wrestling will always be taking liberties with our heights and weights.

Jerry and I had gone back and forth a few times, but, as the undersized underdog, and face, he always found a way to outsmart me.

Until I caught him for good. One day, one taping in early February 1992, the Horowitz chicanery came out on top. With means not entirely clean, I finally took him down for the belt.

Fans booed. I waved my arms, and then used them to back-pat myself down to whatever kinds of heat I could get. Barry Horowitz had been a Winner, and he'd tell you himself. Now he was a champion, and nothing would change that.

Well, except Ben Jordan. Somehow or another, he just managed to get me in the ring two weeks later, and somehow escaped with the belt. I managed to grab it back from him later than month and feuded with him for a while, but Danny Davis scored the title from me that April.

Ben Jordan: In this business, you pretty much know it's somebody else calling the shots. You always want to be the top dog and the champion, but it takes a lot, a lot of politicking and stuff like that. It was no problem with him beating me, and then we turned around and did a rematch.

Big deal. A few days later, I was over in Ohio, losing to Tito Santana and Koko B. Ware on the same day. That was pretty much my last hurrah in Global.

Some wrestlers need to be the champion to maintain their identity in the ring. Most of us don't, relying instead on just putting out a strong product, and I'm proud to be a member of that group.

Another Near-Fatal Moment

Actually, perhaps the scariest moment of my career happened in Global, and it was nowhere near the ring.

Another Near-Fatal Moment

I had helped his new kid get booked at Global, and I'm just going to call him John. That's not his real name, for reasons that will become clear *very* shortly, and you wouldn't know him anyway. Global's people had inquired if I knew any new babyfaces that were working in Nashville, and I mentioned him. I'm almost sorry I did.

His people skills were a bit problematic, and he was just a *bit* of a prima donna. That's OK. Lots of guys are like that before they get too far into the wrestling business and find out how long and hard those dues can be to pay if one walks in with the wrong attitude. He might have learned better and come out OK.

Just before Christmas of 1992, John was driving back home. I was about three-fourths asleep in the passenger seat, and Eddie Gilbert's brother Doug was in the back.

Just before I finally dozed off, I heard something resembling a worn-down chainsaw nearby. Figuring that Doug had dropped off, I turned around to glance at him.

And his eyes were wide open. It was John.

Driving us down the highway, he'd gone into a near-coma at the wheel. Now we were going about seventy miles an hour with a driver in the Land of Nod.

As we ran through one mile marker after another and were about to smash right into a ditch, I went absolutely crazy. I wasn't ready to die, and if I did, it sure as hell wasn't going to be in the midst of the holiday season, out on a pitch-black road in the middle of the night. If we had crashed and gotten hurt, we'd be out of luck. Cell phones weren't much around yet, and no one was going to happen by at the time of the wee morning.

If I'd been in the ring, I'd have been in full-blown shoot mode, and I wouldn't have given a damn. I proceeded to beat the living piss out of John, Doug screaming terrified encouragement from the backseat. Painfully shocked back into awareness, the genius managed to bring the car to a stop. We were all physically OK, although I don't think any of us could breathe for about an hour.

I kept up a steady stream of profanities at him until we got back to town. If Doug or I had been as deeply out as he was, or if he wasn't a snorer, we could have hit anything, flipped over, whatever else could have ended more than our careers.

Now we had another issue to handle. What to do about the damages to our rental car?

Doug had the good idea to run it through a car wash before we returned it. But when we got it back to the airport, they threatened to sue us for the damages.

After so much time on the road, though, I had learned a thing or two about this sort of thing. Ever so diplomatically, I explained to them that they couldn't prove we'd done anything, and they'd lose my business and wind up in court if they kept playing this game. The car rental company was well acquainted with my dealings, and we got right out of it.

I saw John a few times after that, but I never spoke to him. Once I finished up with Global, I never saw or even heard of him again in the business. Don't know why, don't care why. The careers of fucking idiots who almost end my life don't take up too much of my mind.

A New Addition!

Spousehood and parenthood are never easy for those in the wrestling business. It's a sad toss-up that the higher you make it, the worse it gets for your homelife. If you're just competing locally, you get to stay close to your friends and family, but you typically don't make squat in the financial sense.

If you are lucky enough to make it to the biggest leagues, you might be able to bring in a living wage and maybe even more. But you're on the road for about eleven months a year altogether, and when you do come home, it might be for a day or two. Maybe. Holidays, anniversaries, birthdays, you're almost always on the road, and you're lucky to have time for a quick phone call. Even when you go out of your way to make time for these calls early, it's still pretty frustrating. You miss more than any husband or father would even want to.

A New Addition!

So that made it extra difficult for Michael when I married his mom. Here came this new guy, who, nice as I hope I am, would only be around maybe every other weekend, while still being his mom's new husband. He'd have to get used to a new stepdad that he'd only see every once in a while. The pro wrestling lifestyle has caused far too many a divorce, along with some serious separation issues between parents and children. Now he, as the high-speed hormonal emotion machine called a teenage boy, was getting shoved into stepchildhood, with a guy he'd have extra trouble getting to know. That just made a difficult situation so much worse.

And it was tough for a while, not that he or I would have expected anything different. His biological dad had played in a bar band, singing cover songs. I was as far as one could get from him, in personality, profession, everything. Michael didn't care much at all about wrestling, so having a guy who was on TV all the time as his new stepdad wouldn't be much of a deal to him.

Not that I was the most simple to learn to know myself. I just knew what I wanted for him and for his mom, and he didn't always agree with that. Those waters were rough and rocky for a while. But eventually he and I did reach more of an understanding. We weren't going to agree on anything or even most. That's still the case today. He and I drove each other up the wall sometimes, and still do every once in a while. But he eventually did come to see that I did have her interests at heart. I watched him mature into a heck of a student, a trade school graduate, and a certified plumber. It ended up going pretty well.

Then, in the first months of 1992, we got some news, on the way to the most unexpectedly welcome of adjustments, so to speak.

Diane and I had been talking about having a new child, and we'd sure as hell been trying, but we tried not to worry too much about it. We didn't take it as seriously as some couples might. We knew we were happy, and if Michael was the only child we got to raise, that was fine. If something else never happened, well, that was just how it was supposed to be. It's up to nature with this sort of thing.

I was bouncing back and forth between being one of the biggest stars in Global and enhancing upcoming WWF talent, but I remember that I had a rare weekend off. I was sitting on the couch of our house in Nashville, watching TV or something, when Diane came strolling in. The cat she was about to let out of the bag was the size of a tiger on steroids.

She was pregnant. Per usual, I had no real idea how to react, at least not yet.

But we were thrilled. It had been the three of us for years, and we were fine with it. Now she and I would have our own new special bond, and Michael would get a younger brother (we didn't know the gender yet, but that's how it eventually turned out).

I tried to stay involved in what little time I was home. I went with Diane to her doctor's appointments. I looked after her as much as I could. Fortunately, she didn't need too much extra help, as her pregnancy went pretty smoothly.

As Christmas of 1993 rolled in, we were scheduled to get an early present. Her due date came around, and we had to hurry up and wait, and wait, and still wait some more. But a few days before Santa Claus brought toys to kids all over the world (yes, I still celebrate Christmas, despite being Jewish!), he brought us a little boy one early Wednesday morning.

I can remember holding Josh for the first time. I was scared. I was proud, I was overly cautious, terrified that I'd move wrong and hurt him. My wife did most of the childcare. Diane was always better at that sort of thing.

Like any new father, I was terrified, but also full of hope. Hope that I'd be as good a father as I'd tried to be as a stepfather. Hope that I could keep doing right by my family. Hope that I could be everything he and they needed.

And, maybe a little selfishly, hoping that I could really take advantage of my new chance. My second chance.

Because, over a decade before, far before I even knew Diane, I had already gotten a shot at fatherhood—and it hadn't gone well.

My First Daughter

Still far on the outside reaching toward the wrestling world, I'd taken the marriage plunge before my teen years were even over. I'd found my soulmate in Donna, and I just knew this whirlwind was going to keep spinning for decades.

The honeymoon period, for me at least, didn't last much longer than our actual honeymoon.

Even for a teenager, I had already formed my wrestling goal, no matter how many people asserted that it would never happen. I knew one part of that was staying home at night and staying sober while doing so. No matter what I had planned for the next day, even if there was nothing there, I hardly ever left the house. Some would call that sensible.

Others, like Donna, called it the epitome of boredom. Eventually, she stopped waiting for me to grab her and lead her into my wild side, where rules don't apply and the edge becomes the most attractive place to live and dance.

That didn't happen. I'm not sure why she believed it would. Maybe I'd inadvertently given her some clues. Maybe she thought that, right off the bat, I'd be a world-famous wrestler, living at high speed without a cause or a clue, and then she could hang out with some renowned names. She might even be my valet and become the heartthrob of young male fans across the nation.

Wrestling has never worked that way, and it shouldn't. It takes time to learn to put on a great show, to work the crowd, to give interviews, to play the backstage game. Fans see some of the greatest wrestlers on TV, people who make their job look easy. It's not. It takes education far from the classroom, and no one should begin anywhere near the top.

Donna didn't feel that way. And she got tired of waiting. I eventually found out that part of the reason she'd married me was to get out of a bad situation at home, and now she was ready to rock and roll, in every sense of the term.

Wrestling Is My Gimmick

More and more, she'd ask me to go out and party. More and more, I'd say no. Soon, she stopped asking me and just went out herself. She'd come home all hours of the night, drunk, sweaty, still smiling. I didn't have to think very hard to figure out what, or who, she was doing out there.

But then, in the fall of 1978, we found out she was expecting. We were going to be parents. My family name would live for another generation.

Maybe we subscribed to that old fallacy about childbirth stabilizing a shaky marriage. Maybe anything. But even after Melissa was born in April 1979, things got bad again. Before I went up to Tennessee to wrestle, it was over.

I left Melissa behind, and I always felt bad about that. I was just a kid myself. I didn't know how to handle this. I was angry at Donna, first for running around so much, then costing me a ton of money and getting us thrown out of our apartment.

Maybe I took that out on Melissa. Her mother certainly didn't help there either, spending the years I was away brainwashing her about what a horrible person her dad was.

For over ten years, we hardly talked, and even then, it was mainly a quick phone call here and there. Her mom did what she could to keep us out of contact, and I guess I didn't try as hard as I should have to get around her obstacles.

Donna got divorced and remarried, a few times I think, and I'm sure Melissa saw quite a bit she shouldn't have and learned many things the wrong way.

One day in 1995, my phone rang. It was Donna's grandmother, whom I hadn't heard from in years. It took me a minute to figure out that this wasn't a prank call.

Donna was dead.

I later found out it was something of a one-two punch. She had a colossal, dangerous cyst on her ovary, and it may have burst and caused her to go into septic shock. Of course, the cocaine in her system hadn't been too helpful either.

And as sad as it may sound to say, I felt almost nothing when I heard the news. I wasn't that upset, mainly because I wasn't that surprised. Didn't even think much of Melissa. It was like reading the obituaries page of the newspaper, or seeing on the TV news that someone you didn't know had died. Donna was little more than a stranger to me, as was Melissa.

I also learned why they'd called me. Not to deliver bad news to someone who deserved to know. Not to lighten the blow or offer condolences.

They called because, in their mind, some foul play had happened, or so they said. They tried to tell me that someone had done this to her. They thought I was a famous, rich wrestler who could just drop out a ton of money to pay some lawyer or detective to drum up a bunch of noise and look for something that, even then, I knew damn well didn't exist.

Of course, I said hell no. I never even considered going to her funeral.

After her death, Melissa went to live with her aunt, who kept shutting me out. She came over a few times, but she was always cautious about opening up to me. She'd heard enough horrible stuff from certain people that she felt she couldn't trust or believe me much.

Now a husband and father myself, I tried to stay in touch with her, but never could like I wanted. But she did OK, got a good job managing a hotel, and adopted a two-year-old girl named Lauren. Then, in 2016, I got another call.

Not from Melissa, or from her aunt. Her boyfriend was on the phone.

He told me Melissa was sick, and not for the first time. Unbeknownst to me, she'd beaten lymphoma in the past. But now it was back, and she wanted to talk to me.

My wife and I went to pick her up. It was horrible, but nice in a way. We didn't go crazy at the "reunion," because we didn't want to freak her out. We could tell she was sick, but she didn't look all that bad. Certainly not like she had cancer. Surely not like she was about to die, which she was telling us.

She wasn't going to stay there. Not with her boyfriend or his family or her mother's family. She was coming to stay with us, and her little one, now about ten, was coming with her.

It was great having her around. I finally got to know her better. My wife and kids loved her to death. We didn't spend much time talking about the past or feel any need to apologize or anything like that. We just felt that there was no real hatchet to bury, just a chance to catch up.

All the while, Melissa often said that she wasn't feeling well, or she was just tired. We didn't think she was that sick. We figured she'd turn things around. She smoked once in a while, but never drank. Took fine care of her little girl.

Right around Independence Day of 2017, Melissa seemed more sluggish than usual. She said she wasn't feeling well, but that was common enough that we didn't really react to it.

On the morning of July 6, Melissa was sleeping in my son's room. Diane went in to wake her up.

She called to Melissa. She shook her.

I remember Diane shouting for me. I'd known her long enough that I could tell that this was something unusual, and something horrible.

I came running in. Melissa was cold. She'd been gone for some time. Hadn't seen her thirty-eighth birthday.

I don't really even remember much after that. My daughter had just died in my house, and my wife and I had been the one to find her. Maybe I'd been in denial about her health issues, but this was shocking. That was all that was real at that point.

I'm sure I freaked out. I'm sure I lost it. I don't even remember when I finally came back to reality. Fortunately, Diane kept it together enough to contact the right people to come and help us. The police, the medical examiner, the coroner. For me, it just all seemed like a merry-go-round of strangers.

The only saving grace was that Lauren happened to be with Melissa's ex-husband that weekend. I can't imagine how horrible that would have been, to see (or, God forbid, find) the only mother she'd ever known suddenly gone.

As much as I hadn't gotten along with Melissa's aunt, I'll give her credit; she did a great job taking care of all the funeral arrangements, even though I offered to help. Melissa was cremated, and her aunt got her ashes.

That was OK. I don't think I'd have wanted them. But what happened next was far from OK. As far from it as anyone could get.

Losing a kid, especially doing so right in front of you, as had happened to my family, isn't even possible to handle. I was about to find out how impossible. I was about to nearly toss my entire life away as well.

Almost Losing It All

I'd been awake for a while, but hardly had the strength to roll over. Eventually, I managed to make it, and glanced at the clock.

It was about 7:30. I didn't even know if it was a.m. or p.m. And sadly, I didn't care. I didn't care much about anything at that point. This was a common occurrence for me, and it would stay so for a long time.

I wasn't sick. At least, not in the sense that I could have gone to a doctor and found a cure. I wish I was lucky enough to have the flu or something like that. At least those things have vaccines.

My illness was in my head. Those ailments can be the toughest to get rid of, and you can't control it if they decide to come back and hit you even harder. Sometimes they lessen, but still stick around.

I couldn't stop asking. Couldn't stop wondering.

What could I have done? Did I do the wrong things? Why hadn't things gone better for Melissa and the rest of my family? Was it my fault? Would this have happened if I'd paid more attention to her? Had I been a deadbeat or something? So many others. So much that I couldn't know.

I'm sure every parent who loses a child asks things like this. But the most frustrating questions are those that can never be answered. You keep hoping they will, that the solution will just come to you one day, from without or within, but it never does.

You also expect, or at least you hope, that the pain will one day end. Not completely, as it never does for anyone who's been through this. But you believe that it will at least lessen.

Maybe it does. But it still hurts so much that you don't notice the slightest improvement. I know I didn't, for a very long time.

My days consisted of laying around, using the bathroom, occasionally eating. For far too long, that was all I had going for me. I didn't do anything physical. Didn't go to the gym. Didn't tan. Didn't see a doctor.

Nobody could help, mainly because I didn't let them. My wife and son would come around, and I'd react like a caged lion, snapping at them. I was sure they couldn't help, so why should I even let them try?

I had nothing. That may not have actually been true, but it's certainly how I felt at the time. I was pissing off my family, to the point that I expected to lose them. I don't think I'd have put up with someone who was treating me like I was being towards them. Someday I might actually get out of bed, only to find an empty home waiting for me.

I'd been out of the wrestling business for a while, and I was getting too old to go back on the road anyway, so I couldn't find solace amongst my mat brothers in the locker room like I had in the past. What few friends did reach out to me, I responded the same way as I had to my family, either brushing them off or ignoring them completely.

I was sure I was losing my family, my mind, everything. Once in a while, I didn't even want to wake up the next morning. If this was all I had to look forward to, I hoped I wouldn't have a future.

The first weeks turned into a month. Then several months. I got past a year. More than a year. About two. I'd always had a Type A personality, facing down issues and solving them as best I could, but I'd never been up against anything like this.

There's never going to be one simple, sudden solution to this sort of thing. I found that out the hard way. Only time eventually healed my wounds, as much as anything could. There wasn't one step I could take to feel better, one moment where I was like, "Hey, it's time to get OK."

I started off slowly. I wasn't going to see a shrink or be put on some antidepressant medication or something like that, but I started taking some new vitamins. I'd been feeling ill for much of the past years, but that might have been my pitch-black mindset just tricking my body.

My depression had played hell with my sleep for the entire time. I was lucky to get in a few hours at once, and it got to where I was afraid to do so, because I didn't like the dreams I was having. I learned some ways to deepen my sleep a bit and actually feel rested up.

Just to get a fresh start on a few things, I found a different chiropractor. I hadn't exercised worth a damn for the entire time, but I managed to drag myself outside, which itself was almost monumental. I'd start doing cardio, a little more each day. I'd drop down for pushups, another total that kept increasing. My neighbor had a weight set that he let me use, and I eased back into that as well.

Once I could get up the spine to drive a car, another frustratingly difficult battle, I managed to go back to the gym. I picked a new one of those as well.

I hadn't even hardly watched wrestling since I'd gone down, and the thought of even doing a meet-and-greet or seminar had been unthinkable for far too long. But I eased back into those as well. I showed up for some indy shows. I got back to as much normalcy as I could find. And I was lucky enough that my wife and son stuck with me all the way through.

Even today, I'm not all the way back from losing Melissa. I don't think I ever will be. Outliving your kid is something you never recover from. I'd like to think that I've come as far back from it as I could have.

I also haven't heard from Melissa's daughter since Melissa died. But as rough as it may sound, I'm not exactly torn up about that. Lauren went to live with Melissa's ex, who'd helped Melissa adopt her. He had a family, young daughters included, for her to live with. I'm not related to them and never knew them at all, so I don't care to hear from them now.

Too Many Sad Endings

As much as Eddie Gilbert, and, to a smaller extent, his brother, were considered the faces of Global—at least, once the Patriot left—it's easy to gloss over just how fast their federation time ended. Both of them were with the company for less than two years, and left around the same time I did. Eddie was great with a wrestling book, but he wasn't much of a team player. He didn't like to listen to others with a different idea of putting together a good wrestling show. He didn't mind taking blame if things didn't work, but he sure loved credit when they did, and even the possibility that others might share or steal some of it ticked him off royally.

Pay was also an issue. Not at first, but as shows went on and attendance and ratings started to taper off, it became tougher and tougher for the bosses to pony up the green they'd guaranteed. Perhaps that was one of the reasons why our next little incident happened.

He might have been *this* close to becoming the next star of the Universal Wrestling Federation before it closed in 1987. He'd make it near the top of the United States Wrestling Association, winning the tag title with Jeff Jarrett a few times. Now, with a few years of experience and a hell of a look for the business, Jeff Gaylord was ready to hit it big in Global.

Oh, he'd make some big hits, all right. But not the one he, and certainly not Eddie, were hoping for.

I had just finished a match at the Dallas Sportatorium, and was walking back to the dressing room. I'm not sure why; maybe my match had been off the charts, or perhaps I'd been awful, but I was in a zone that evening. That happens to me sometimes. It probably happens to every wrestler. You get so into things in the ring that you can't always immediately leave that mindset behind when the match ends.

No, you could have fired a gun right in front of me at that second, and I wouldn't have reacted. Unless I had to.

Too Many Sad Endings

As I made my way down the hall, I noticed, barely, that Eddie Gilbert was behind me. He wasn't trying to talk to me, so I just kept going.

Then something that looked like a torpedo with a brown wig came flying right past me.

It (as I would later learn, he) landed all over Eddie, and started whaling him. Two, three, four, however many times, Jeff lit him up like a firework. Equipped with pretty significant advantages in height and weight, Jeff used Eddie as his personal punching bag.

I turned. I couldn't believe it. People started screaming.

Fortunately, for Eddie at least, a huge crowd ran in to break things up, led by Doug, who whacked Jeff with a soda.

As it turned out, it wasn't even a personal thing. Apparently, Eddie had taken another promoter's advance, then decided not to show for the event in question. You don't do that. The guy had slipped Jeff a few bucks to send Eddie a message.

Ironically, later that night, I actually drove home with Eddie and Doug. It was one of the few times I'd traveled with Eddie. Despite his face being a beaten mess, Eddie insisted on driving us home. Maybe he wanted to show that things weren't as bad as they looked.

Then Eddie turned to me.

"You were near it," he asked. "How come you couldn't help?"

Well, I could have ranted for an hour about that. I could have told him that the place simply had become too crowded too fast for me to step in. If things had been different, I'm pretty sure I could have taken Jeff out, as he was never much of a tough guy outside of the ring.

Second, I wasn't that great of a friend of Eddie. I didn't have a problem with him, but not to the point that I was willing to step in front of a punch, kick, or flying chair for him.

Finally, and most importantly, I hadn't stepped in because, with what I learned later, I didn't entirely disagree with Jeff. I have never been paid for a show or appearance and not shown up. That's not cool. This is what happens when people in wrestling fuck each other over for money.

Yeah, I could have taken that one and run in a few different directions. But I didn't. I don't even remember what I said. Probably just spat forward some cop-out formula and turned over to go to sleep. It wasn't worth the effort. What happened hadn't been because of me, and I could already see the writing on the wall as far as me leaving. Why go out of my way to impress a guy who I might never see again? Of, if I did, wouldn't be in a position to control my career?

Soon after, he and I would both be gone from the company. I'd never work with him again, but not for reasons that I'd ever want.

In the midst of a WWF road trip in February 1995, me and the crew were hanging out in the ever-popular jaunt of an airport.

Suddenly, Jeff Jarrett stepped up to us. We could tell that something was wrong.

He told us that Eddie had died. Just thirty-three, a few years younger than me, he'd had a fatal heart attack at his Puerto Rico apartment.

Heart failure, heart condition, enlarged heart, just about always brought on by years of self-abuse. That's been on the autopsy for the overwhelming majority of the premature deaths in the wrestling community, so common that we're hardly even surprised if they happen anymore.

But who can we look to for that? Who gets the blame? The wrestlers themselves? The business? Usually, it's a little from each column. Some guys get caught up in the party lifestyle, riding the highway in overdrive, full of parties and substances that either stay illegal until we're twenty-one, or never become legal at all, and never were. Eventually, that catches up with almost everyone.

He's known best today as the guy who kicked off the career of "Stone Cold" Steve Austin (although how big a role he actually played in Austin's training is always going to be debated), but Chris Adams got shoved to the moon in Global after I left, scoring the heavyweight title twice. I didn't work with him then, but we hit the mat when we got to WCW a few years later.

I regretted it. I don't know if he was just in a bad period, if his years of booze abuse were catching all the way up with him, or something else, but the match was one of the worst of my career. Since I've been a wrestler, there have been very few times when I didn't walk up to my opponent after a match and thank them with a handshake, but he was an exception to that rule. His unprofessionalism went outside the ring as well; he was supposed to pick me up at a hotel once, but forgot (or "forgot") to show up, and I ended up missing a flight, which could have gotten me in serious trouble.

In October 2001, as drunk as usual, Adams and a friend got in an alcohol-induced brawl at the friend's house in Texas. His friend, who had been the best man at Adams' wedding just a few weeks before, got a gun and shot him. The law decided that he'd acted in self-defense. Adams had flirted with disaster one too many times.

And then you have guys who go too far for too long with things designed to heal, and will if we use them right. Painkillers, prescription drugs, even steroids can help us out if we use them right and get them from the appropriate people.

Of course, there are those who don't do any of that stuff, and still pass away. Sometimes, it's because of wrestling itself, and little on the performers themselves, if at all. Owen Hart was one of the cleanest fellows in the history of the business, and his May 1999 death in front of thousands live and millions on pay-per-view was all on wrestling itself. It showed that this line of work had gone way too far, and had been for far too long. Wrestlers had been dropping out of the stands and rafters for years, and this sort of thing was bound to occur sooner or later. Fans come to see what we do in the ring, not stunts that people like Owen, and so many others, should never even be asked to perform. There's no reason why Owen isn't here today, maybe still putting on a show for his fans.

But it can happen to anyone. You never know. I could walk out of the gym this evening and get hit by a truck as a meteor lands on my head. Death's going to get everyone, one way or another. Sometimes you can't blame the business or, to much of an extent, the individual. Sadly, that's happened to a few of my closest friends.

When I showed up in the WWF in the early 1980s, Vince McMahon, Sr., was running the show. But driving the ring trucks, setting things up, doing a million things at once with the rest of the ring crew, was a teenager named Joey Marella.

He was one of the friendliest, funniest guys the business ever saw, something I learned from travelling with him as we both tried to break into the WWF mainstream. Joey never really wanted to be a wrestler, though he'd nearly gotten drafted into pro baseball, but he ended up as one of the WWF's top referees, even as the man in the ring as Hulk Hogan and André the Giant battled it out in the main event of *Wrestlemania III*, one of the most famous matches in history.

And Joey probably could have used nepotism to manipulate his way up in the company. No one outside of the WWF, and even many in there, had any idea that his dad was none other than Gorilla Monsoon, an icon of the business.

Until tragedy shoved it into the spotlight. On Independence Day 1994, Joey and Harvey Wippleman were driving home from a night of refereeing in Ocean City, Maryland, when they crashed into a guardrail and a tree on the New Jersey Turnpike. Harvey, who'd been wearing a seatbelt, would barely survive, but return to the WWF. Joey, who hadn't been, was gone forever.

Then, and only then, did his family history come into the public eye. Everyone knew his dad, and many people knew Joey pretty well, but when the wrestling world found out the two were father and son, everybody went crazy. That was actually pretty commonplace back when it was easy to keep secrets. When Owen Hart showed up in 1988, the WWF went so far as to hide him under a mask and call him the Blue Blazer to keep anyone from finding out he was Bret's little bro.

For Joey, I did my grieving in private, like I always do, but I still hurt from that today, especially when July 4 comes around, for both him and Melissa.

Just over five years later, Gorilla joined his son at New Jersey's Lakeview Memorial Park. Many said he'd lost much of his own passion for wrestling after the loss of his son, as anyone certainly would.

We'd worked together all over Florida beforehand, and Brady Boone and I battled all over the WWF in 1987 and 1988, rooming together at the same time. The company labeled him as Billy Jack Haynes' cousin early in his WWF career, work-wise, but that didn't work too well getting him over. Neither did the Battle Kat gimmick that only lasted for a few months in 1990.

Still, like me, he worked like crazy to have a good match, no matter how few times he'd come out on top (sometimes over me!). And someone else had noticed just how hard Brady worked, handspringing and backflipped around the ring and doing victory rolls everywhere.

Sitting at home, watching Brady do his thing, another future world champ and Hall-of-Famer could feel his own career getting started. He did Brady's moves on his own friends. He soon broke into the business, and got some help from Brady early on. Three decades later, he was still working Brady's moves in the ring (including on Brady himself, once down in Florida in 1996), one of wrestling's long-time tribute mannerisms.

His name is Rob Van Dam, a guy who never forgot where he started.

And with Brady, neither will I. By the mid–1990s, we'd both end up in WCW. He'd lost his hair and beard, and switched his wrestling tights for a referee's outfit. By this point, very few in the audience were probably much aware of his past between the ropes.

But even then, he'd find a special way to say hello to the wife and kids that he never stopped talking about. Usually just before his matches started, Brady reached up and pulled or rubbed his ear. It was the Boone family secret connection.

Right before Christmas 1998, I was doing a program with Chris Kanyon in Florida, and Brady was there refereeing. He'd just counted me out at Palmetto's Manatee Civic Center (now the Bradenton Arena Convention Center), and we'd headed home.

Either the next day or a few days later, I showed up for the next show. I figured that Brady would be with me between the ropes again.

Then someone told me that Brady had never made it home from the shows. Just as with Joey, he'd been killed in a car accident. Another close friend gone.

End of Global

My whole journey was less than two years, from Day One to when WCW signed me, from when I was nineteen years old

Wrestling Is My Gimmick

> to twenty-one. I was at home, and I got a call that Global was ending. I was thinking, "What am I going to do now?" That same day, Magnum T.A. called me. The Patriot, Scotty the Body (later Raven), and I got contracts with WCW.
> —Buff Bagwell

The hardest thing for every new wrestling promotion isn't getting started. That's actually not that difficult. You get a location to do your shows, hire enough workers to perform, get some bookers to lay out the show (who are hopefully not the wrestlers themselves), and obtain enough licenses for everybody to perform. It's hardly simple, but anyone with deep enough pockets and the guts to put them to work can do it.

And a major key to success with any promotion is television. A few more dollars, knowing the right people, landing a deal there, it's a major accomplishment, and a very admirable one.

Things tend to get off to a great start in situations like that. There's a new promotion, something for fans to look at aside from the major ones, the veterans. It's pretty easy to get publicity when one is starting out. Wrestling has been one hell of a boon to several TV channels since long before cable television was even a thing.

And, for a while, it usually pays off. People come running. People love wrestling. Always have, always will, in one capacity or another. The new promotions tend to score high ratings, heavy attendance, strong merchandise sales, everything (we're not mentioning pay-per-view here, because that's not part of this discussion. It's a whole separate thing, and one bad pay-per-view has put a huge halt to many upcomers).

But, see, that's called a fad audience. It's about fans coming to see something new just because it is, in fact, new. Not because it's actually good. That's an important distinction to make, and it's caused many promotions to firework and fizzle out. Promotion higher-ups get it into their head that a very successful beginning will lead to a long period of just as much success and probably more, and that the people and the deals and the dollars that are around now will be around forever, if not increasing.

Doesn't happen. It doesn't work that way, because people don't think about next year, next month, tomorrow, hell, even this evening.

People have the right to expect that they'll keep seeing great shows. Especially on TV, they deserve to see what's happening now move into next week and the future. One great show in the ring won't make a great TV show last. There must be a strong, continuous thread that makes audiences say, "I can be sure that this is going to be a great program, and I'm going to come back next week to see it. There's enough here that I want to watch this, even when I have so many others to pick from."

They usually don't. The shows lose focus, quality, and ultimately viewers relatively quickly. People, both fans and wrestlers, go back to where they started, like the WWF and, in the 1990s, WCW. These promotions have demonstrated strong reliability (and larger paychecks), though at perhaps varying levels, and people return. The big promotions tend to kick things up a notch at their first sign of competition, and that's typically enough for people to trust that they'll keep being great.

Once TV ratings go down, they're hard to recover. It's tough to get people re-interested in something once they go away from it, especially when plenty of new options have probably popped up since then. And TV stations and executives aren't known for their patience. The firework fades, the TV deal is lost. With so little leverage left, the promotion usually fades away until it's all gone.

Now, don't think I'm writing all this to criticize those who have failed at this. I've never wanted to work much behind the scenes, and I don't have a clue about what it takes to carry success as a wrestling TV program. I could not begin to do what the brains behind these promotions have tried to do, no matter the levels of success. It takes a hell of a lot of guts to even try that, and those do deserve a hell of a lot of respect. I'm just discussing why these things happen, not to play Monday morning quarterback and say, "Here's what they should have done…," or, more irritatingly, "Here's what I would have done." I hear that garbage all the time from people who don't have the first damn clue how to run a show, many people who have never gotten anywhere near the business, and I give it the exact time and attention it deserves: zero.

That's happened to many promotions, some I've worked for and some now. Enough that it could fill up a few chapters of this book, and more time that we have to discuss here. My point is, in the fall of 1994, Global's lifeline ended. The tickets stopped selling, the TV ratings went away, and the federation couldn't survive on flash appeal alone. ESPN even cut pro wrestling away permanently after that, except for the classics.

To be fair, I was already gone at that point, and had been for years, although I felt terrible for those who had been loyal enough stuck it through and now had few places to go. Some of them eventually made it to the big leagues, and I was proud of them. Marcus Bagwell, Raven, Bradshaw, Sean "X-Pac" Waltman, Cactus Jack, Charles "Godfather" Wright, Booker T, and so many others jumped from Global to the bigger leagues. Some would up as world champions. A few made it all the way to the WWE Hall of Fame.

Ironically, one of the first to jump had been one of the first federation faces, the Patriot himself. Doug Gilbert had put on a mask, called himself the Dark Patriot, and taken the title from him, and the Patriot eventually made it to WCW, where he and Bagwell became tag team champions. He'd even get a big push in the WWF, although many felt that he was rushed a bit, just there to put an All-American face against the Hart Foundation's anti–U.S. sentiment in 1997.

Still, even after beating Bret Hart on TV and headlining the *Ground Zero: In Your House* pay-per-view against him in September 1997, Del Wilkes' wrestling career, and his life, didn't have a happy ending. A few months later, a triceps tear put him on the shelf. I saw him soon afterward, and he gave me some sadly surprising news.

He was done. No more weightlifting, no more wrestling, no more gym time.

Del battled drug addiction for the next few years, and looked to have come out on top. He moved to South Carolina and started selling cars, and I tried to stay in contact with him. But then he stopped returning my calls.

I think he just got wrapped up in nothing to do. The effects of drug use can keep hurting your mind and body long after you find sobriety, and I believe Del still struggled with depression. When my agent called me in June 2021 to tell me that Del, just in his late 50s and a newcomer to grandparenthood, had died of a heart attack, I was saddened and shamed, but not really surprised.

Going Around and Around (and Around!)

If it wasn't one thing, it was another. And if it wasn't that, it was about ten other things.

Global. The WWF. Indy shows. I spent the first chunk of 1992 getting passed all over the place like a misdirected package.

Not that I'm complaining about it. I got lots of paychecks, albeit nothing steady, and my reputation spread all over the place. But if I'd had the time and tools, I would have built myself a cloning machine and sent my copies around.

And then things got even tougher. I didn't say worse, but tougher.

Someone let me know about a new promotion that Jim Cornette was starting back in Tennessee, calling it Smoky Mountain Wrestling.

I was a little iffy at first. I'm only human, and every wrestler deserves a break once in a while. But, hey, I knew how smart Jim was. It was pretty close to my hometown, so travel wouldn't be much of an issue. And no one was going to ask me to work for free.

Starting out working with my old friend Tim Horner, I'd soon battle Brian Lee all over the promotion.

That was the first time I'd meet Chris Candido as well. A few years later, he'd become part of perhaps the biggest highlight of my career.

Still, if I had to pick a highlight of working for Cornette's promotion, it would be my ring wars with a man named Paul Orndorff. Mr. Wonderful himself.

Working with him was nothing new; we'd hit the mat during my first go-round in the WWF and on the indys. Still, when one of the biggest draws of the 1980s specifically requests to work with you, it really makes you proud. A fellow gym rat and former amateur mat man, like me, Paul had contacted Jim because he knew we could put on a show.

And we did. He'd been working as a face for a few years now, and I was glad to be a heel again, especially if it meant I could work with him. Paul had always shown me a ton of pointers on succeeding in and out of the ring, and I knew I'd learn something.

Firing off one cheap shot after another, I gained the upper hand and fist. As I backed Paul up against the ropes, he told me to throw him out of the ring. And once we got there, Paul all but demanded that I gun him headfirst (face-first, actually) into a nearby camera. Watching it later on, I was proud of how great the visual looked.

As did the ending. Back in the ring, Paul lifted me upside down for one of wrestling's most legendary piledrivers. He dropped me smack on my head, knocking me so far out of consciousness I could hardly hear the fans cheer and chant his name.

No, not really. I never felt a thing. It takes some serious talent to take one of wrestling's most devastating moves and make it harmless, but Paul did it.

Back in the WWF

By the summer of 1992, the WWF had seen me getting over with both Global and Smoky Mountain. I was winning, the fans were cheering, I was in great with all the wrestlers. I was becoming a hotter and hotter commodity. Maybe all of that could sell me a few more tickets for them than I had in the past.

Or maybe WCW was thinking the same thing, and might just grab me and push me up and over there. Either way, the WWF figured it was time to make a move.

At tapings one day in Louisville, J.J. Dillon happened to notice

Back in the WWF

me in the restroom. He mentioned my accomplishments elsewhere. I took a shot.

"J.J.," I asserted, at least hoping I had the slightest bit of leverage, "you give me a contract, and I'll never go anywhere."

That was true. I wanted the money, yes, but the security of full-time work was just as big a priority for me. If someone else I'd been working for at the time had made me a similar offer, I'd have grabbed it as well. But then and there—well, not right there in the bathroom!—the WWF handed me a new deal and more guaranteed folding green than I could have gotten anywhere else at the time.

As hectic as my schedule was and continued to be, those few months were some of the easiest of my career as far as in-ring work went. Right around then, the company started dumping about the entire roster, along with a few local fellows from whatever town we were in, into forty-man (or however many fellows they could gather) battle royals. Such a great way to get everyone a payoff.

Battle royals are some of the simplest matches to perform. Basically, at the start, it's just a bunch of guys walking and talking and punching and kicking. You don't want to do anything flashy at first. To begin with, the crowd has so many different people to focus on that nobody's going to notice. Second of all, you don't have room. The whole time you're in there, you're worried about getting an inadvertent smash in the back of the head by a flying elbow or dropkick. It's brawling in the middle of the ring, and people trying to power each other over the ropes, on the ropes and corners. People just want to see you methodically knock the shit out of each other and try to toss each other to ringside.

Once the numbers thin out, then you can show your individual stuff. There are few enough people in the ring that the fans can see the standouts. That's when things can get really crazy.

I was a ways away from making my *Royal Rumble* battle royal debut, but I'd have a blast with that. Later on, one of the highlights of my WCW career would be the three-ring *World War 3* pay-per-view at the Palace of Auburn Hills in Detroit. Sadly, I only got to the event in 1998, the fourth and final time the company would start the War, and I didn't win. Every time I think about that match, I wish that someone would bring it back, along with the similar *Battlebowl* event that WCW held for a few years. I'm sure I'm not the only one who enjoyed being in the midst of these events.

Elsewhere, I was back to getting Bushwhacker battering rams and the occasional Doomsday Device from the Legion of Doom. Just before my program with Owen kicked off, I had a few matches with his older brother, then the proud owner of the Intercontinental strap. Tito Santana and I opened many a show. Sgt. Slaughter choked me out with his Camel Clutch. I only worked with Kerry Von Erich a few times, and he was a hell of a nice guy, but that discus punch of his nearly broke my jaw and sent me to dreamland.

Yeah, it got to the point where I started counting the people I hadn't worked with. The list just kept getting smaller and smaller. After a while, as far as I could remember, there was just one guy there, who I kept hoping and hoping I'd finally get the same shot that so many others had.

All I wanted was a chance, just one go. I know virtually everyone in the Federation wanted the same opportunity, but most of them had already had it, and I felt like I'd earned it.

Just one time in the ring with Hulk Hogan.

Look, I knew I wasn't going to headline a pay-per-view against him or anything. Maybe not even a major show. But many times, he'd come out after the taped part of a show for a dark match, one that only those in an attendance would see, usually against a heel the company was trying to push. Sometimes it led to the opponent's getting a longer program with Hogan, sometimes not.

But I think he and I could have done something special. We were both from Florida, so we'd have both had some hometown fanfare during a company trip through the Sunshine State. It could have inspired every wrestler with a dream of battling the best.

Ric Flair had given me a hell of a match during his champion days, and he would do so again later in my WCW career. Hogan had been counted out against Lanny Poffo back in 1989 on *Saturday Night's Main Event*. It would have been nothing for him to get in the ring with me, even if I'd have ended up taking his legendary legdrop (like there would be any other outcome!).

Never happened. Hogan was a good guy backstage, although I didn't really spend much time with him. Still, I never heard anything about him wanting to work with me, even for a one-shot deal, or the decision-makers letting us put on a show.

But he was gone for good—well, for a few years—by the summer of 1993, and I still had plenty to work against. Not long after that, Owen and I tore it up at *Summerslam*.

And a few months later, I'd get another pay-per-view shot. And this one would mean a hell of a lot more.

I Get "Knighted"

Like almost everything else in my WWF career, to that point, my biggest pay-per-view splash came out of nowhere on a whim. Up until literally a few hours before the show began, even I had no clue I'd be a part of it.

As I would be for every pay-per-view of my career, I was there early. You never knew when you might have to suddenly step in, and I, like everyone else backstage at the Boston Garden the day before Thanksgiving 1993. The whole roster was there, although we knew only a few of us would actually get into the *Survivor Series*. But injuries happen, no-shows and contract disputes tend to pop up at the worst of times, and we were ready to sub in.

Well before the show, at least one major change had sent the company scrambling. Not long after losing his first WWF title, Bret Hart had plunged into a huge feud with Jerry Lawler, and Hart had enlisted his entire family, including his dad Stu, to show up to fight the good fight. It wouldn't have been the main event, but many fans had undoubtedly grabbed the show to see Lawler finally get a series of Hart attacks.

Then came a monkey wrench that threatened to derail the entire angle, if not the show itself. Lawler had suddenly found himself in legal trouble involving an underage girl, and the angle with him and

Bret would be on the backburner for over a year, although something that would turn out a hell of a lot hotter would be found to take its place.

Now it would be Shawn Michaels in Lawler's spot at the Series, and the consolation prize suddenly shined as bright as first place.

Wrestling is full of that "hindsight 20/20" garbage, but many people truly thought that after Marty Jannetty got launched through the window of Brutus Beefcake's "Barber Shop" set by Shawn in 1991, making the Rockers' breakup about the most explosive divorce in wrestling history, he might actually come back and be bigger than Shawn. With all that babyface sympathy behind him, there was reason to figure it might be Marty who'd go to the top of the federation, win the big matches and the titles, headline the big pay-per-views, make it all the way through.

As crazy as that seems, three decades later, when Shawn did absolutely everything and Marty's career fizzled out (to the point that wrestling jargon refers to the lesser-successful member of a squad as "the Marty Jannetty of the team"), people who believed that shouldn't be ashamed. Wrestling's like that. Shawn just had more pizzaz for the business, more entertainment ability. Most of his biggest moments came as a heel, but some were as a babyface as well. Marty as a heel would not have worked. Shawn had the drive and talent like very few others.

He and Hart had main-evented *Survivor Series* a year before, and Bret had managed to hold the upper hand since then. But just as Owen and fellow Harts Bruce and Keith would be there to back up their big bro, Shawn was coming with reinforcements as well.

So what would all this have to do with Barry Horowitz? Well, like I mentioned before, I first figured, very, very little. How fortunately wrong I'd be.

Because Lawler had been the object of destruction amongst the Harts, he'd be the focal point of his team. Rather than put him out there with three lesser-known guys, however, the Federation gave the King his own trio of Knights to do some bodyguarding. Now it would be Shawn with the three men in masks, and armor made of tights.

And, according to rumors I still hear today, one such masked

I Get "Knighted"

man was scheduled to be none other than a legend who I'd been cheering for as a world champ since my high school days.

It was to be Terry Funk.

Bret Hart vs. Terry Funk? Hell, Bret and Owen vs. Terry and Shawn? That could have headlined pay-per-views itself.

But none of it would happen. Again, this is simply what I've heard. Apparently, Terry called Vince McMahon and informed him that he wouldn't be up in Beantown that day.

Why? Because his horse was sick. Terry loved his animals, and that horse might have cost him six figures. It wasn't like he needed the Federation's money at that point either. Many of us wish we could prioritize ourselves like that.

Still, there might have been another reason. As each Knight lost—yes, no one thought anyone on the heel team, except maybe Shawn, had the slightest chance of still standing at the end!—he'd be forced to unmask. Bret didn't want that. Vince didn't want that. Terry was against that, as his making such a cameo would have taken the focus off the match's real angle.

So now the company had to recruit some new Knights in little time. Fortunately, there was a slew of locker-roomers ready to knock each other out of the way for a spot in battle.

Legendary veteran Greg Valentine stepped into the blue costume. In the black getup would be none other than Jeff Gaylord. I liked Jeff. His sense of humor could crack anyone up, and while he was never a great worker, he tried as hard as anyone.

After the incident with Eddie ended Gaylord's Global career, he'd headed back to the USWA, and was now trying to break into the WWF. Unfortunately for him, that wouldn't happen, as Jeff's work ethic didn't produce enough results to impress the right people.

And, I learned from Pat Patterson, I'd be taking Terry Funk's place in red.

I couldn't believe my luck. Desperate to hide the Knights' identities, they ordered me to shave my beard. I would, after all, be wearing a chinless mask, and no one could notice me. They tucked Greg's hair into his mask. If anyone had any tattoos or other distinguishable marks, they were covered up very fast.

Working as a heel was certainly nothing new for me, but this was going to be different from the Barry Horowitz persona. I was there to do a job, and I don't mean getting pinned for the umpteenth time, or not just that. I had to be stoic, there to ensure that my team captain would be safe.

No jawing with the fans. No cheap heel tactics. And, it was sometimes tough for me to remember, no back-patting when I got into the ring. I wasn't Barry here. I was as much a robot as a wrestler.

Despite the issues that would soon develop between them, Bret and Shawn were still getting along great here, and all of us quickly laid out the match in less than an hour. Things would eventually focus on Bret and Owen, but there would still be time for some fun before that.

As I stepped through the backstage area before the match, I noticed some wide-eyed, pint-sized fellow standing by the door. I didn't know if this guy was even a wrestling fan, but even if so, there was little chance he'd know it was me under the mask.

Armed with some significant advantages in height and muscularity, I maneuvered toward him. He turned around and looked at me like he had seconds to live.

"Hey, shorty," I growled. "Get out of my way." He scurried off in terror.

It was Ray Combs, none other than the then-host of *Family Feud* and the guest announcer for our match. It's tough for me to even think about that without grinning.

Originally, the match would have been at least as much storyline as talent. Lawler would have been hiding behind us three Knights as the Harts mowed us down one by one until he was standing alone. Shawn chose to take a different tactic, starting things off himself and wrestling the majority of the match for his squad. Everyone hoped that fans would be so taken by our collective ability that they'd forget about the Lawler-Hart issue.

And we think they did. The majority of my time in the match was spent against Owen, but the entire family got a chance to tear the living hell out of my legs—another tough part of the match was having to wrestle with a very basic moveset, as doing anything Horowitz signature-based might have given me away as well. I managed to stick around for almost half an hour in the match, longer

I Get "Knighted"

than Jeff, but Bret eventually slammed me down with a spinebuster and planted me in the Sharpshooter for the quitting.

Of course the Harts would win, but Bret would accidentally cause Owen's elimination near the end. Those two would have a feud that would go for years. Owen would beat Bret at the next *Wrestlemania*—commonly called one of the greatest opening matches in *wrestling* history, not just the *Wrestlemanias*—only to see his older brother win the title later that night. The rest of the family would be involved in Bret and Owen's legendary cage match at *Summerslam* later that year. Owen would cost his brother the world title at the following *Survivor Series*. The two simply went to heights they could never have reached without each other, and took the Federation up with them. I don't think the company would have gotten to the same heights if Lawer and Hart had remained the main event.

Funny secret for fans of the WWF at that time—they might have seen quite a bit of me without even knowing it still today. I'd keep the Knight outfit on for the rest of the year and some of the next, although sometimes my colors would change. I'd be the Red Knight one night, the Blue or Black one soon after. I don't think I was ever on TV doing this, but sometimes I'd be by myself, usually losing to Marty Jannetty. And while long-term tag team wrestling has never been a forte of mine, once in a while, Steve Lombardi would become another Knight and step into the ring alongside me, where we'd typically fall to Men on a Mission.

Early in 1994, I'd welcome a fellow named Thurman "Sparky" Plugg to the company by losing to him in South Carolina. Like most wrestlers, he'd zip through the gimmicks before hitting it hardest as Hardcore Holly. I spent the majority of the year working with him and another WWF newcomer called the 1-2-3 Kid—yes, the future X-Pac himself! Reno Riggins and I came *this* close to beating the Headshrinkers for the federation tag titles. And then there was...

Oh, hold on a second here. I've touched on the beginning of my love, borderline *need* for country music, one that still stays with me today. Listen to it all the time, just as I have for decades.

Around this time, though, I got to take a step farther into the genre. Here's where I happened to be in the right place at the right time around a few very right people that reached right out and pulled me into a dream come true, handing me my own special spot in country legend.

A Part of Country Music History

As I scribbled a few chapters ago, country music had been my main such interest for years. You'd catch me listening to it on planes, in locker rooms, in hotels, everywhere. I'd be watching it on TV at home. I think it's all but legally required for any country fan to have a favorite Garth Brooks song, and mine, probably like a lot of his fans, is "The Dance." But not for the reasons you might think.

If you look at the lyrics, or listen to the song on the radio, it's a tale of a guy who was in a great relationship, only to see it end, though for the right reasons. That's an unusual tact in music, but it's a hell of an uplifting song.

But if you watch the full video, it's a whole separate impact. Between clips of Garth himself belting out the dance, there's a montage of people who paid the ultimate price for their dreams. The crew of the Challenger shuttle, President Kennedy, Martin Luther King, even Lane Frost, killed by a bull in the midst of competition in 1989, two years after he took a world title in the sport. Seeing the song, rather than just hearing it, hits you twice as hard, and it still lifts me up today.

Just a few years ago, I was driving home from a show, with, per usual, the genre on the radio. Then I heard Miley Cyrus' voice.

It certainly wasn't the first time she'd been on there, but I hadn't heard this one before. Whereas Brooks had told us about a dance, this one was about a trip upward. Yes, I'm talking about "The Climb," which just about anyone who's had trouble getting off the bottom of the corporate ladder, let alone to the top, can relate.

A Part of Country Music History

"There's always gonna be another mountain," she explains. "I'm always gonna wanna make it move. Always gonna be an uphill battle. Sometimes I'm gonna have to lose. Ain't about how fast I get there. Ain't about what's waiting on the other side. It's the climb."

In a business like wrestling, when everyone, those who stick around, lose all the time at the start, but come back to pay their dues, these words are pretty accurate.

Nothing happens fast in the business, and it shouldn't. If you're main eventing, let alone winning a belt, a month after your first match, you haven't paid your dues. You haven't learned nearly enough. And these are the people that are *much* more likely to let their egos get out of control—and, when they eventually lose the title for whatever reason, have trouble rebounding, so much so that they end up quitting.

On my rare occasions off, I might even venture out to a concert every now and again.

My family and I had just *happened* to migrate to Nashville to work for Jerry Jarrett in the 1980s, and we might just live back there someday. One day in 1994, we were hanging out at the Nashville Fairgrounds for the Summer Light event, which eventually became the Country Music Association Festival. Six figures' worth of fans showed up to watch, and hopefully meet, some of the biggest names in the genre.

Tammy Wynette noticed us, and, like most people who met him back then, fell straight in love with Josh, holding him, chatting with him, gushing over him. Honestly, I think Josh had more girlfriends before his first birthday than I did in my first couple of decades.

In the far distance, I saw another fellow strolling through the crowds. I'd heard him in some opening acts recently, and he'd done pretty well, but I didn't know his name or any of his songs. Apparently, neither did anyone else; while fans were all over many of the celebrities at the event, as much or more so as I'd seen fans attack everyone from Hulk Hogan, Bret Hart, and the rest of my top ring colleagues of then, this gentleman made his way across the entire event without a single autograph request, as far as I saw. However, his involuntary anonymity would disappear very soon.

Then a gentleman that I'd seen quite a few times stepped forward.

Wrestling Is My Gimmick

"How are you?" he asked. "I'm the lead guitar player for Joe Diffie." His name was Lee Bogan, and next to him was Keith Burns, another member of Diffie's band.

I tried to keep my composure as Bogan explained what a fan of mine he was. But then he inquired as to whether I'd like to be a part of Diffie's next video. And my head nearly blew straight off, taking my then-country-appropriate mullet right along with it.

Yeah, I figured I could budget my schedule for such an outing. Actually, if they'd needed me to go over right then and there, I'd have been off like a world-record sprinter.

Everyone met up at a closed drive-in movie theater in Lewiston. As Joe, Lee, and the rest of their band told the story of a young man and his trucks in "Pickup Man," a huge crowd, mainly pretty ladies and rednecks, gathered behind them, singing and clapping along.

It felt like we filmed the song a thousand times, but enthusiasm was never a problem for anyone. Seated on the bed of a red pickup, wearing a black tank top, I was right at the head of the group—and even managed to work my back-patting gimmick into the production.

Even with over thirty of his songs on the *Billboard* magazine chart in less than fifteen years, "Pickup Man," would arguably be the top one of Diffie's career, making it to the top of the chart for a month straight. Wrestling fans today still ask me about it.

In November 2023, just over three years after the COVID virus stole Diffie from the world far too soon, Post Malone, Hardy, and Morgan Wallen did their own version at the Country Music Association awards.

I stayed friends with Bogan after that, and he got me into quite a few more shows. A favor I did for one of his colleagues would end up becoming a career highlight for me.

Some wrestlers get managers to add some heat, one way or another. Others are more in the mentoring sense. Sometimes workers will show up and find themselves left off the card, usually at an indy show, and the promoter's nice enough to let them walk out alongside a performer, just to get them a paycheck. I've had quite a few managers during my career, some for longer than others.

And if you asked me my favorite, there's absolutely nothing to argue about.

A Part of Country Music History

Oliver Humperdink, very far and away. I learned a ton from him. The patience that he showed with my inexperience was almost saint-like. He was wonderfully articulate about the old school of wrestling, how to get heat, everything. When a lot of veterans would have busted my chops or ignored me altogether, and many did, he reached out when he had very little to gain; if his managing of me hadn't worked out, there's a load of other people they could have put him with, and he'd have been just as effective. I regret not keeping in touch with him before he passed.

Yes, no question as to the main manager for me. If asked to name my favorite individual experience with a manager, however, that's a different answer.

I personally didn't have many managers while working the independent circuit, but this one stands out for a couple of reasons. See, sometimes people don't realize that no matter how famous you get, no matter how many people like and know you, you've still got your own dreams and wishes. Things that you just hope you could do, if only once.

With the help of Diffie and a couple of promoters, I made that happen.

I was working an indy show at some small Tennessee town not far from Nashville, and one of Diffie's guitarists told me he'd always wanted to be part of a wrestling show. I went to the show runners with his request, and I was kind of surprised at how quickly they said OK.

He put on a plaid, nerdy suit, taking snobbishness to the extreme. He named himself Faron Square (get it?). He did every single thing right that night.

I was a heel, and he helped me grab all kinds of heat. He battled the fans, some of which were certainly trying to figure out why this guy looked so familiar. He did it all. I'm sure years of performing in front of wild audiences helped him in that regard, but I've worked with many with much more wrestling-specific training that weren't as effective at managing as he was.

He helped me cheat to win. We got booed out of the building. And then he thanked me for helping his dream come true, and went right back to strumming the guitar.

Wrestling Is My Gimmick

You don't get a lot of chances like that, but they're amazing opportunities when they do arrive. That's definitely one of the most memorable experiences of my life, not just my wrestling career.

Oh, one other flashback here; that person that was still an unknown (at least, to me) back at the start of this chapter, the one still looking for a way into the country music world at that event in Nashville? His star went into the stratosphere very soon after, with a fandom that believed in a *hell* of a lot more action, if not a little less talk. People loved him, and he certainly "loved this bar"! When he asked, "How do you like me now?" generations of music fans answered in the high volume affirmative.

Yes, it was Toby Keith himself, who rose out of the country genre and into the mainstream for about a quarter-century, and I was proud to count myself in his fan group for one album after another.

Ironically, he'd even take a few brief steps into wrestling. Every country music fan watching in the first days of Total Nonstop Action wrestling in June 2002 wanted to climb in the ring and help Keith put an American boot in the ass of Jeff Jarrett, hardly a sufficient punishment for someone with the audacity to interrupt a live show of "Courtesy of the Red, White, and Blue"! A few years later, millions of WWE fans, particularly those of the male persuasion, had a new reason to envy Keith on a *Raw* episode, as none other than the Bella Twins handed him a specially made WWE belt and then walked him to the ring.

Sadly, just as I made my way toward the finish line of this book in February 2024, the music world's heart broke when Toby passed away. Right around the first time I saw him, he'd explained to a betrayed lady of her boyfriend, "He Ain't Worth Missing."

Toby, however, was, and will be forever.

In the Ring and Out of Trouble

Back to wrestling, and back to 1994. Per usual, I spent the majority of my ring time, at least at the matches' endings, on my back, either on the mat or getting nearly torn in half with Lex Luger's torture rack. I was doing comedy matches with Doink the Clown. I was losing to Virgil, who sadly also passed away as I was finishing up this piece. But my Global pal Ben Jordan had found a spot in the WWF, and he put me over quite a few times.

Ben Jordan: The WWF would periodically call for guys from Tennessee, and they'd fly us to New York or Dallas or Ohio once a month for them. A guy from Memphis one told me, "Make these people believe that you think you're about to win this match. Go out there pumped up," and I always did, and someone once said, "Ben Jordan's an overconfident jobber." I was like, I'll take that. Barry always came in there showing that he was gonna give you a good match, a good try. Guys don't always go out and show that.

We had a match at a high school in Nashville. We wrestled for thirty minutes straight, which was nothing to Barry. I was like, "Oh my God, how am I going to remember to do this or do that?" He laid out the match, and we went out there, and I got back to the dressing room, and he gave me the biggest hug, and he said, "You did it!"

In 1995, I was working my shoot job as a state inspector for the highway department. Then I got pinned under a concrete pump truck by an eighteen-wheeler. That took me out for about a year. I never went back to the WWF, but I started doing tag wrestling in Tennessee, Kentucky, and Alabama. I never got back into the shape I was in. Barry gets me motivated, getting me back to the gym, and helping with my diet. He still calls me, always encouraging me to get back into gym and get after it.

Wrestling Is My Gimmick

Yes, 1994 was a pretty good year for me on an individual level. But not everyone was as lucky.

For a few years, rumors had been making their way around the locker room, usually in whispered tones, about steroid usage. With some of these guys as big as they were, I'd have been nuts to think it wasn't happening, up to a point. I used to joke and chat about it with the guys from Demolition on road trips.

I'd tried not to pay too much attention to it. I never saw anyone have the drugs, let alone use them. No one was stupid enough to even ask me if I wanted any. I wouldn't have been a shit-stirring rat and run to the bosses or anything, but I'd certainly have laughed in their faces and walked away.

The only sort of interaction I ever had with the drug issues came up in the form of a pair of prepositions.

Once, just before a show, two people—one I don't remember, the other I won't name—came up to me.

"Hey, could you piss test for me?" one of them asked, holding out a cup. "Just piss in this, and I'll sneak it into the test."

Clearly, this guy wasn't squeaky clean. Maybe steroids, maybe cocaine or just marijuana, which you would get fined over back then, but something that was going to dirty up his urine.

Still, I'd give him some credit. It took a set of balls to ask for this kind of help. I didn't show, let alone admit it, but I was impressed in a rough sort of way.

So much that, for one of the guys, I did it. But only once or twice. I was afraid I'd get in trouble, and the guy never had the decency to show a little appreciation. No saying thanks, nothing. Quite frankly, he'd been a prick before. I'd hoped he'd changed, either with time or me doing him this favor, but he was still an asshole, so I stopped helping him pretty fast.

But compared to the boss' troubles, this guy could have been crossing a street.

A few years before, Dr. George Zahorian, a ringside doctor who'd been working for the WWF, was convicted of illegally supplying anabolic steroids. But then he started talking, and the company's foundation shook faster and faster.

It came out, quite quickly, that the doctor had been dealing to wrestlers and to Vince McMahon's office—keep in mind, though, that steroids had only become illegal in 1990, and the company had begun drug testing the next year.

In 1993, Vince McMahon had been indicted for both possessing and distributing steroids. The next summer, he went on trial. Forget the WWF; he could have lost his freedom.

And there were several locker room voices convinced that one or both of these things were going to happen. Suppose he was convicted and went away? Who would lead the company? Would enough advertisers and partners leave to put the entire company out of business?

And if certain people could nail Vince on this, they may not stop there. They could have gone to WCW to look for the same things. And they might even find something. If they did, could the same things happen there? Then, not only would we be unemployed, but the only other game in town would end as well.

Well, they didn't. After Vince was acquitted in July 1994, the Feds decided that if they couldn't catch the big fish, hunting for minnows wasn't worth the time and money. But a dark cloud would hang over the business for a long time, and it's shrunk, but still there today. We keep hearing about wrestlers suffering all kinds of horrible, often incurable health effects from excessive steroid usage, and many, way too many, such as Eddie Guerrero, have died from heart issues, a common effect of those that stay on the gas for too long.

But to give credit where it's due, while most in the high offices had been too busy worrying about Vince's legal issues to care much about the in-ring product, those there were putting on some of the best shows in history. Bret and Owen were battling for an hour at a time in Ironman matches about every other week, it seemed. Razon Ramon and Diesel, close friends backstage, squared off for the Intercontinental title across the country. The Undertaker had been out for a while, but he was back, and doing what he could with Yokozuna.

Earlier that year, I'd been back in Japan, mainly battling Terry Funk's older brother Dory or Steve "Dr. Death" Williams in tag matches. Over in America, I was doing the same stuff against the Bushwhackers and the Smokin' Gunns. By myself, however, something very strange started to happen.

At that point, and until 1997, *WWF Raw* was following the

same format as the other TV tapings, both there and at WCW—as in, doing one live show, then taping a few weeks' worth of episodes immediately afterwards. In my singles debut on *Raw* in May 1993, I'd come out on top of Phil Apollo. Granted, it was a dark match, seen only by a small Manhattan Center crowd, but I was proud of it.

Then I started scoring more *Raw* battles. I was up against Lex Luger. Razon Ramon. The 1-2-3 Kid. And still so many more with Doink the Clown, who beat me quite a bit over that period. This was when Doink had first started out, and Matt Borne did an outstanding job of making him into an evil clown. Borne worked as hard as anyone ever had with a character to make the clown a terrifying creation, and I, like most people, felt the character really lost something when Doink was turned face later that year. I'd work with Ray Apollo's Doink at some point, and the character today keeps showing up all over the indys, but no one's ever touched the job Borne did with it. They were just light copies; his Doink had some depth. He was another one who became his own biggest hindrance to a great career, with the drug habit that shortened more than his time in the ring.

While *Raw*'s crowds hadn't reached the size they would in a few short years, people were cheering for me. They'd get loud when I got ahead in a match. They'd boo when I got beaten, or even beaten down. I could feel and hear myself winning over more and more fans per taping, and I wasn't the only one.

Early the next year, I headed down to Texas and put over a newcomer named Chris Candido. That's all he was back then—just Chris Candido. No real gimmick, no manager, albeit with a hell of a lot of athletic ability and enthusiasm. I didn't think much of that match just yet.

That would change soon. Everything would, and would forever in my career. But there's a little bit more to this piece before we get there.

Lenny Lane, former WCW cruiserweight champion: I wrestled Barry in Iowa in April 1995, in the third match of my life, right before they were gonna start the program with him and Candido. I was trained by Eddie Sharkey, after the first month, I showed up at a show, and Eddie's like, "You gotta work the show tonight." I was like,

"What?" Nowadays, you can't get a spot on a show, cause everybody shows up. But back then, if somebody missed, either somebody was gonna work double or somebody was going to get left off. I'd done two matches un two months.

Eddie called me and said, "We're doing TV tapings for the WWF." I said, "No way, I'm not ready." He said, "Oh, yeah, you're a natural. You're ready." So I went down with a truckload of other people who'd been in the business for a while. The guys were like, "You're so lucky! You're going to get paid, but you're not going to work. You're too new." Then we show up, and I was the first match of the taping, against Barry. Eddie said to me, "If they ask you, say you've been in the business for three years and had about a 100 to 150 matches." I don't like to lie, but that's what you do in the wrestling business.

I used to watch Barry when I was younger. Here was a guy who's an established star. He followed me around for about a half hour, before the match, explaining it to me. Barry and I went over this match. I was on top of him in the beginning, and then he does a comeback, and then we go home. They were saying, "If you mess up, we might have you go out there again." I was controlling the match when it started. I think I had him in an armlock. But then (referee) Dave Hebner leans in and says, "Go home!"

I was like, "Go home?" I didn't know what that meant. I thought it meant to let Barry go. We're gonna get out of the ring, we're gonna do this again like they mentioned earlier. Barry said, "Do this!" Then he hit me with the Northern Lights and beat me.

When you're learning wrestling, you learn the moves, but you really don't know the reasons for them, or transitioning into the moves. What I learned from him that night is the psychology of why we do moves, and why a match goes a certain way, depending on the push. I was just glad the match was done, and everything went right, so it wasn't until afterwards that I appreciated what Barry said.

I knew psychology in wrestling, but I didn't know how angles were set up out there. If I'm setting something up with another person, I have to show that I have the ability to go with this person, so I guess when Barry, the way he was telling me, it looks like I beat him up, so how can he beat Candido? I finally told him, "Listen, Barry, I haven't been wrestling for three years. I've been in the business for two months, and this is my third match." We had a good laugh over that.

Finally Moving Up a Bit

Through the late 1980s and early 90s, Jeff Jarrett had won, oh, I don't know, about *a million* titles in the USWA, probably second only to Jerry Lawler himself. I was personally on the losing end of one of them when in freelance mode. Wearing the same Red Knight outfit that I hadn't gotten to wear alongside Lawler at *Survivor Series*, he and I made it to the finals of a USWA tag title tourney in October 1993 before falling to Jeff and, ironically enough, Brian Christopher, who, at that point, everyone was only *pretty sure* was actually Jerry's real-life son.

Not long after showing up in the WWF, Jarrett scored singles gold there, upsetting Razon Ramon for the Intercontinental belt at the 1995 *Royal Rumble*. At the time, I was ticked that I didn't get a spot in that show, but the WWF experimented by having participants come in every minute, rather than every two minutes like usual. The result was a rushed mess, with hardly enough getting enough space and time to put on much of a show. It might have been just a ploy to have Shawn Michaels and Davey Boy Smith become the first and last two in the match, but it didn't go over well, one reason why it hasn't been tried since. I wouldn't have minded being on the show, but in hindsight, I don't think it would have benefited me much.

I was still losing to Doink a lot. As I landed in California for the March 13, 1995, *Raw* at the Stockton Memorial Civic Auditorium, I expected more of the same, if not from the clown, then maybe Davey Boy Smith or Mabel.

But that was not the case. Just before the show began, I was informed I'd be facing Jarrett.

Finally Moving Up a Bit

As 1995 kicked off, I got ready for some of the biggest WWF happenings of my career.

Hey, cool! A title shot on TV, especially the biggest company show? Not bad! Yes, I'd be losing, but that was a heck of a lucky break for me.

Then came something else. I'd even get an interview.

OK, now this, this was momentous. In a show that was still an hour long, even the champs didn't get much of this. Even Jim Cornette sounded shocked on color commentary. Maybe he was mad that I didn't stay long in his Smoky Mountain promotion!

Wrestling Is My Gimmick

"I've got three things going for me," I assured an equally incredulous Vince McMahon. "I'm sure of myself, I'm confident, and I've been talking to Double R, the Bad Guy, Razor Ramon." Only in wrestling could a guy beat the hell out of you one week and be your personal pep talker the next, but this is how it is in our world.

"What's your win-loss record?" Corny rhetorically quipped? "0-forever?"

"There's first time for everything," Vince counselled. Maybe we'd pull the biggest swerve in *Raw*'s then-short history.

I gave Jarrett a bit more than he'd expected. I tossed him around with backslides and small packages. I rolled him up from the side, a move that would make history for me later that year.

We went back and forth more and more, but I was winning, nearly tearing off his left arm. And the crowd was responding. Even a hip-toss got me some cheers.

"Sometimes, the conditions are right, a guy competes over his head and over his ability," admitted Cornette. "Barry Horowitz may be doing that!"

I did, for a just a little while. As you probably know, I didn't win this one. But the ending was different than most. Rather than my opponent overcoming my courage and outsmarting me, it was me who damaged my knee when I slammed it into his face. Jarrett managed to lock on his figure four, and I was out.

Unlike most of my opponents, this guy needed some luck to win, and audiences could tell the difference. Maybe the next time I'd step into the ring, or shortly thereafter, I'd be the one holding the four-leaf clover.

I was still trying not to get my hopes too high up. Maybe the company had just done that to be nice. It might have been a small thing that everyone would forget about, a tiny piece of the puzzle that was actually geared toward the Jarrett-Ramon program. I kept my mouth shut and head down about it; if something was going to happen for me, more people might have to go a bit out of their way, and they weren't going to if I started blasting my own horn here.

Not long after, those Body Donna videos I mentioned way back at the opening started hitting. Skip and Sunny were going to show up and get us all in shape, or damn well wish we could be as good at it as them.

That May, the company took a long jaunt up to Bret and Owen's Canadian homeland. All over Alberta and Saskatchewan, I graciously welcomed Skip to the federation with one loss after another. And, yes, with Sunny on the mic, he was getting booed quite a bit. All according to plan.

But while it may not have been part of the predictions, I was getting more and more cheers. Fans were rooting for me, regardless of whom I was fighting. When you just get cheered for battling one or two opponents, it's usually because fans just want to see *someone* beat them, regardless of who. But even when I was heading out there with the biggest of names, like the Undertaker or Shawn Michaels, or the soon-to-be big names like Helmsley, people were still chanting my name. They didn't just have an issue with my opponent. They liked me as a performer. Experienced ears and minds behind the scenes could tell the difference.

And then, with a little bit of help from a few people, I finally stepped into history.

Hitting It Big with Skip

> From the perspective of my brother, I would ask him what it was like working with Barry Horowitz. He was like, "Dude, I love Barry Horowitz. He was really fucking good." The two of them could talk, get a finish, go out there, and it was good. "Working with him was like a night off in a way."
> —Jonny Rea, brother to Chris Candido

"Barry! Barry! Barry!"

The chants kept coming and growing. They'd been there since before I lost my match with Jarrett, and they were still there.

As my program with Skip had rolled forth, and, "Barry! Barry!"

resounded across Canada, it was clear that people even out of America knew me. They liked me. I was getting over with them.

But would they get a little bit more? Would they have a new reason to raise those chants and cheers a bit higher? Maybe they were chanting in a joking, maybe even sarcastic sort of way: "Let's cheer for this guy, even though we know he hasn't the first prayer!"

Maybe. But certain people were watching, and certain decisions were being made.

Fred "Tugboat/Typhoon/Shockmaster" Ottman: The wrestling business is an ego-based business, more ego-driven than others are. You got the whiners, you got the criers, and everything. But if you work hard enough, they're going to do something. Even nowadays, it's hard for guys to realize that if you have a hundred guys or more than are under contract to wrestle, there's only so much TV time. Once they're pushing people at different levels, you got to wait your turn, but when you're in front of the cameras, you bust your ass and perform and give them something to talk about, because between the writers and Vince (McMahon) and the people that are surrounding Vince, those are the people calling the shots.

At a Milwaukee house show in early June, road agent Blackjack Lanza found himself suddenly enthralled.

Sunny and Skip were getting booed like crazy, but that's expected. It's good. It's what heels should do. The new guys in town, they were making one hell of an impression, and fast. On their way. But before, during, and slightly after the match, my chants had been about just as loud. I was still getting over. I'd had one big match recently. Why not a few more?

That's what Lanza figured when he reported back to the front office. He told them about the show's attendance, the merchandise sales, and, maybe most importantly, especially for the wrestlers, who was over and who wasn't.

R.D. Reynolds, owner of *WrestleCrap.com*: They would do those TV tapings for *Superstars* and stuff back in the day. Those *Superstars* shows would be five hours of nothing but jobber matches, and then twelve Brother Love shows packed in there. So I'm sure if I was in the back, and I was a star, and I could say, "Oh, I'm going out with Barry Horowitz. Great. This guy knows what he's doing. There's not going to be any problems," and I'm sure if that guy, if you have talent in such a way, these guys were gonna say, "Hey, Vince, the next time you come to Florida, let's make sure Barry Horowitz is on the card."

Now Lanza told them that I was finally over enough. Pat Patterson jumped on board with him. So did Vince McMahon.

There in Pennsylvania, I'd wondered if Kevin Nash had been playing. Then came the meeting with Patterson and his folk.

They'd shown their confidence in me. Now it was up to me to come through for them, in a way I hadn't been allowed to in so many of my outings.

Me already in the ring, Skip and Sunny showed up and assured everyone that this would be just another act of simplicity.

"Here's what's about to happen here," Sunny blared, "another victory, one more, for the Body Donnas."

Wrestling legend Jim Ross decided to zing back.

"Hi," Ross sniggered on commentary, pulling out his sarcasm and sense of humor like we never saw enough of. "I'm J.R., and this is Gorilla ... and we're *not* the Body Donnas."

Sitting next to him, Gorilla Monsoon sounded confused.

"What *are* we, Jim Ross?" he pontificated.

"Well, that's probably up for debate," Ross smirked as the match began.

Skip flipped me over and tossed me around a lot, but I kept coming back. Slamming him, body-dropping him, a few uppercuts. I got in more offense in the first minute than some enhancers do in a week of matches. As I armdragged him around, the crowd got as loud as it had all night.

Then I patted my back and mocked his jumping jack skills. Not a good idea.

He slugged and tossed me down.

"He ain't nothing but a loser," he roared at the fans. "He ain't never won a match in his life!"

Wrestling Is My Gimmick

"Why don't you let us do the commentary?" Ross fired. "You do the wrestling. It works out better that way." Clearly, even a guy whose role it is to be impartial couldn't stand this loudmouth.

Skip kept me down, slams, dropkicks, everything. But as I tried to raise myself off the mat, it was clear I wasn't done.

He'd thought I was, ignoring me while he suddenly decided to put on a pushup display. Ten seconds later, my career (and, I'd like to think, wrestling history itself) had changed forever.

I crawled up next to him, grabbed him around his head, and flipped him over, rolling his shoulders to the mat in a three-quarter nelson grapevine, the very ball-and-chain move I'd worked so hard on all the way back in high school and college. Fans probably figured he'd kick out, lose his cool, and stomp me into the ground for the win.

But he didn't. The ref dived down and slapped the mat. Then again. Then again.

That's all you need.

Arms raised and jaws dropped. Cheers went roaring all over the arena.

"Horowitz wins! Horowitz wins! Horowitz wins!" Ross roared as I jumped around like I had springs in my shoes. I couldn't help but think that his enthusiasm crossed the line from scripted to real (the best kind of "shoot" in wrestling, if you will). "Can you believe it? Horowitz has just won his first match in the WWF!" Who gave the first flip if that wasn't true? Between him, me, and the fans, it was tough to tell who was most into things, and I think, deep down, Chris was flying himself.

"I don't believe it!" Gorilla responded. "Holy smokes!" Even I was feeling the same way.

The crowd kept cheering. Sunny jumped back into the ring and shouted into her mic, but people could barely hear her. Referee Dave Hebner followed me back to the dressing room, raising my hand all the way. In one of the shorter matches of my career, Barry Horowitz had pulled off one of the biggest shockers the game had ever seen. Even today, if fans go on the Internet searching for "Biggest Upsets in Wrestling History," my win is on most such lists.

For that one brief moment, I was the hottest real name in wrestling.

Hitting It Big with Skip

Ironically, Chris would get some revenge later that very day. Remember, these were the days where we'd tape a month's worth of TV shows in a single time and place. My win over Chris actually wouldn't air until the second week of July, and our next outing would hit the small screens even later than that.

In my second battle of the day, I finished up with Hunter Hearst Helmsley pedigree-ing my head through the mat. The crowd wasn't as against him as they would be during the future Degeneration X days, but he got booed.

When Skip came out and whaled me into the mat, however, the boos grew and grew. And I knew I'd be back.

A month later (but only a few days later in TV time) in Indiana, Skip geared up for the biggest match of his WWF career, at least thus far. After just a few months with the company, he had a shot at the Intercontinental Title—and all he had to do was take out Shawn Michaels. In the ring for an interview, Chris and Sunny explained how they planned to break the Heartbreak Kid.

There was just one problem. Those "Barry! Barry!" chants were still around, and fans couldn't wait to see me get back at him.

And I got revenge. As Skip looked to recover from a beating, I stepped to ringside. Before I could give him a taste of some medicine from the last time out, though, he jumped back in, and right into Michaels' legendary superkick and a loss.

Still, we weren't done. Elsewhere at the taping, Skip had already promised to make me pay. In ten minutes or less, he'd put me down for good—and if he couldn't, he'd admit defeat. I didn't even have to win the match to come out on top.

Well, that was exactly what happened. We hit each other with everything but bags of popcorn, and, with a short time left, it looked like he'd make good on his guarantee. But I kicked out, he rolled out of the ring, and the referee raised my hand as the buzzer sounded.

Gearing up for another yet TV battle with Skip, I headed into the back room of an arena one day. I don't mean the dressing room; most of these places have a huge ballroom-type place where everybody can hang out and chat. Go over their matches, their plans afterward, their adventures the night before, whatever. I happened to be lucky enough to meet someone new that day.

Wrestling Is My Gimmick

As a kid in Florida, I'd grown up watching Bill Watts tear it up all over the south, in and out of the ring as a wrestler and a promoter, mainly in the Universal Wrestling Federation. In the early years of my career, I'd have loved to have worked for him.

Well, now I was getting the chance. Vince had just brought Watts on as part of the booking team, and if there was anybody who could push us even faster in the right direction, it was this guy. Not everyone had liked Watts' storylines, but I thought they were great. He knew how to put together not just a great match, but a lasting series that could keep audiences turning in. I knew I'd be OK if he were around; Watts loved guys like me, Bret Hart, even Skip, guys who had the athletic side of the business down and didn't worry about being flashy and doing things just for attention. If you showed the sizzle outside of the ring, you'd damn well better have Filet Mignon–level steak to back it up between the ropes.

And that extended outside the shows as well. You had a character in the ring, and, up to a point, you stayed there outside the ring, even outside the arena. If you were a face, you didn't spend time with heels in your personal life (and this was even before fans threw everything you did on social media two seconds after it happened!). You didn't travel together, you didn't room together, you didn't dress together.

You also conducted yourself with the same toughness. Watts wanted people to believe that everything that happened in the ring was full-blown realistic. You had to be tough to work for him, and not just between the ropes. If you were out somewhere and somebody started trouble with you, like a drunk who wanted to show off for his friends by squaring off with a wrestling champ, you better win, no matter how many guys you had to take on. I can't speak for everyone, but for guys like me who didn't live the public life, let alone spend time in bars on the road, that wouldn't be much of a problem. I knew I wouldn't have trouble working for Watts.

But in any case, again, he was all about realism. With Pat Patterson and Jerry Brisco looking on, Watts and Skip were standing there, discussing Skip's match with me. One of us was going to give the other a smack that Watts wanted heard in the upper rafters.

As we chatted, Watts was facing me, with Skip standing behind him.

"Now, listen," Watts explained, "when you do a slap on TV, it's gotta be there, or it's going to look like a bad punch that couldn't break an egg. Here's how you have to do it."

Then he spun around like he was on fast forward—a hell of an accomplishment, considering he was six and half feet tall, over 300 pounds, and almost sixty years old—and absolutely *decked* Skip. I mean, he almost slapped Skip's face around to the back of his head. Skip didn't know whether to cry, shit, or fall backwards. His eyes were as glazed as a load of donuts.

Then Watts went right back to discussing the match with us. I was probably too shocked to hardly breathe, but he fortunately didn't notice. I got the impression that this was a pretty normal practice for him during his decades in the business.

Whatever, it worked. Skip and I went out there and had a great match. We even knocked each other around more than usual, although I don't think either of us used anywhere near the force that Watts had beforehand. We loved it, the fans loved it, and Watts seemed to love it. He certainly didn't say anything to us, which was always a good sign.

As we recovered in the dressing room, Skip came over to me.

"That slap was so hard," he admitted, "that I wanted to cry afterwards." I told him I was shocked that he hadn't.

But we laughed. We moved on, and we kept having great matches.

Sadly, Watts' time in the WWF would be short. As it turned out, he and his new boss were a little too similar. Back in the south, his show had been *his* show. He made the decisions. He called, and occasionally acted out, the shots. Of course, he knew how to delegate, any effective boss does, but the buck, the bucks, and the authority they brought, stopped with him.

To be fair, the success he had down there certainly gave Watts the experience and the credibility to say that. Wrestling's full of promoters who think that walking in with a ton of money makes them qualified to not only start or take over a promotion, but run it all the way to success, and those people almost invariably lose their money and talent *very* fast.

You did things the way he wanted, or you jumped on the SH-3 highway and motored right out of the UWF's Oklahoma homeland.

Quite a few people did, and not all were lucky enough to make it all the way over to Carolina, up to New York, or any of the other big promotions from there. Watts didn't mind being questioned once or twice, but handing him a hardcore challenge, let alone an order, was asking for a brawl in several different senses of the world.

Yup, just like Vince himself. He ran the show, he ran it right, and you adapted to his methods, and his authority, or you weren't going to be there. He and Watts agreed some of the time, maybe most of the time, but their ideas were far enough apart that Watts wasn't going to have the same authority he once did. Watts wasn't going to be anyone's supporting character, and had been smart enough about his past, at least in the financial sense, that he didn't need to be there anyway. Just a few months after he'd started, Watts was gone.

But, certainly aided by his impromptu clocking demonstration, Skip improved. We improved together, and our program kept drawing.

This was going well. Very well. As well as anything I'd encountered in my WWF tenure.

So well, in fact, that there was only one place for it to continue.

My Pay-Per-View "Debut"

The 1995 *Summerslam* wouldn't be my first WWF pay-per-view; that had come in the 1989 *Royal Rumble* in a non-aired match with Jim Powers. It wouldn't be my first non-dark match, as I'd been one of Shawn Michaels's infamous knights later that same year, against Owen and the rest of his family, at *Survivor Series*.

But it would be my first aired supercard match as Barry myself. And I'd pick up another first soon as well. Before that, however, we need to make a quick detour.

He'd only been with the company a little longer than Skip, but

My Pay-Per-View "Debut"

Hakushi had made his own impact pretty fast. As they always did, Owen and his brother Bret were putting on some of the top matches in the country, but company officials had decided to break off Bret, who himself had just dropped the federation title the previous November, and stick him into a program with the newcomer.

And just as he could with almost anyone, Bret turned the battles into highlight reels, making Hakushi into a main event threat and even battling him at some pay-per-views through the spring and summer of 1995.

That feud had been going for some time, and, as we sold out *Monday Night Raw* that August in Massachusetts, it looked like the Japanese would be the next in a long line to restore his courage with a big win over me.

Things went pretty fast for the first few minutes, him flying around and me looking for a way to bring him back to the mat. But someone got a little too impatient.

Skip stormed to ringside, looking for a close-up view of my next loss. As heels of wrestling tend to do, he got a little overconfident.

Not content to just watch, he jumped to the apron. I sent Hakushi slamming into him, then rolled my opponent up for the pin.

I was done, but Hakushi wasn't, giving Skip a nice beating of punishment before clearing him from the ring. Perhaps his sights and thoughts were changing as well.

And now we get to *Summerslam*.

My name and my back-patting had been making a mark on fans for years, but for the first time, the WWF handed me a little more character depth, in and out of the ring. Suffice to say, it was pretty far from the typical wrestling persona.

Preview graphics for the match had me looking a bit different than fans had seen me. Honestly, I didn't even look like a mat man at all.

Jewish people aren't specifically known, legitimately or otherwise, as tough and intimidating, ready to hand out the fisticuff beatings. Well, the fans already knew I was the exception to that rule (or "rule"). So they decided to make my faith a part of Barry Horowitz the performer in another way—the high-class intelligence that Jews have! Or that we're *supposed* to have!

Wrestling Is My Gimmick

Huge glasses. Dress shirts. Calculators. Even a pocket protector. A *pocket protector*? Yeah, that's what us brainiacs do. Clearly, from these photos, I looked like I'd rather be standing in front of a university advanced calculus class, not a wrestling audience. Come to think of it, it wasn't all *that* different from my early student days.

You know, it's funny—Bill Goldberg was still a ways away from wrestling stardom, but can you imagine if WCW had started him off like that?

There's typically two reasons to do this, to give someone a gimmick that others, especially those unfamiliar with wrestling, might look at it and scoff.

One is to punish those with an attitude backstage, those that show that they're not going to be team players even before they've really earned their spot in a lineup. If people piss and moan and whine, or even break character in the midst of the show, their spotlight is going to dim fast, and they end up having to work twice as hard.

I'm not a fan of that type of discipline, but I was going to make damn sure no one could ever apply it to me. I was going to personify the other common reason to get this sort of persona—a chance to prove that, no matter what, I was going to work my ass off at it until it got over. A chance to make the fans love it regardless.

I'd been around some real prima donnas who'd look at something like my nerd character and say, "Hell, no, I ain't doing that shit." I'd heard many utter exactly that.

And management's response was invariably, "OK. Then stay the hell home." Either you worked hard with what they gave you, or you didn't get to work—and therefore, your paychecks and business reputation would drop fast. I didn't care. I was getting paid. I was getting a push. I was going to show anyone who looked down on me that the rib was on them.

For almost a century, the folk tune "Hava Nagila" had been welcoming Jewish couples to marriage and kids to their teenage years; the WWF put together an updated upbeat mixed up version of the song for my entrances. Only in wrestling could one encourage others to, "Let's rejoice and be happy!" just a few moments before whomping someone into a pinfall.

My Pay-Per-View "Debut"

Stereotypical? Maybe, but not in a bad way. Not over the line to insulting. Less is more in wrestling, and character development can't and really shouldn't go all that far. The in-ring work is what brings fans to the arenas and gets them to turn on the TVs. Fans don't really want or need to know much about the people they watch, only enough to know who's worth cheering and who isn't. The company gives fans a little bit of a character as a starting point, and it's up to the wrestler to personify the persona. Fans knew from my name and the star on my tights that I celebrated Passover and Yom Kippur, so why not go a little farther with that?

But it didn't go so far as to making a mockery. They didn't ask me to do my interviews in Hebrew or wear a yarmulka or wave the flag of Israel. I wasn't told to get on the mike and scream about antisemitism. They might have pushed a little with the stereotypes, but not overboard.

Pittsburgh fans loved their mat action, and that night at the Civic Center was no kind of exception. Hakushi finally pulled the fans all the way over to his side early on by slipping past the 1-2-3 Kid—years away from X-Pac!—and some fellow named Hunter Hearst Helmsley made his first pay-per-view showing by Pedigree-ing Bob Holly for a victory.

Soon I had to take on Skip, and the fans were as behind me as they'd been since I'd beaten him the first time. I was going to deliver.

You can't really explain this sort of thing, or at least do it justice while trying it out. When you're at a pay-per-view, you just work harder, even if you don't always realize it. You brings things up a notch, and if you're lucky, you'd don't even realize you're doing so. A red-hot crowd that's going at high volume blasts your adrenalin up a few notches as well. House shows and TV tapings are great, but this is what they build up to. If you didn't succeed on those, both with your opponents and the fans, you wouldn't have won a spot on a special show, especially not on a *Summerslam*, which by this point and still today many fans see as the company's biggest annual show, aside from *Wrestlemania*. If people are judging you on a scale of one to ten, you give them a fifteen or twenty. It's like how NFL players move up their game from the regular season to the playoffs to the Super Bowl.

That night, I did. And so did Skip.

I stayed on the offensive for most of it, but, not exactly surprisingly, Sunny kept stepping into the action, both literally and figuratively. Many fans probably thought that the ref would get bumped, then she'd KO me from behind and give Skip a quick condescending pin.

But that would have thrown a roadblock into our momentum. I knew that, Skip knew that, and the people behind the scenes knew that, which is why we'd quickly agreed on the finish. My earlier victories and the pops they'd received weren't just going to be a one- or two-win wonder.

With Skip out freezing cold on the mat, I went up top, not a common move for me. Sunny shoved me down, and Skip handed out a massive suplex. But I'd have some outside help of my own.

Out came Hakushi. Was he mad at Skip for costing him his match to me early, or was he so impressed by the Body Donnas' ability that he'd swerve me and join them? In wrestling, the scenarios were equally likely.

He stepped up to the apron and leaped right over Skip's head, then charged out of the ring. Just as before, I caught the distracted blonde fellow with my pseudo-legendary small package, and held him down for the win.

Weeks before, Jim Ross had been the one to blare, "Horowitz wins!" This time, it was none other than a fellow named McMahon on commentary.

The crowd went as crazy as they had all night. I was jumping all over the place, and, as only wrestlers can know, this was no act.

Because it didn't even end when I got back to the dressing room. Chris was as high on life as I was, as we couldn't stop congratulating each other for the match. I just sat there, people walking back and forth in front of me. Some of them offered handshakes and congratulations, but I couldn't tell you a single one even today.

I've never done drugs and never will, but there's no way one of them can give a man a high like this. We'd told a perfect story in the midst of a perfect storm. When the fans, the backstage folk, and even the opponent who did it for you are rocking and rolling, it means you couldn't possibly have done more right.

We'd believed in ourselves, and people had believed in us—our match had actually gotten more time than Diesel's main event battle with King Mabel!

I sat there with a grin on my face that could have stretched over to Philadelphia. The next thing I knew, a full hour had passed, and I hadn't even taken off my boots!

Jonny Rea: My brother loved his experience with Barry. At the time, he was such a sponge. For him, doing a program with a guy like that, who was also serious about wrestling, who was also a smart guy, who was a legit tough guy, Chris didn't mind putting him over at all.

Skip and I spent the next month going back and forth. And Hakushi got into it too. We made vignettes of me showing him all the great things about America: where to shop, what to eat, how to drive. We even got to do a commercial for Karate Fighters action figures. It was the first time I'd ever gotten to do something like that, and it was fun. He'd start to take my place in the feud, downing Skip while I was squeaking out wins over Mabel's fellow Man on a Mission, Mo. Skip and Sunny started costing me losses to King Kong Bundy, a great guy who I wish I'd gotten to work with more often.

By that November, I was defeating Skip again, and then came our next pay-per-view outing.

Now we were in Maryland. Now we were at *Survivor Series*. And we were starting the show.

The 1-2-3 Kid had just gone bad, and managed to piss off his real-life close friend Razor Ramon, so we knew that would be a focal point. But the crowd didn't seem to care. As my teammates Marty Jannetty, Bob Holly, and, of course, Hakushi, battled Skip, Kid, and their team, all anyone could hear was those "Barry! Barry!" chants. Even after a few eliminations, and while Skip and Hakushi went at it, people kept wanting to see me—and you better believe I encouraged the hell out of it, clapping and patting my back on the apron! Even Vince and the others on commentary had to acknowledge the noise.

It would be almost fifteen minutes before I got in, and those chants kept coming. Kid and I mixed it up for a few minutes. Then Rad Radford—soon to rock ECW as Louie Spicoli before becoming one of far too many to pass away too soon—knocked me around for a while.

Wrestling Is My Gimmick

But as ironic in ways only wrestling can be, he just *happened* to decide to mimic Skip's pushups from before—and just as not-so-way-back-when, I packaged him down for the pin.

Now Skip and I were face to face, and I whaled him from turnbuckle to turnbuckle. But Kid tagged in behind my back, dropkicked me from behind, and pinned me. Marty would take Skip out soon after, but Sid Vicious showed up to distract him and leave Kid as the only one left standing.

I couldn't know it at the time, but my WWF career was already winding down. We'll go over that in a future chapter, but Chris and the roles he played in my career deserve a little bit more exposure, a little more thanks.

Once our program and respective WWF careers ended, both of which would happen the very next year, Chris and I didn't see much of each other. He and newcoming Body Donna Zip (Tom Pritchard) won the tag team title at *Wrestlemania* the next March, which might have been him getting his just due for his program with me, but that clearly didn't do much for him or the company, as Chris was gone that fall.

He was off to ECW, and I was doing my own thing elsewhere. We'd eventually become co-workers again very briefly in WCW, but never worked together in the ring.

We didn't meet up, we didn't talk, we didn't communicate. That's what happens in wrestling; you get way too busy to keep up with people in other companies. Sometimes you don't even get to hang much with the people you're working with.

Jonny Rea: Me and my brother would be going to the mall, and people would be running up, patting themselves on the back like Barry Horowitz, and running away. They thought he was gonna get pissed and beat them up. My brother would just laugh. He laughed about everything. He was like, "Why do fucking grown men really care about shit like that?" People were like, "Hey, Skip!" and pat themselves on the back and run away. My brother would start laughing, like he didn't give a shit. All these years later, people were still breaking his balls. He'd be bouncing around in the ring, and people would start chanting "Barry Horowitz!" He'd jump on the second rope, do the pat on the back, and the crowd would laugh.

My Pay-Per-View "Debut"

Once we both headed out of WCW, I believe I only saw Chris one more time, I think at an independent show in Florida sometime in 2001. By that point, I was on my way out of the business for the time being.

But I'll never forget that sad night in April 2005.

I got a phone call, an e-mail, maybe even a text. Probably from another wrestler. I don't even remember. I've kind of tried to forget.

"Hey, did you hear about Chris?" I think it said. If someone asks you a question like that, especially about a person you haven't seen or talked to for years, it's almost certainly bad news.

And it was the worst.

A few days before that, Chris had been working a pay-per-view for Total Nonstop Action wrestling. In one botched move, he was left with a double-leg fracture and dislocated ankle. Showing just how tough and dedicated he was to the wrestling business, he had plates and screws put in his leg the next day, then came right back to the TNA taping to help his friends. A huge cast on his leg, he was going to war at ringside as his pals won the tag title.

But a few days later, everything was gone—for him and for so many he'd touched in wrestling. Chris had started to feel ill and made it back to the hospital. He'd never see another sunrise.

Right down next to Owen Hart and my friend Mike Graham, who I'd lose to his own hand a few years later, Chris's death loss hit me as hard as any I've experienced in the sport.

It's sad to have to keep track of and rate things like this, but in a business such as wrestling, you get used to having to say goodbye far too soon. Any of us who have been in this line of work for long enough have probably lost a few loved ones, or at least highly respected ones.

I'm proud that, nearly two decades after we lost him, the wrestling business still remembers Chris. Fans he entertained, wrestlers he worked with, wrestlers who imitate his style, and wrestlers he helped train—like, say, a fellow called Dwayne Johnson, whom Chris defeated in the WWF before he became The Rock! If he were still around, I'd think he'd be an even bigger star than back then, now that the business focuses less on giant musclemen and more on those with some strong tactical skills.

Wrestling Is My Gimmick

For many, memories are all we can really hope for. We hope we're remembered, and for the good reasons. For Chris, I know I will, just like so many others. His characters might not have been the most upstanding, but he sure as anything was. For those who make it in the business, it's company first and individual second, and if Chris hadn't done that, I might not have found much elevation in the games—and neither might have many others.

Hakushi and I kept teaming for the rest of the year, and sometimes we'd come out on top, usually in six-man matches. Sometimes we'd beat Skip. Sometimes we'd even come out on top of a squad with Sid, or Isaac "Not Kane yet!" Yankem. Usually we'd go on first and get the crowd going. I scored my first pay-per-view tag team win at *In Your House* the next month in December, as we teamed with the Smokin' Gunns to knock down the Body Donnas, Yankem, and even former two-time company champ Yokozuna. Things like that, along with the battle royals I discussed earlier, are some really great ways that promoters get more and more people on the roster to the show, and get them paid.

Yes, once in a while, you get a reminder of why wrestling was the right career choice. When you see the bosses going out of their way to be nice just because it's right, it's a wonderful thing.

My biggest example of that took place far from the major federations. Actually, it was far from America.

For years, a fellow named Otto Wanz had been after me to mosey down to Austria and be a brief part of his shows. Wanz had won the American Wrestling Association title for a while right around the time I was breaking into the business, and was one of the top wrestlers in Europe for decades, but he'd moved on to promoting a few years before.

He'd heard of me, he'd seen me work, and he wanted to show me off. He never really told me specifically what about me had stood out, but I didn't really mind. He just made it clear that it wasn't about who I was or who I knew or who I was related to, just about what I could do in the ring.

It was 1992 or 1993 that he put me on a plane over the Atlantic, then put me in an amazing downtown hotel and ensured I had the greatest food and first-class cappuccino that would normally cost upwards of $20 a sip. Once, I was waiting in line at a restaurant, right behind two WWF superstars with a hell of a lot more audience appeal and recognition than I had.

The chef called for them to get a table. Otto stepped in.

"No," he said. "Barry's next."

I got to work out at some gyms that had helped spring the bodybuilding career of a fellow named Arnold Schwarzenegger, who credited Wanz with getting him into the sport to begin with. Then Otto handed me a spot in the main event, and had me beat his top star for the title. I even got to take it back to America, as long as I brought it back to lose a month later.

When it was time to leave, he picked me up in his Mercedes in the middle of the night and drove me three hours to the airport. He even handed me an extra $50 (this was three decades ago, so worth even more so today) and told me to go grab some food and souvenirs.

The same sort of thing happened on a different continent.

While I was still bouncing back and forth between Global and the WWF in the summer of 1992, Ted DiBiase stepped up to me one day and said he thought I'd be a good fit for a tour coming together for All Japan.

Of course I said yes. I'd been there a time or two before, and I knew I'd have a great time.

But I also knew that Japanese fans are different than those back in America. Not better or worse, just different. If you went over there, they expected you to wrestle. They wanted the scientific type, pretty much all the time. They weren't much for guys who just kicked and punched all the time, and they didn't go for cheap heat. I wouldn't be patting my own back over there.

A guy like the Ultimate Warrior might get over like crazy here in America, but if he went to Japan to put on his single-digit move arsenal, he'd be laughed at and booed and back on a plane home later that night. Doink the Clown might have gotten over as an evil heel, but ever since he'd gone good and on the side of comedy, they wouldn't want him either. You *wrestle* wrestled over there, or you didn't stay.

DiBiase's friend Stan Hansen had been one of the biggest American stars in the Lady of the Rising Sun, and he'd mainly been a brawler himself, but he had enough charisma to get over with the fans. Being twice the size of most of the stars over there, they were as awed by him (as well as my old friend Steve Williams and Terry Gordy, for the same reasons) as when Godzilla was tearing their town apart.

Just like Otto, the promoters made sure we foreigners had some great hotels to stay in, food to eat, everything. Once we got to the rings, however, we were on our own.

My first night there was something of an initiation. If I could make it through this, they'd keep me. The promoters had brought me over because they knew I could wrestle, but they couldn't have known if I was going to piss and moan if someone gave me a good whack, or throw a hissy fit about having to do a job. So they started off the tour (ironically, on July 4 of that year) by teaming me up with Stan and Johnny Ace, himself a common American sight over the ocean, in the main event of a show in Kanagawa against Kenta Kobashi, Toshiaki Kawada, and Mitsuharu Misawa. These guys were three of the greatest in the business, not just in their own country, and they'd be passing back and forth or teaming for just about every major title in Japan for decades.

They knew Stan very well, as he'd be right in the middle of the title picture himself. Johnny had been there before as well. But this new guy? Well, let's just see if he's worth our time.

I got in there with Kawada, and he started giving me some good whacks. They don't worry much about making things just "look" good over there. Guys are getting hit because they're getting hit.

Then he stepped back, hopped up, and spun-kicked me right in the face.

I grabbed my mouth, and I wasn't selling. He'd landed a blast unlike few I'd felt in my career.

I saw blood on my hand, and probed further. Then I reached into my mouth, and felt that my entire tongue had been split in half.

It hurt like hell, but now I was pissed. That can help you overcome the pain.

OK. He wanted that, we could try it that way. He better not be surprised at what he was about to get back.

I fought him off and shoved him back into the corner. Then I blasted him with three European uppercuts. No need to worry about visuals. He was getting hit because he was getting hit. I was giving as stiff to him as he'd given me, and maybe a little more.

Kawada was cool. He respected me for fighting back, and he didn't have a problem getting hit. I'd keep working with him and his teammates in singles and more tag matches during the trip (I'd also battle future WWF Hall-of-Famer Abdullah the Butcher over there as well). I was in a house show almost every night, usually in the main event. I worked several dozen matches that month alone, which didn't bother me too much, as it wasn't much more strenuous that the American schedule. When the welcoming crew realized that I'd take their beatings and lose to them without complaining, they put me on the winning side of a few matches, and I didn't have any more in-ring issues.

Except with the guy who'd actually pulled the string to get me there.

Maybe Stan felt that he should be the center of his matches. Maybe he wanted to be the only American with much spotlight over there. Maybe he just felt that everyone should be as reckless as he was.

Over the span of less than a week, I'd go back and forth from teaming with him to battling him and Ace, usually with me teamed up with the Patriot. Sometimes Stan would feel I was getting too much performance time, so he'd literally pull me out of the ring and tag himself in. Once, I was outside of the ring, and he blasted me with a chair so hard in my shoulder that it gave me a stinger than numbed my entire side for about two scary minutes. Stan didn't really care if anybody got hurt; either way, he was touring like crazy in Japan and making a ton of money.

Still, I think I proved myself pretty well to the All Japan crew. Just a few years ago, Stan came up to me at a wrestling convention in North Carolina. Surprisingly, he was there to apologize.

"Look, I'm sorry," he said. "I know I was this and I know I was that."

"Yeah," I replied. "I'm glad you manned up."

I don't know what response he was looking for, but that wasn't it. He got upset with me. A few decades before, he might have started blasting me.

Whatever. I didn't care, and I was going to get my shit in at him. But I'd call my trip over there a highlight of my career, and the majority of the people there, in the ring and backstage, some of the nicest I've worked with and for.

Everyone who spends any extended period of time in wrestling can tell you a few sad, depressing, or angering stories about this business. But when you see people doing things like that, the bad memories disappear very, very fast.

I went over to Austria and came back to America with a new title.

A National Award!

By *Wrestlemania* the next spring, I was falling back down into the WWF shuffle, losing to everyone from Savio Vega to Tatanka to Duke "The Dumpster" Droese. Still, I had a few more career highlights that season.

I represented my company in a celebrity softball game. Near the WWF's headquarters in Connecticut, myself, Michael Hayes, and Henry and Phineas Godwinn rocked a Fan Fest event with our

A National Award!

rendition of "Sweet Home Alabama." Lynyrd Skynyrd might have challenged us to their own tag team battle if they'd been there to see it!

The night before the biggest show of them all, I was fitted for a tux, sitting in the crowd at Anaheim, there with the rest of the company to celebrate the Slammy Awards, just about as prestigious as the Oscars or the Grammys in wrestling-land. They name last year's top wrestler, best newcomer, finest manager, and greatest match, among others.

But some of these awards don't exactly come with honor.

There was, for example, the Most Embarrassing Moment award. 1–2–3 Kid's foray in a Diaper Match was up, as was Helmsley getting tossed into a hog pen by Henry Godwinn. And then there was furious nominee Skip, whose loss to me had won him a shot at the statue.

Well, it didn't happen. Jerry Lawler being forced to kiss Bret Hart's feet and then chew his own toes at the previous summer's *King of the Ring* was the unfortunate winner.

Would I do better? Maybe so. My Skip win had a shot at the Biggest Shocker of the Year, up next to 1–2–3 Kid's heel turn and Goldust's debut. As fans had waited years to see my moment and no one had seen it coming, many figured it would win.

But it didn't; the award went to Shawn Michaels' collapsing after getting a good kick from Owen Hart, who gleefully accepted the award on his "behalf," as Shawn was out with an injury.

Big deal. It's been almost three decades since, and from what I keep hearing from fans all the time, what Chris kept being reminded of, and everything else, my specific moment looks to have outlived all the others, with time, if not the award.

And around that same time, I'd get an even bigger victory. Aside from breaking in the Ultimate Warrior at the start of his reign and narrowly falling to Jeff Jarrett, I hadn't gotten too close to the title picture.

Still, ever since 1972, *Pro Wrestling Illustrated* had been handing out its own annual awards, and unlike the Slammy, these awards are for *everyone* in the business, not just the WWF. Some awards had been added and subtracted since the inception, but others had stood the test of time. Most Popular, Most Hated, Match of the Year, Tag

Wrestling Is My Gimmick

Team and Wrestler of the year ... and Inspirational Wrestler of the Year. Here's a chance to go a bit beyond the entertainment aspect of pro wrestling and, once in a while, turn to those who just might have been role models as more than just skilled performers. People who showed the true great side of wrestling, the time, the effort, the sweat, the tears, the pain that one entails and overcomes to make it somewhere in the business. People who win this award aren't really judged by flashy moves, great interviews, even wins. They just show that they are willing to give a little more to a tough business than most, and can show it in all kinds of ways.

Ron Simmons, who'd overcome so much to become one of wrestling's black pioneers, had won it before. After overcoming a serious knee injury to make it to the top of the business, Sting was a past victor. Even Cactus Jack, considered one of the hardest workers in wrestling history long before anyone knew the name of Mankind, had scored a plaque. All of these guys, and many other winners, would one day snare their own spot in the WWE Hall of Fame.

Point is, I certainly didn't expect to be ranked alongside these guys. But that spring, I'd gotten something special in the mail from the magazine. Then a phone call came from one of the editors. They needed something back from me, and they needed it the next day. A long way from e-mail, I improvised like crazy.

I roared into a small, family-owned photography studio in my Nashville hometown and gasped out what I needed—fast! The photographer set things up, and I stepped into the studio.

He had no clue what was going on, or how to handle this at all. I'd just barged into his place, and now I was walking out to see him—in just my wrestling trunks, oiled all up, and pumped up like I was about two seconds from storming the ring again.

Then I held up my plaque and smiled. He took a few shots, and I mailed them in. That March, millions of readers learned of my being named the Most Inspirational Wrestler of 1995. I was a runaway winner, although how those votes are counted or how legit they are isn't really my place to know or guess.

What an honor. What a thanks from a group I'd never really expected it from. I had always worked hard, never complained about losing, busted my tail as a heel and face, and now another someone, or someones, was saying thanks. Very few men from the wrestling world could ever say that. Just one more reason to thank and remember Skip.

Done right, he and I could have kept working and drawing for another year, at the very least. He was hot, I was at a career high, the fans loved it. We could have kept making some amazing things happen in the company.

But, as we touched on before, it wouldn't last. Not my wave in the WWF, or even my relationship with *PWI*. Sadly, things were about to go back to normal.

Moving Down in the Ranks

For over three decades now, that *Pro Wrestling Illustrated* magazine we just chatted about has published its annual list of the top five hundred wrestlers in the business that year. It's called the *PWI 500*, and it's quite the honor to be listed.

How? It's a mystery. Ticket sales, big wins, working for the major promotions, headlining pay-per-views, or at least showing up on them every once in a while—all sorts of factors in play here. It's a wonderful thing, especially for workers of the smaller federations, who get a chance to see their name get out and their chances go up.

And ever since it started in 1991, I've been in the top ten every single year and ranked first a couple of times!

Just kidding. But I have made the list more than once. When I was rocking and rolling through Global in 1992, I almost got into the top hundred.

As anyone into and even most people *not* into wrestling in 1997–98 could have guessed a few months in advance, Stone Cold Steve Austin was tops in the 1998 list. The inferno he'd been lighting for years had propelled him to the top of the wrestling game at

Wrestling Is My Gimmick

Before he made it to the WWE Hall of Fame as Rikishi, I helped break the Sultan into the federation.

Wrestlemania that year, and many even today call him the top star in the history of the business.

Yeah, everyone saw that coming. But flipping through the pages of *PWI*'s "Top 500" edition that year brought one of the biggest digs of my career.

There's a huge color shot of him twisting my neck, a huge smile on his face and me screaming in agony. The only match we ever had, we'd battled right around the 1996 *Royal Rumble*, one win that shoved him towards being *King of the Ring* a few months later.

"It's tough to believe," the caption condescendingly blared, "that

Moving Down in the Ranks

just two years ago, the WWF had Austin facing foes such as *Barry Horowitz* at Madison Square Garden!" The italics and exclamation point were theirs, not mine just for this book. Like that was such a dark spot on his career.

Real nice, guys. Very professional. Way to insult a guy just to maybe sell a few issues, if they did at all. Wonder if they would have done that if I was still winning big when the magazine hit the newsstands.

Unfortunately, I wasn't. But give me a minute.

When they told me I'd be in the 1996 *Royal Rumble*, I was thrilled. When I learned I'd be one of the last in the ring at the Selland Arena in Fresno, I was overjoyed. As one guy after another bolted out to the ring (and some flew right back out faster than others), I waited and waited. I'd be number twenty-six out of thirty.

Just before me, a newcomer charged out. White boots. No goatee. No glass breaking. And, most importantly, hardly any crowd reaction.

At this point, people backstage may have been doubting this guy who they'd dubbed the Ringmaster. They'd stuck him with legendary heel Ted DiBiase as a manager, but as over as Ted had been as a hated competitor, fans didn't care much about him on the outside. For this wrestler, it might quickly come down to a gimmick change or a release.

Fortunately, they picked Option A. By that summer, the fellow had ditched Dibiase, gotten some serious mic time, and starting winning over more crowds than the majority of the faces. Ringmaster wasn't a very intimidating moniker. Stone Cold certainly would be.

Of course, Steve Austin would go on to be wrestling's biggest star. But not yet. Still, when Austin hit the ring, he'd be doing battle with Diesel, Shawn Michaels, and another newbie named Hunter Hearst Helmsley (not cool enough to be labeled Triple H just yet!), all at the same time. Just a few years later, this matchup would look very different.

Also there were Owen and a large scary-looking guy named Kama. Years later, he'd become the Godfather. Every guy in the ring at that moment would end up in the WWE Hall of Fame, as would Rikishi and Isaac Yankem, the future Kane, who'd follow me in. Maybe someday I'll join that rank myself.

Wrestling Is My Gimmick

Jumping in, I didn't fare too well against Diesel. Owen and I went at it, and then Shawn started tuning me up.

"If Horowitz wins this match," asserted Curt Hennig on commentary, "I quit! You'll never see me again!"

"Really?" a shocked Vince McMahon responded. "Never thought I'd be rooting for Horowitz, but I might be now!" But Curt needn't have worried; moments later, Owen backdropped me to the arena floor.

And unfortunately, as quickly as I'd fallen from the ring, my star outside it began to fall as well. With Skip moving on, Austin moving up, and everyone else jumping on the rising wave of pro wrestling, I was hardly afloat. I did lose to Austin, then another to Helmsley, as well as Goldust and just about everyone else. I slipped past Owen for one win in that time and came out on top against Isaac Yankem, but my losses kept piling up for the rest of that year and then on into the next spring.

Along the way, though, came an especially memorable moment for me. Ironically enough, it's because I didn't do anything.

For the first time in WWF pay-per-view history, the October 1996 *In Your House* event would *not* have the champion wrestling. There were a couple of reasons for this. Shawn Michaels had won the belt at the previous *Wrestlemania*, and could carry a mannequin to a great match, but the company hadn't been able to build up a new strong heel for him. His friends Kevin Nash and Scott Hall had left for WCW, and, for a time, it looked like Bret Hart might be following them (had he, the WWF may have gone under). Steve Austin's star was just beginning to rise, not quite to the level that he'd be seen as a world title threat, although that would change. The same could be said for Mankind. The WWF had tried to turn Davey Boy Smith into the next monster, but it hadn't worked out.

So, rather than putting Michaels against a random opponent at the top of a pay-per-view, where he'd almost certainly have had a great match that very few would remember, the WWF instead changed the event's focal point. Mankind and the Undertaker had put together some amazing showings already, and now the company was putting something new together—and naming the entire show after it, *Buried Alive*.

Moving Down in the Ranks

It's tough to think of a more appropriate match for a guy literally named the Undertaker than one taking place in a makeshift graveyard, with the object to toss your opponent into an empty grave and then bury him there, and he'd come out on top. What happened afterward, however, would be the lasting image of the event.

Backstage before the show, I was hanging out with some colleagues, wondering if I'd get something to do. But I didn't expect this.

See, the crew had built the match's grave with huge loads of dirt, but they added a small room below it, large enough that a few guys could crouch down on small chairs. That might have been OK for a little while, but they would be down there since before the audience arrived. Basically, imagine sitting in a tiny teepee-type place for about five hours.

I went down to take a look at the creation. Just as I leaned over to see it, someone—I'm almost certain it was Jake Roberts—snuck up and tried to shove me into it.

Not sure what happened there, but I turned into a statue. Ever hear those stories about people who suddenly turn into superhumans, like an average-sized person suddenly being able to lift a car off of a victim? That was me. A speeding Mack truck couldn't have shoved me into that shaft.

I told everyone there was no chance in hell I was going down there for two seconds, let alone five hours. I've usually been pretty good about fighting off my claustrophobia if the need arises, but it was hitting me as hard as ever here, and I'd sit in the dressing room all night before I'd be assisting on this.

So, some others did. The Undertaker won, but he was knocked into the grave, seemingly out of it. Then Terry Gordy (under a mask and called the Executioner, although everyone knew it was him) came out to save Mankind. Those two, Paul Bearer, Goldust, and that Helmsley guy came out to fill in the grave almost all the way.

Were things going too far here? How could this be part of the show? How could the Taker stay down there so long, buried under all that dirt, and survive?

Well, he did. Lightning somehow made its way down into the Market Square Arena, and just happened to land right on the grave—and resurrected the Undertaker, his gloved hand eerily making its way out of the ground.

How? Well, he'd been lowered onto a shelf-like platform, and pulled back out of the dirt before it fell, right into the room I hadn't wanted to visit. Then the guys who had been coerced into being down there had helped him up and back to life.

My old friend Tracy Smothers came up to me afterward. He'd been one of the helpers.

"Barry, I'm not claustrophobic," he gasped, "but be glad you weren't down there!"

But when it came to actual ring work for me, there was nothing. The calls and the bookings started to taper off. I'd show up at television tapings and not see my name on the schedule. I had known my contract was coming up, but I'd been hoping someone would walk up to me with a new one.

They could have kept me going. They could have pushed me with someone else; Owen and I had worked together enough that we could have drawn some green, and I know he would never have had an issue putting me over. The company had repackaged me, sort of, and they could have done something else.

Maybe they just didn't want to. Some questions in wrestling, many questions in the business, you'll never get a straight answer or even a curved one. The best you're going to get is, "We don't have a place for you." Anything further than that, and they're setting themselves up for a lawsuit. Me, I was never really told anything at all. By the time I got back from a Kuwait tour in April 1997, I could see the writing on a wall, even if the company's words weren't extended.

No farewell tour, no big goodbye, just being quietly drummed out of the company. That's just the way that this works for wrestlers.

Tim Horner: Barry had the chain and cinder block around his neck. Once you get beat, beat, beat, everybody else is like, "Well, we're supposed to beat him too." We all get the limelight sometimes, it's just that some guys get it more than others. Some of the guys he worked with, and I worked with, we had to carry them, and they couldn't carry our bags. We're working to get them over, and they move up cause they're friends with someone and they make all the money, and we're still second or third match. I was working as an agent in the WWE in 2006, and you'd have guys in the back for four hours to go over a five-minute match. I would say, "Y'all couldn't have worked back in the day."

R.D. Reynolds: Since he lost all the time, people would say, "OK, this guy lost all the time, and now we're supposed to take him seriously? I've watched this guy lose for eight years, and now I'm supposed to get really behind him and flip a switch?" It was an uphill battle to come back from.

But no one makes it in a business like wrestling by sitting around hanging onto grudges and chomping on sour grapes. And I'd had my dream fulfilled. I'd worked with some of the best the business ever saw. I'd worked for both Vince McMahons. I'd been paid for every booking I'd ever done, and pretty well. I know how many guys would have died for that spot, and many, even just as talented as me, would never be lucky enough to get the opportunity. You've got to take the bad with the good and know that the good usually comes out ahead.

Back then, the WWF wasn't the only game in town, and, while Global had long since gone down, I still had some old stomping grounds down south.

I had to make a living just like anyone else, and I knew I could make a contribution there, same as I had in the WWF. Business is business, and I had no issue with working for my old employer's rival to provide. That's all it is for a wrestler who moves over—just taking care of your family. Not backstabbing your former employers.

World Championship Wrestling had treated me great when I'd been there for a few months in 1990, and hoped they would again.

I had to make a few phone calls, and of course they knew of me. They knew I'd work as hard for them as I ever had, and that I wasn't going to walk in with a list of demands. They had a few small booking issues with me, but they said they'd find a place. Before the next Halloween, I was back in WCW.

Landing Back in WCW

And what a great start I got down south.

The WCW did indeed remember me, and they trusted me. They knew that I was a good investment, and they treated me like a stock on the way up.

Like I said, I'd had to wait a few months before I could actually put my name on a contract. But they were so confident that I'd bust my tail for as long as they asked, they actually paid me for the months I had spent waiting to sign.

In the middle of October 1997, I headed down to Fort Myers for my debut (yes, I was out of the WWF just weeks before the infamous Bret Hart–Vince McMahon *Survivor Series* screwjob, and thank GOD I hadn't had to sit there and watch that happen). My first match—well, for that tenure—would turn out to be a great experience as well.

When you're at, or especially below, the middle of a card as stacked as the one containing my battle with the Disco Inferno, it's not uncommon to suddenly learn that your match has been gutted. Not removed all the way, if you're lucky, but torn up by time. You go in there with the expectation that you'll get ten or fifteen minutes, only to be a few steps from the entryway and have someone walk up and say, "Oh, we need you out of there in five or six." And sometimes that even includes each wrestler's entrance. By the time the bell rings, you're going to have to be on fast forward to have any kind of substance in your match.

Hell, that sometimes even happens in the middle of a battle. You'll be building up, when suddenly the official gets a shout through his earpiece. Then he runs up to you and says something like, "Hit the finisher and go! Boss's orders!" Then everyone starts falling all over their feet, trying to salvage something into an ending that you just don't want to be TOO anti-climactic.

And you can't do anything about it. Like I said, they normally do this in one of the first matches, the ones that don't factor into company storylines as much as the ones at or near the main event. Those that are less important.

To their credit, those that change the schedule might have a legitimate reason for doing this. They may need to add something to the main event. A star in the midst of a push might require a little extra time to show his stuff. Or they could decide to suddenly add a whole new match, interview segment, or something else to the show. Sadly, WCW would get a reputation for last-minute, seat-of-the pants booking, and this wasn't great for the workers' stability. But try to fight back, and you might come across as a bratty kid, a pain in the ass more concerned about himself than the company. Not fair, and usually not the case at all, but that can happen. You certainly can't control what people think.

As I stepped into the company with a shot at Disco's TV title, we would be one of about twenty battles at the taping. We knew we weren't going to get a full-blown Ironman Broadway or something, but we knew we could give the crowd something that would stand out amongst the multitude of matches.

But we almost didn't even get the chance. Just a few minutes in, someone called down from backstage, telling the ref to tell us to get done and go. I think the audience probably saw me sigh and put my head down at hearing that, knowing that I was already off to a rough start in my new company.

But the Inferno man wasn't having that.

"No, Barry," he whispered to me. "We're going longer."

My face and my enthusiasm lit right back up. I was going to show those who'd signed me up just how hard I would work for them.

We went right back to the battle, and the referee might have been a bit surprised, but he stayed in character. Disco and I only stuck around for a few more minutes (which can obviously make a huge difference in a wrestling card), but we gave the crowd someone special.

Disco took a risk for me that night, as well as for himself. He'd only been the champion for a few weeks, and the company could have used this as an excuse to yank the belt right off him. And, yes, he certainly got some heat from the decision-makers. But he made it quite clear to them that we had gone on because he had wanted to, and because he was confident we could make it work, as we had. I respected that a lot, and I still do.

Lenny Lane: When I went to WCW, and they brought him in, we started traveling together. One night, we put self-tanner on each other, ordered pizza, 'cause it was our cheat day. I invited the pizza guy in, and he's trying not to look at me. I'm like, "How much is it?" and he's just looking down. I'm like, "Man, this guy's weird." Then I realized Barry and I both have thong underwear on.

Going from the WWF to WCW was about like switching to a different trailer in the same park. Nothing enormously different. The WWF had a few more rules and regulations, but nothing that was a major adjustment. I knew almost all of the guys there already, and I'd never had an issue following the rules anyway.

Ironically, though, even with less control from the bosses, WCW didn't have nearly the ribbers and pranksters than I'd encountered with my previous employment. Curt Hennig, wrestling's unofficial king of backstage chicanery, was around to do his thing, but he had fewer "colleagues" than back in the WWF.

As welcoming as the wrestlers were, and would continue to be, I can't say much the same about the ones running the show. Back in the WWF, Vince McMahon had always been a man of his employees. You could come to him about ideas and issues, and he'd do what he could, as long as it didn't hurt the business. That's not to say, of course, that he would necessarily follow everyone's suggestions, or that he was OK with people just randomly running up to him or barging into his office in the midst of a tirade—there was a set of rules to setting things up, and you worked on his schedule—but I never heard of him being rude to an employee who needed a meeting. He never came across like, "You're not in the main event, so you're not as important as those that are!"

About then–WCW head Eric Bischoff, however, I can't say as much. Not long after I arrived, I happened to encounter him at the former Sun Dome in Tampa (which, since my days of working there way back in Florida, had been changed to the Yuengling

Center). I went up to him and thanked him for giving me a contract.

He looked at me like I had just filled his living room with hippo manure. He hardly said a word. Within a few seconds, we were both glancing all over the place with nothing to say. Definitely one of the more awkward interactions of my entire career.

By the beginning of 1998, murmurs were starting to amplify across WCW, and then, slower but surely, the wrestling world as a whole. Eric Bischoff had lit a match flame under this guy, and it was reaching campfire size on the way to a brushfire. Soon it would be an inferno.

The man in question would start off as just that, a man. But soon he'd be seen as everything but a monster. A force that many were too scared to even attempt to stop. One opponent after another had fallen under his trail of destruction, which lengthened and strengthened every match.

Soon all of wrestling would know him, many in a terrifying way. And for my first match of 1998, my new year wouldn't get off to the happiest of starts.

Catchphrases are old hat in the wrestling world, and the simplest has always been the best. This man's was simple.

"WHO'S NEXT?!"

It would be me.

Getting Struck by Gold

There's a time and a place to show your technical skills and put out a competitive match. There's also a way to conduct yourself when you're working with a guy who's going all the way over.

As in, get creamed, lay down, and get out. That doesn't hurt you if you do it the right way.

Wrestling Is My Gimmick

Like about everyone else in the business at that point, I wasn't too familiar with Bill Goldberg. He hadn't gotten too much wrestling training, and WCW had pushed him hard and fast. Too fast, according to some of the guys, who felt that he hadn't paid enough of his dues to justify it.

That's not to say I felt that way, as, like I've written before and will continue to, I don't get involved in my co-workers' pasts or personal business, or backstage issues. I just saw the *Saturday Night* mat battle in Georgia my next match as a job to do, though a different one than I was used to playing.

At this point, the fans weren't even sure what to make of this fellow, not making too much noise as he strolled to the ring. Clearly, that would change soon, and in abundance.

Patting my back, I was facing and mugging for the crowd. Then, as I turned around, he hit me like the many running backs he'd whomped during his time in the NFL. One jackhammer later, a twenty-second match was done.

It's little things like that that can show the difference between face and heel. If he'd attacked me with my back turned, fans would have probably had a problem with him. Only heels do that. The nanosecond that it took me to turn around made a pretty big difference. It's a big reason why he got a much louder ovation after the match than for his entrance.

By that May, he was already moving up, enough to score some main event spots. Our next encounter hadn't been supposed to happen.

I wasn't even scheduled for *WCW Thunder* that night in Nashville. The card layout had had Goldberg destroying some Japanese wrestler. But on the day of the show, the guy hadn't bothered to show up. All day, up until the show was actually going on, people were calling all over the place, looking for him. It was, after all, the main event!

I don't know if the wrestler thought that a quick loss would kill his credibility, or if he was just scared. In any case, like always, I was backstage, ready and able to sub in. At the last second, I was asked to.

But the situation was different than before. This time, he came out with the United States title. This time, the lights went out before

Getting Struck by Gold

the bout, and the crowd knew it was the sign to get as noisy as the show's title. Fire and fireworks erupted around him as he methodically strolled forward.

And this time, in heel mode myself, it was me attacking him before the belt. He didn't so much as drop a drop of sweat, knocking me right down and tossing me straight into a powerslam.

Then things started to replay from our first match: a spear, a jackhammer, and a pin. Still, I actually lasted three times as long with him as I had before, which added up to a *full minute*!

Bill always gave 150 percent in the ring, and things paid off, as he moved up to the world title, the face of the company, and a household name in wrestling for years. Even when he took time off from the business for over a decade, WWE fans certainly remembered him when he came back in 2016, enough that he even won two titles there and was a member of the Hall of Fame's class of 2018.

He had a reputation for being reckless in the ring, although I never got hurt with him, albeit in less than two minutes of actual action. Bill was a good guy out of the ring too; in Miami, he told me his dad had been a big fan of mine, mostly because I was Jewish.

Yeah, let's go ahead and talk about that.

Wrestling can make it tough to walk the line between person and performer. Most choose to go all the way out, using a new name, a new personality, even a mask to become something other than a person. They create a character and they become it as long as the show goes on. They're not "real" personas, so people don't expect them to have much in the way of realistic personal lives. Some do this over and over until they finally find something that hits hard with the audience, like Glenn Jacobs, who fell short with one gimmick after another until he launched to the stratosphere with Kane. Sometimes guys even go the other way, like Kevin Nash, who ended up getting much more over as himself than as Oz, Diesel, or anyone else he'd portrayed.

Yes, using your real name in the ring (or a realistic variation, as we'll see in a moment) can be rare and risky. But when you do, your personal life often gets more incorporated into your ring portrayal than it would if you were, shall we say, a "fictional" creation. That's why my Judaism was a pretty large part of Barry Horowitz the performer.

Wrestling Is My Gimmick

With Goldberg, it was different. Except for his last name, almost as Jewish-sounding as my own, his faith was never too big a part of his persona, although he never tried to hide it. When it comes to religion, wrestling's always been a bit iffy. It's easy to find wrestlers with a deep devotion as people, but they usually don't bring it into their characters. Colt Cabana doesn't use his Judaism in his ring presence over in All Elite Wrestling, nor did my longtime friend Dean Malenko.

And please don't think I'm jealous of Goldberg for, not necessarily intentionally, becoming such a mainstream focal point for the Jewish faith in wrestling. That's just not the case. But when people make him out to be the most famous Passover-celebrator in the business, that's crazy. That honor needs to go to someone who meant and did much more for wrestling than he could.

I'm talking about Randy Savage. Yes, the Macho Man himself, who I worked with all of one time in Alabama in 1988, is a runaway winner for the unofficial title for Most Famous Jewish Wrestler of all time (his father was Catholic, but his mom was Jewish, thereby making him a Jew, according to Jewish law). Had he been more devout as a person, or maintained his real name of Randy Poffo, that fact might be more publicly known.

We've seen mat men portray priests, ministers, even cult leaders, and, in keeping with wrestling's longtime satirical nature, they almost (intentionally) come off as self-righteous and irritating. If I, or Goldberg, had gotten into the ring wearing a yarmulke and started reading from the Tanakh, the Jewish Bible, fans would not have enjoyed it much. Probably not in the sense of, "Let's boo this guy, but pay to see him lose!" but more of a, "Let's just ignore this irritating jerk until he goes away!" sort of thing. Obviously, that's the wrong kind of heat.

With me, it was always pretty subtle. My faith was shown in my music and the Star of David on my tights, but I didn't bring it into my in-ring persona, nor did I mention it in interviews. I've never really heard any anti–Jewish slurs from fans, let alone anyone involved with the promotions. Sometimes, though, when I'm at a meet-and-greet or something, fans come up to me and say things like, "I'm Jewish, and you inspired me to be an athlete. Some people think Jewish people can't or won't do great in sports, but I'm trying, and doing good, and I learned some of that from you." That's of course one of the more uplifting aspects of my career.

And as heelish as promoters have wanted me to be, I have never been asked to do any kind of anti–Semitic angle for the purpose of a wrestling show. I'm sure that no one in the WWE or WCW would be stupid enough to try that, but some of these independent promoters might be obsessed enough with shock value to tell me to go out there and badmouth my own faith.

If one were to do so, I'd have demonstrated my entire wrestling arsenal on him right then and there, all for the backstage crowd. Then I'd have walked right out, never worked with them again, and not regretted it for a second.

Working with the Flairs

About a month after getting my first Goldberg squashing, I landed my first shot at Ric Flair in over a decade. He didn't wrestle much on the Saturday morning shows, but he and I did battle there, and the fans got one hell of a thrill seeing him. I personally thought our battle back in Florida was the better outing overall, but for a *WCW Worldwide* match, it was pretty good.

My next interaction with his family, however, would be very different.

David Flair was one of the nicest guys in the locker room, and he had the look for the business. Still, like many second-generation stars of any sport, he was expected to live up to the standards of his predecessor, even surpass them.

Ridiculous, and totally unfair to him. Who exactly in the history of wrestling could even approach, let alone top Ric Flair when it comes to wrestling ability and passion? I could compile that list without needing both of my hands, and I'm sure others would contest whatever selections I came up with anyway. But no matter what David did, he was always going to hear, "Great job, but your dad was better." That's just how the naysayers are, expecting David to reach his dad's level just because he was his son. I know if it were me, I'd get out of the business fast if I kept having to deal with that.

So I wasn't too surprised when David didn't stick around long in wrestling.

Sadly, his younger brother Reid, who I think the WWE very much wanted to turn into a star, had too many demons himself, becoming one more victim of wrestling's drug culture. But not long after, their sister Charlotte came blasting onto the pro wrestling circuit, racking up title after title and a *Royal Rumble* win and becoming part of the first women's match to headline *Wrestlemania* in 2019. Heck, maybe it *is* possible to match Ric's ability and devotion!

But getting back to my next program, WCW was quite obviously willing to do just about anything to shove David over, and if that meant openly hurling kayfabe out the door for a hot half hour, that was what they were gonna do.

And I would be a part of it.

In mid–May 1999, in the Kansas Coliseum, I believe the same spot where they filmed part of the 1989 Hulk Hogan debacle *No Holds Barred*, fellow enhancement talent Scott Putski and I strolled down the hall of a *Thunder* segment, discussing our hopes to get a spot on the show. Suddenly Ric, a few of his Four Horsemen buddies, and some bodyguards surrounded us.

Putski was told to take a walk, and he eagerly complied. Then Ric informed me that he needed to talk to me. Actually, the conversation would be a bit one-sided.

"It's really important that my son look good out there tonight," he said, sounding like a mob boss impressing upon a newcomer. "Do Mongo and Benoit need to impress on you how important this is to me?"

Remember, I was Barry Horowitz the performer, not the person. And the performer knew on which side to butter his bread.

Working with the Flairs

I assured him this would not be an issue. Our mat battle would become one of the most ... interesting of my career.

Everyone knew David was way out of his league. That was sort of the point. He didn't try to be something he wasn't, portraying the plucky upcoming with much more enthusiasm than ability.

And I had to make it all look good. I'd settle for moves that looked awful or missed altogether. Every time I hit him with a big move, Benoit, Arn Anderson, Steve McMichael, or somebody else would be right on the apron, letting me know in loud tones that this wasn't my match to win.

Like I said, though, it was all a joke. Things like this even let the fans know that this wasn't a serious match, just a bit of comedy. Wrestling's old-timers would probably have woken up and spun in their graves if they saw us doing so much to expose the business, but we saw it as a way, if only for a few minutes, to push entertainment above sports in the business.

So when I had to actually sit there and assist David to put on his dad's legendary figure four, then *act* like it hurt me so much that I just *had* to submit to a move I'd helped with, no one thought much of it. With things like this, you just try to keep the fans entertained. You do the right kind of comedy to make them laugh, even if they're laughing at you. If they're still responding to you at the end of the match, or the "match," you've done enough.

But I was flattered that they would even ask. First of all, it showed that my name still had value; if fans weren't already aware that my specialty was losing, my fall wouldn't have made that much of a difference. Secondly, I'd been picked because the pickers knew that I could pull it off. If it had gone too long, or I hadn't reacted right, an entire segment would have been wasted, and no one likes to waste time.

Sadly, just a few days later, wrestling would enter some of its darkest days.

The Night We Lost Owen

I should have already been asleep. I should have missed the news. Should never have heard about it, not then.

Packing my bags on the evening of May 23, 1999, I could only hope I'd doze off long enough to get some sort of freshness for my just-past-dawn flight down to Augusta the next day.

With the TV blaring soft, soothing noise in the background, I finally climbed into bed. I welcomed the weight on my eyes. I reached over to grab the remote control, finally ready to snooze for a few very precious hours.

I had it pointed at the TV, and I think my thumb was even on the power button. Then, seconds into the news, I saw a familiar face.

It was Owen. I'd been away from him for a few years, but I'd have welcomed another chance to put on a show with him.

Right away, I knew that something horrible had happened. News shows don't hardly give coverage to professional wrestling, even for great reasons, let alone make it the top story. If this was happening, it wasn't a happy beginning.

Seconds later, I found out how sad. How heartbreaking. In front of thousands of fans at the Kemper Arena in Kansas City, and millions more watching the *Over the Edge* (what a sadly prophetic name for the event) pay-per-view, Owen had been killed. Being lowered from the rafters into the ring for his match—itself nowhere near the main event—something had gone wrong, and he'd fallen into the ring to his death. Over and over, I saw clip after clip of him doing his thing, as enthusiastic as he'd always been, with memories like these all we would ever have of him again.

I sat there in the dark, maybe hoping I was already out and was about to wake up from a nightmare. I couldn't feel anything. I couldn't think anything.

Owen, with so much of a career left—hell, at 34, so much of a *life* left—was gone forever.

The Night We Lost Owen

And for what? A ridiculous stunt that added nothing to the show? Something that was basically a glorified photo opportunity, done just to get some spectacle attention here and there?

It was ridiculous. Fans had been watching the Blue Blazer run to the ring, jump off the ropes, get all kinds of ariel for years. Everyone knew what he could do. Everyone had seen Owen, with and without the mask, putting on a show since his career had begun. Something like this wasn't going to impress anyone, or even really entertain them.

You know, by that point, even the "enter from the ceiling" was already wearing thin. Sting had been making it a trademark. The Undertaker had done it. Hell, just over three years before, Shawn Michaels had come rappelling down from the top of the Arrowhead Pond before headlining *Wrestlemania* against Owen's own brother Bret.

I don't know how I got to sleep that night. I hardly remember getting up the next morning and making it to the airport. Sitting on the plane, feeling it take off and land, is a blur. I can't even remember much of it today.

But that's one more obligation you meet, one price you pay to be a wrestler. The show always goes on. Hell, Owen's own death didn't even stop the pay-per-view (Jeff Jarrett, one of his closest friends, not only did an interview right afterwards, but wrestled in the very next match), and so many of his friends had to go out and talk about it on national TV in their own tributes the next night on *Raw*. I never considered staying home from the Augusta show, and I don't think anyone else in WCW did either, despite many of them being Owen's friends and former co-workers. The WWF performers probably had it tougher than we did.

I landed at the airport in Tampa. I ran into a group of wrestlers discussing the tragedy of the night before. Sting came up to me. He'd been dropping from the rafters for years, and sometimes escaping from New World Order attacks by going back up. That's not to say he necessarily enjoyed or wanted to do such a stunt, but WCW had had him flying around on pay-per-views, *Nitro*s, everywhere. Like everything else in the company, it was becoming too much of the same thing, but, again, the WWF hadn't realized that until it was too late.

"I'm going to tell Eric Bischoff," he asserted to me. "I'm not coming down from the rafters tonight, out of respect for Owen."

And he didn't. That got phased out of wrestling pretty quickly, although Sting did descend for one of his final matches in February 2023 for AEW, which Owen's family had approved ahead of time.

At *Nitro* that night and at a *Saturday Night* taping the next day, where I sleepwalked through a match with Evan Karagias, all I noticed was how quiet the locker rooms were. People just kept asking each other what they had seen and what they thought, along with how much they'd enjoyed knowing, watching, and working with Owen. It was as if everyone was hoping that someone somewhere would find the right words to say, to reassure everyone and lead them to comfort.

But no one did. No one could. Still can't. There's never going to be an explanation of why Owen didn't live long enough to win more titles, see his kids grow up, everything he deserved. Wrestling had gone too far, and it took the loss of one of the nicest guys it ever had to learn that.

WCW Winds Down

It's funny how often fans remember more, or at least the different aspects, of a wrestler's career than the wrestlers themselves. One day in the middle of the New World Order explosion that carried WCW past the WWF for years, I was going toe to toe with someone in the ring. Then came the guys in black and white, and the infamous theme music that many fans claim sounded just like a porno movie soundtrack.

They grabbed my opponent and started handing out a beating. Punches, kicks, slams all over.

But surprisingly, they didn't touch me. The Order was hardly known for diplomacy, especially towards those not at the top of the card, but they didn't do anything to me. Either they destroyed my opponent, celebrated, and left, or they let me leave during or right after it.

That depends on who you're speaking to.

Notice how I didn't name the day, place, or opponent. It could have been a house show, TV taping, or something else. The specific NWO members (some say inducting too many newbies and creating several other factions severely watered down the product. I don't disagree) were not listed as well, though most people tell me that Kevin Nash was in the lead.

Know why that information was missing? Because I don't remember a shred of that moment. But invariably, almost every time I do an appearance at a convention or show, one or more fans always bring it up. It's important for quite a few people. It's amazing, in a great way, how a single incident from my career keeps standing out for so many, even if I can't recall it to save my life.

My WCW wasn't much different from the WWF one. I knew what I was there to do. Putting over everyone from Bobby Eaton to Glacier to Perry Saturn. But I did have at least one moment that, while it was, per usual for *WCW Saturday Night*, a short but sweet outing, carried quite a bit of personal meaning for me: I got to do battle with my old training buddy Dean Malenko.

Joe Malenko: When you're in the moment, you're not really thinking about those subtle nuances. "Oh my gosh, isn't it amazing that twenty years later, this is where you're at?" You're really just experiencing the moment. There was no ifs, ands, or buts. My brother and Barry were definitely going to have a great match. I had a match against my brother, and even though I could have reminisced and ruminated and done all these things, I just went in there and said, "OK, I have to have a good match."

Hey, check this: ironically enough, I'd been in the business so long that I was now putting over the same guys, in different federations ... playing different characters!

The same guy who'd pinned me back in Global as the cautious Handsome Stranger was now cocky NWO follower Buff Bagwell.

Wrestling Is My Gimmick

When I'd lost to Virgil in the WWF, he was the upbeat underdog who hardly spoke. Now he was the angrily outspoken Vincent, also in the NWO. In the WWF, Marty Jannetty was almost 100 percent known as one of the Rockers, but in WCW, he was trying to make it in singles competition, under not just his own name, but his own new persona.

Still, I did win a bit, going back and forth with my buddy Johnny Swinger. We were getting ten or fifteen minutes in the ring, which is long for a main event on TV, let alone a midcard match.

Johnny Swinger: Even as a kid, I could tell he was a good wrestler. I knew I wanted to do it too. You could definitely tell he was a skilled wrestler, and lot of guys in his position weren't. You could tell. I'd met Barry in 1995, when I went to WWF to do some TV matches. But we really met in WCW when I was a full-time talent. A lot of wrestlers wanted to go out and party and chase women, and he wanted to work out. I wanted to do that too, so we were a perfect match. I wasn't one of those people that went out to the clubs and celebrated, and neither was he. The fact that the work was paying off was enough for me.

In 1997, I got a three-year contract with Ted Turner. I still think about that. J.J. Dillon told me they hired me and the Kiss Demon, and that was it for the year. It was a lot harder to get in back them, and they didn't put people on TV unless they were really ready. I got a good break early on. We had some good matches in WCW as well. If you couldn't have a good match with Barry, you weren't having another one with anyone. He's on a list like that for a lot of people, along with guys like Brad Armstrong and Bobby Eaton.

One of my favorite moments came out of character. Diamond Dallas Page, who'd quickly join the diligent resistance against the NWO, was standing in the ring doing an interview, assuring his rising fanbase that WCW would win this war, and he'd lead the company there.

Suddenly came the attack. A group of men wearing huge riot masks and black gear came barreling in from the dressing room.

But these were the dirty kind of cops. The men suddenly rushed ol' DDP, yanking out their nightsticks and going to work. This guy wasn't doing any problems solving tonight. One blow after another (a dozen) rained down on him, leaving him the next beatdown victim. Obviously, the NWO had more outreach than the WCW locker room.

Oh, the point of recounting that? It was me behind one of the shields. No one would know it, at first at least, but it would become one of Barry Horowitz's most aggressive outings. Just as when I'd been a *Survivor Series* Knight, I was a mindless brute, all about the aggression. It had been so nice of WCW to give me a spot like that.

Unfortunately, they didn't give me many more spots. I started off pretty strong, doing *Nitro, Thunder, Saturday Night*, house shows, all kinds of events. But then my numbers started to fall back. A *Nitro* here, a *Thunder* there. One *Saturday Night* match (we sometimes taped several months' worth of shows in a weekend, so it was common for me to have several per taping). Down to the point where I was only working two to three dates a month.

Still, I couldn't complain. My pay stayed the same, and WCW let me do independent shows on my frequent off days, so I was making great money. I was doing one- (or, once in a while, two- or three- or four-) shot deals mainly around Florida, but sometimes as far away as Canada. Sometimes I'd walk right into these promotions and get a title shot my first day on the job. Sometimes I'd even win a belt!

That was really cool of the other promotions, and of the fans who came to see and cheer for me, knowing I'd be in and out of the area. Some might say that titles only matter if you win them in the big leagues, but I disagree. Winning a belt means that someone felt you deserved it, and no one makes a decision like that without listening to the public, whether it's the fans outside his door at a show, those writing the wrestling newsletters ("dirt sheets," as those on the inside refer to them), or the ones cheering on TV. You're just grateful to get the booking, and a belt adds something special to your résumé.

But then someone in WCW had a new idea, one that could have scored for me in the same way that the Skip program had.

A newbie called Allan Funk (no relation to Terry Funk, like anyone could have made that mistake) was rubbing some people the wrong way—in character, not the person. He'd eventually become the irritatingly flamboyant Kwee Wee, his campy sliminess irritating in ways like Lanny Poffo's Genius character or Adrian Adonis, but when he showed up, he was simply "Angry" Allan Funk (WCW was labeling me "Bad" Barry Horowitz, to give you an idea of how hard they were trying).

Our first meeting on *Saturday Night* was typical. I was stretching beforehand, and he walked up to introduce himself.

"I've been watching you for years," he said. "Let me ask you a question."

"Sure," I responded. Was the recent WCW Power Plant grad looking for help breaking into the business? Advice on how to take a body slam, or reverse one?

"You think you're *ever* gonna win a match?" he smarmily smirked.

Yeah, same old stuff. I guess he thought I hadn't heard this gibberish a few thousand times before. I informed him I'd be winning that very night, and stormed away. As it turned out, he'd be my opponent.

When he openly cheated to beat me, payback was going to happen.

Allan Funk: The match was pretty solid. Getting five or six minutes was pretty good TV time, especially for a kid like me. I was excited to start working that, and then they told us that we'd be working an angle together for *Saturday Night*. I was pretty fired up, because everybody knew who Barry Horowitz was. For a young kid coming up, you couldn't ask for anything better than that.

I started distracting him into losing matches. He'd do the same things to me. We got interview time. We were filming vignettes. Week after week, this program was building into a solid part of WCW programming.

And then it all disappeared.

Barry was one of the guys that I grew up with watching on TV, so it was great to work with him. They always told us back then, "Yeah, we're gonna do this. We're gonna do that." But they never finished it. No reason why. Those of us from the Power Plant, we were just happy to be on TV. We were like, "We're getting TV time. Let's look at it as a positive thing," not knowing that we were screwing ourselves in the middle, cause there was no rhyme or reason for this. They never really explained anything. Barry and I did a couple of things, where I did a run-in. We did a couple weeks' worth of stuff, me and Barry, but nothing ever came of it, which sucked, because it would have been cool to have that run for a couple of weeks or months. But they just let it fade away. At that point, WCW didn't have anybody who was definitely in charge. Everybody was kinda up in the air, with Bischoff, Vince Russo. Bischoff was supposed to come in and buy the company, which I thought he already had, and then Vince buys the company. It was kind of a whirlwind back then.

Wrestling Loses WCW

I never got a phone call, never heard a thing.
To this day, almost a quarter century later, I still haven't.
The WCW was going down for the last time. Too much money lost, too many bad decisions made, just too many things wrong. In early 2001, a company that had entertained for generations just vanished.

And nobody notified me at all. Not the people who'd brought me in, not the bookers, not my colleagues who had been wrestling more often lately than myself, no one. Even though I'd been in the midst of an angle that was just starting to really warm up, it was almost like I wasn't even there.

Yes, the federation's falling was a terrible thing. Many people would be out of work for it. Most of these people had worked like crazy for the company and had nothing to do with its going down. The bosses had made some bad decisions, mainly pushing the wrong people and ignoring the fans.

Look, I'm a firm believer that bookers should book and wrestlers should wrestle, and the twain just shouldn't meet. That's bad enough when the wrestlers doing the bookings are still active competitors, and free to push their friends and themselves to the front of company when the fans don't want it. But when people with no wrestling ability or experience suddenly feel that being a booker entitles them to a place on the screen, it's ridiculous.

Baseball fans don't go to games to see the owners, general managers, and managers take the field. The owner of a pro sports team doesn't interrupt a game in the middle of a play to grab a mic and tell people how great she is. An NFL head coach wouldn't ask his starting quarterback to sit out the fourth quarter so he himself can play it.

If you're a wrestler, at least one still on the roster, you shouldn't be in the booking room. If you're a booker, you shouldn't be standing in the ring, let alone competing in it.

Look, I knew Vince Russo when he was Vic Venom writing the *WWF Magazine*, and when he was booking and writing for the WWF, and he was a nice enough fellow. I always got along with him, and probably still would today. When he moved to WCW to write and book in late 1999, it was a glimmer of hope for the company. Things hadn't looked great there for a while, and maybe he could help the company get to the same heights WCW had.

But when he started being one of the most-seen people in WCW programming, it was never going to work. Fans don't pay to watch people who just talk all the time; they're there for in-ring action, and if they know in advance that the guy that just spent twenty minutes cutting a promo can't, let alone won't, back it up in the ring, they're not going to care. Just as with Eric Bischoff, who himself never saw a camera or microphone he didn't like, Russo felt that being a decision-maker behind the scenes meant that fans wanted to see him actually battle the wrestlers. Not the case.

Look, when Vince McMahon started spending more time in front of the camera, mainly as evil Mr. McMahon after the Montreal Screwjob, it was for a reason, and, for the most part, done pretty well. His company was so low on heels that there needed to be a *really* bad bad guy, desperate to shut down the upcoming everyman force that was "Stone Cold" Steve Austin, and it worked very well. Austin vs. McMahon became a metaphor for the dream of the individual to topple the uncaring rich and pompous, and caught on with fans like few angles in the business, becoming the driving force behind the WWF's comeback that knocked WCW out for good.

However, Vince was smart enough to do the majority of his fighting from behind the microphone, mainly tossing one obstacle after another in the path of Austin to keep him from making it, rather than doing it himself. If Vince did step into the ring, it was usually for a reason, although his winning both the 1999 *Royal Rumble* and the world title (if only for a week) later that same year was pushing it.

Interviews and backstage skits have their place, but they are simply not what attracts fans. If these things don't lead to a payoff in the ring, they fall flat. This was a huge issue for WCW once Russo and Bischoff took over. You'd have over half a TV show, sometimes more, taken up by vignettes that would often not even lead to a match, let alone a program, and fans just got bored.

Still, nothing was worse than what eventually happened to the WCW title in 2000. First, there was the ludicrous decision to give actor David Arquette the WCW title. And if that wasn't enough, Russo put the belt on himself later that year. Just sad. The WCW crew didn't know whether to laugh or cry, and many probably went back and forth, for several reasons. To his credit, Arquette not only disagreed with the title change, but donated his entire paycheck to the families of wrestlers who had recently passed or suffered career-ending injuries, including Owen Hart's family. No one has any right to call him anything but a great guy in this.

Many have accused Russo of taking too much of the sport out of wrestling and replacing it with entertainment, but these things were just ridiculous. It made fans think of WCW as a joke, a company that didn't even take its own world titles seriously. It made wrestling look so easy, like anybody could do it, and even make it to the top just like *that*. That was an insult to every wrestler who'd spent years working on the craft.

The WCW would stay around until the next year, but if it had disappeared right then and there, no one would have cared.

That's not to say that the in-ring product was the main reason for its downfall. People spend so much time watching people like Russo and other decision-makers that they automatically make them the face of the company, and pin the blame on them. That's not fair to

Russo. Many issues were taking place that no one knew about until the company went down, like overpaying people guaranteed money, spending millions on celebrities that no one was paying to see, and everything else.

I'm not a big computer guy, so I wouldn't have found this on the Internet unless I'd (finally!) heard about the decision from someone else. Now I could start looking into more independent bookings, working elsewhere, taking advantage of other options now that a big one was gone.

But I was certain I'd be brought back to the WWF. When Vince McMahon bought it, everyone was cautiously optimistic as well. Maybe WCW would get its own show, and a team of qualified bookers behind it. Maybe *Smackdown* would become the next *Nitro*, and turn back into the show that had stayed ahead of *Raw* for years before Vince and Austin captured lightning in a bottle. Maybe we'd soon be operating under a slightly different name with a vastly improved product.

That didn't happen. Why, I can't say with any credibility. I also can't say why I never got a call to work for a company that I'd busted myself for for years. I would have kept enhancing. I would have worked while other guys sat out their contracts. I could have added something strong to the product, in the same way I always had. I felt that I'd been loyal enough to the WWF that someone there could have reciprocated enough to keep me around for another year, or even a few months, but no one did. Like many others who'd hoped to catch on with WWF in some capacity, I was left right out in the cold.

Never to the Extreme

I've wrestled in more independents than could ever be counted, in countries and continents all over the world, and, at least up through the end of the 1990s, all the major federations.

Never to the Extreme

Except one. I've often been asked why I never showed up in Extreme Championship Wrestling.

Well, it's not an easy question to answer. Getting heat or cheers, to the extreme on both sides, has never really been a problem for me, so that's not the issue.

I know, I know. People certainly don't look at my in-ring work throughout my career and think of me as a guy who could get as hardcore as Paul Heyman and his crew that rocked Philadelphia and elsewhere through the 1990s and early 2000s. It's still tough to believe, not to mention very sad, that WCW and ECW both disappeared so close to each other in 2001. Wrestling had gone from one of its biggest booms in the late 1990s, the rise of which in and of itself allowing ECW to go from a glorified indy show to pay-per-views and television, to having its guts ripped out in a matter of weeks. As any wrestler who was suddenly tossed into the unemployment line, along with all the up-and-comers who saw their chances to be the next big star all but destroyed, the lights really went out for professional wrestling for quite some time. I was glad to see TNA, Ring of Honor, and finally All Elite Wrestling finally get a foothold in the business, for no reason than a ton of people had a new way to make a living.

But back to the original questions. Why did Barry Horowitz never get hardcore? How come I didn't go to the extreme?

Like I said, there's no easy answer.

One of the last times I ever saw Chris Candido was an indy show, well after ECW had gone down.

"You won't believe this," he snickered to me. "I was working an ECW show, and when I got into the ring, people were chanting *your* name!" Looks like our moment lived longer than some do in wrestling.

"Really?" I answered. "Paul must have heard that, and I still couldn't get a match with you there."

I thought Paul should and could have been there for me. Not because I deserve anything more than anyone else, but we had a bit of a history. I had known him for a long time. He had been one of my first managers, me one of his first charges. I'd like to think that we learned something from each other.

And after all, we are two of the most prominent Jews in the business! No, just kidding, that should never be a factor.

Wrestling Is My Gimmick

Look, of course I wasn't going to go over there and get a plane of glass broken over my head or get slammed through a table or climb up on a balcony thirty feet in the air and go flying off. I don't think it takes a tremendous amount of skill and precision to set someone on fire and then drop them onto a ton of thumbtacks, though I certainly don't look down on those who enjoy that, doing it or watching it.

But that's not really the point, or the points, plural. While I'm not and never will be a big fan of hardcore wrestling, I admit that it will always have a place in the business. I guess I see it as more of an exhibition sort of thing. There's nothing wrong with a long show, a long more technical-based show, with a hardcore match or a women's match or a midget match here and there. A little variety is great for wrestling.

Second of all, if we look back at the glory years of ECW, there were a ton of guys who were outstanding in the technical department. I'm not talking about Rob Van Dam or Tazz or Chris, guys who could have torn things up on the mat (and often did) and made the choice to spend the majority of their time going hardcore. I'm talking about Eddie Guerrero and Chris Benoit and even one of the epitomes of technical wrestling, Dean Malenko himself. These guys were putting on some of the best wrestling (repeat, *wrestling*) matches of the time. This sort of mat war was the exception to the ECW rule, but it was there, and fans appreciated it.

I could have fit right in there. I could have been one hell of a contributor to ECW without needing to get too extreme. Chris and I could have continued our rivalry there, and it's a strong badge of honor when a wrestling feud runs rampant through two federations, and the fans still care enough to remember and cheer.

But I still had a few other options.

Making the Best of It All

I'd manage. I always have. There would always be a place in wrestling for a guy like me, even if those places were fewer and harder to find.

Making the Best of It All

If there was one silver lining for the WCW or ECW alumni who found themselves out of work, it was that the indys went absolutely crazy at this point. Promoters jumped all over the change to bring in guys who'd just been on national TV with one of wrestling's biggest companies. A guy who never got past the midcard in WCW (or WWF, for that matter) can become the biggest star in an independent promotion *very* fast. The smaller the promotion, the bigger the star's name. Fans might not spend WWF-level money just to see you start the show, but they might pay a little less to see you in the main event, especially if they get a meet-and-greet with you at the same time. Smaller costs can pay off for a promoter if a larger crowd can be brought in.

For years after WCW and ECW went down, I was experiencing that very thing. I jumped up to high demand all over the northeast. I was in New York, Georgia, Pittsburgh, even Canada quite a few times.

Often I'd win. Sometimes I'd be in the main event. Once in a great while, I'd even score a title. It's not uncommon for a name wrestler to show up in a promotion and win and belt on the first day of work, especially if the promotion doesn't have a set schedule or location. It's just something to establish fast credibility with the fans, something to make them remember and want to come back when the next show gets booked down.

And in a position like this, there's a bright side to find. Many people, both on the inside and out of wrestling, think that one must be in the big leagues to earn a decent living in this business. That's not entirely true, and sometimes it's not even the full point.

If you come in with enough credibility as a performer, people want you to come and work for them. And the money's not quite as great as the WWF or WCW, but it's almost as good. You learn to make do with just a little less. Considering the alternative might be unemployment, making a little less dough isn't so bad. You just adapt. If you kept control of your finances while you were making the big bucks—and a lot of guys don't, and I've certainly been tempted to give myself too much leeway there at times—you won't have much trouble doing the same things if your paychecks shrink just a little.

You can make decent money on the indys. Wrestling there just makes you feel like you're moving back toward the beginning of your career, and that's not always such a bad thing. The structure of the major leagues might be a little stronger and more focused, but there's many things about independent work that make it just as much, if not more attractive.

First off, there's less egos. Fewer politics. Very little whining and complaining. Pissing and moaning about jobbing in a match can get you a bad reputation in the big leagues; doing it at a smaller show is almost unheard of. If you're going to complain about losing at a one-stop show for a promotion that's struggling to begin with (and with the indys, that's usually a question not of if, but of how much), you're sprinkling cyanide on your career.

Remember that in a situation like this, you're going to be mainly working with guys on the way up, fellows with more enthusiasm than experience. That's fine, because everyone starts there, and it's a great way to move forward in the business with the right attitude. Most guys in the indys have exactly that. So egos are small, politics are almost nonexistent, and it's much more laid-back atmosphere than a TV taping, let alone a pay-per-view.

That's not to say that guys don't, or shouldn't, try as hard in the ring as those that are on TV, only that they're almost all about having a great match, not hogging the spotlight. That's what I've always been about, and it's a major reason why I was a pretty common sight on the indy circuit.

Another one is my ability to adapt pretty quickly. When you're the most experienced performer at an indy show, you're, of course, expected to have a great match. But you're also expected to set an example in the ring, and not just in the bump-taking sense either. You walk into the building, meet the promoter, and hear something like, "Hi, meet your opponent. You two will be headlining the card, and you'll be going over in a seventeen-minute match. Now you guys go and work out the details and the finish."

That sounds like a pretty tough assignment. Sometimes it is. But, again, most of the guys I work with on these shows are eager to learn, and they're usually pretty good listeners.

You approach it sort of like a job interview.

"How long have you been wrestling?"

"About a year and a half."

"How many matches have you had?"

"I think about seventy."

"OK, I'm gonna call this match. We're going to make it basic, but very solid. We're out there to get the match over with the fans, to tell a complete story. It'll be fine, but you got to listen to me." Usually they do, and that's why working the independents is pretty easy.

Well, not always. A few years ago, I stepped into a country music bar near my home. Not to get out on the floor and line dance or maybe grab the mic myself and belt out a few tunes, but, shockingly, to wrestle.

My opponent was a smaller fellow doing a Captain America gimmick. We had the usual conversation beforehand, but once we started, things almost went too far wrong.

As nervous as anyone I'd ever seen in a match, let alone worked with, he was as tense as a statue. I'd try to work him, get him to bump, even bump for him, and he was missing about everything we tried. I finally had to take matters, and his head, into my own hands.

"Listen," I growled at him in the midst of a chokehold, "Your way isn't working. Let's try my way, and this match'll work. I'm not letting you up until you say yes."

He did. We got back to work. And the match turned into a piece of cake, for both me and him. The fans liked it, and I could tell he was proud.

Backstage, he was apologizing like crazy.

"I thought you were going to be like a big star," he admitted, "gonna come in and act like a superstar."

"That's your problem," I responded. "You're green. Don't anticipate that I'm going to act like a superstar. I'm talking to you, I'm laying out the match, do not assume. What you need to do is listen."

I asked who had trained him, and he told me about the learnings that had nearly derailed our match.

"Well, they didn't teach you right," I asserted.

That should have been the end of it. But it wasn't.

Not long after, I got a call from his trainer, almost begging me to apologize to the guy. You'd probably recognize the trainer's name, but I'm not going to say it here, because it's not that big a deal, and he's dead now anyway. Still, he was the type of person that bugged and nagged you until you did what he wanted.

A real noodge, as we Jews like to put it.

Normally, I would have told him to go swim the full length of the Nile with his arms tied together. But I figured it just wasn't worth listening to him blither. I made a short, very short, recording for the guy. The trainer didn't like it, but that was life.

Ironically enough, not long after that, I was going to wrestle another of his protégés, with the trainer himself in the corner. I was ready. If he'd told his pupil to go heavy on me, or if he himself planned to interfere and try something during or after the match, I was ready to knock the shit out of both of them, and they wouldn't have to work hard to sell the beating I was going to hand out.

But it didn't happen, and we had a good evening.

All that planning, all that instructing, all that experience had been coming together for me for years in the ring. But, also not long after the wrestling breakdown, I'd take those same tools to embark on a new path in the business, one that's still going today, over two decades later.

Training: Past and Future

My training career had actually started about a decade before, back around the time I had been Global's top "Winner."

Before I caught all the way back on with the WWF in 1992, I was still living in Kentucky, and the city of Franklin was about to close and probably destroy, an old building. Not much to the place, as it had been going down for quite some time, and many people who drove by probably saw it as one hell of an eyesore.

But along with Reno Riggins, both a common partner and

Training: Past and Future

opponent during my WWF days, I saw an opportunity. Along came the R&B School of Wrestling.

We didn't have to pay rent. We had a ring. We had an office. That's all you need to learn the business—well, along with the trainers.

If you're going to school to wrestle, it takes more than just a one-shot deal, a few hours of work. You're talking a few times a week for six months to a year. Reno and I would show them how to lock up, how to hit the ropes, take a slam, all sorts of things.

We learned a lot, we taught a lot, and we got quite a bit of private workout time. We stayed open for a year, and then had to close the school for the most welcome of reasons—bookings in the WWF started to take off, so we didn't have time to run the place. But we didn't lose any money or anything.

And no, I would not do that again. I love training and teaching, but I would never try to start my own school. I don't have the prowess, or, to be fair, the out-of-ring business talent to do that. But I'd certainly love to catch on with someone else. I always wanted to be a full-blown coach or agent with the big federations after my wrestling career ended. Maybe I still will.

I've been freelancing there for about two decades now. I've trained students all over Florida, in Baltimore, in Buffalo. Sometimes I do a training session, meet-and-greet, and wrestle a show on the same day.

These training sessions probably last about three hours. I spend some time talking about the business, giving them my background. We discuss what to watch for, in and out of the ring. Then I show them more holds, more moves, more slams.

We discuss the psychology of the business. Doing things for a reason and how to react to them. They learn about selling—and selling is about having your physical injuries actually stick around and affect your performance. Too many people think "selling" is laying around, typically holding an injured body part, then doing a regular move, only to go right back to laying and grabbing. That's not ring psychology in any form.

Whatever you do in the ring, even if it's just one extra punch, a facial expression, the most subtle of actions, should have a reason.

It's all got to tie together. Otherwise, a match can quickly deteriorate into a bunch of spots, and it becomes obvious that the competitors are just trying to outdo each other, a contest of who can take the biggest bump until someone finally lays down. That's not telling a story like wrestlers should, and fans can tell.

"You might have been taught by other people," I explain to the trainees. "You don't have to say mine's the best, but at least you have options."

Often I hear something like, "Hey, this guy from the WWE taught me something different, but this is better."

"How many matches did he have?" I ask. "How long was he there?"

"I don't know. Probably a few years, maybe two hundred matches."

"Well, I've been in the business for over thirty years," I reply. "I've had 20,000 matches." Experience is the main enabler for one to be a credible trainer, not popularity or titles.

And not looks. That's something we go over as well. Height alone doesn't make a great basketball player. Muscles and stamina won't send a football player to the NFL, let alone the Pro Bowl. Some guys who look like they just won a bodybuilding contest walk in and expect to pick up the business in a few hours. They get a rude awakening, and often wind up on the mat, gasping for air in a few minutes, usually while people who look a hell of lot less athletic are still cooking.

When you're wrestling, you're lifting a couple times a week, but you're still in the ring, in front of people. You're traveling in the car or on the plane, then you get to the place to do a match. You still try to squeeze in a few workouts here and there. When you can do that four, five, or six nights a week, then you're in wrestling shape, not because you have the gym's top bench press.

At the end, I take a few of the standouts and let them put on their own match, usually for five or ten minutes. They, along with most of the onlookers, are often impressed with how much they've learned.

But getting back to my work in the indys for the next few years after WCW went down, I eventually decided to move on, at least for then. It wasn't anything physical. Years of bumping had taken their toll on me, of course, but that would happen to anyone. I was always pretty lucky that my neck injury never really flared back up again.

No, I just kept running into the wrong people to work with. In independent work, that becomes the rule, rather than the exception. Out of every ten indy promoters, maybe three are good. The rest try to set something up, then suddenly forget to call or pay or anything else. That's just how the business works.

I like to give these guys the benefit of the doubt. I like to think that they just jumped in without checking the depth and wound up way in over their head. They probably saw a one-shot wrestling show somewhere else and say, "Wow, look how fun and fast that was! That only took a few hours, ran smoothly, probably had a great turnout, made some money! I should try that!"

Then they do, and they find out how tough it is. They find out how much more there is to it than what the audience sees. You can't walk into a community college and take a course on wrestling show management. It's about setting up a location, advertising, bringing in the names, establishing trust with so many other people, and paying them. Hoping against hope that the names you sign will actually show up. Guaranteeing money ahead of time and not relying on high ticket sales to bring in enough overhead to pay everything off. An indy promoter who has never lost money doesn't exist.

Wrestlers who are already established aren't going to work on faith. "Sure, just work for me now, and I promise I'll come up with your money later on, probably by this weekend!" Then you never see a dime. You go through that once, and you don't let it happen again. People call you and say, "Hey, I'm putting on a show next month, at this time and place." Then they never call, even to tell you that it's cancelled or there isn't a spot for you anymore.

Then you get a little power. Something extra at the bargaining table. You probably don't go back and work for them, but if you do, you demand half up front. Then you raise your normal price for a little inconvenience fee. And, hey, why shouldn't you? You could have lost another booking. You could have showed up drunk or high. You could have given your word for three hours, then left after one. You held up your end of every deal. If they can't or didn't, they can't help you out.

Wrestling Is My Gimmick

They call me and say, "Hey, I'm putting on a show in three months."

I say, "Here's my price. You'll put me up in a hotel room and pick me up at the airport. You can track the phone when it's landing. Don't leave me stranded."

Then that's it. I don't keep calling them to touch base. I rely on them to come through. Sometimes they do, sometimes not. If they send me the confirmation, the flight information, I know they're good. No one's going to pay $400 or $500 for a plane ticket and then stand me up.

Well, that did happen once.

About twenty years ago, I got a call, a booking, a plane ticket to Toronto. Then I get to the airport, ready for my next show.

And nothing. No one there to pick me up, no messages left for me, not a thing. I called the promoter, and he didn't answer. I had just flown all the way up one country and into another to get stood up. Some guy had just spent probably four figures on a plane ticket, and he'd have no one to show for it.

But, as I always do, I found a silver lining in the cloud. I could have just turned around and gone home. But I happened to know another promoter in that area, and gave him a call. As luck would have it, he was also running that weekend—two shows he got me put on. I got to spend the weekend in a great hotel, noshing on steak dinners. I ended up making more that weekend than if the original guy had been there to get me anyway.

Yeah, that was luck, fate handing me a good hand. But I knew I wouldn't always be so lucky. With me being almost fifty, it was time to get away, at least for a while.

One evening around then, I walked into the Manatee Civic Center (now the Bradenton Area Convention Center) in Palmetto. I'd worked there during the early years of my career home in Florida. I'd been in that ring for the WWF and for WCW. Now it was just to be a one-shot deal for an independent show.

My opponent and I had one hell of a match. I was leapfrogging, dropkicking, everything. I reversed him, hit him with one of the best Northern Light suplexes of my career, and pinned him, right in front of my wife and son.

Finding a New Path

I don't know if that was my last independent match, but if not, it was certainly one of them. Wrestling was running too low on honesty, on job stability, and most importantly of all, on work. It was time to reach back to what I'd learned in my too-brief college career and get something out of the degree I didn't get.

As you can probably guess by now, my sabbatical wouldn't last forever. But it's a very important part of my story.

Finding a New Path

There's always a ton of sad stories about those who hit it bigger than anyone ever dreamed and end up losing it all. People who, usually all of a sudden, start making more dough in a few months than in their entire lives combined to that point, and spend, waste, or give it all away just a few years later. People go from millions to so far in debt that the government has to come in and bail them out.

And, not surprisingly, athletes are a common victim of this. At least, the public and the media portrays it like that. It's so simple to find stories of rags to riches and right back to rags. Wrestling doesn't have as many millionaires as the NFL or NBA, but even the highest-paid in the business are vulnerable to the same traps that cause other pro athletes to wind up in bankruptcy court.

It's about too much too soon. It's about going from barely scraping by to living a mile above your means. You can buy or build the biggest, flashiest restaurant or nightclub in the state, but there are restaurants and nightclubs all over town, and getting people to pick yours over all of them and keep coming back, is a job too tough to even comprehend.

You think anyone can tell the difference between a Rolex watch or necklace that costs $10,000 and one that costs a hundredth as much and looks as good? Nobody can. Nobody cares. If you want a car, buy a nice one, a nice *one* and drive it until you can't anymore, then go get another *one*. Who needs a Ferrari for every day of the week and a Jaguar for Sundays?

All a $40 million house the size of Miami's Hard Rock Stadium adds up to is marathons of housekeeping and repairs, not to mention four- or five-figure water and electric bills every month. Even if you can pay off a mortgage with one fell swoop, these expenses will be around forever. Along with that, you're just sending a message to everyone who sees your obscenely huge possession: this person's got a ton a green to toss around, enough that he can show it off like that! Why shouldn't I try to get some of it? He's got a hell of a lot more than he needs, more than anyone needs, so it's only fair that others should as well. That's why our entourages often suddenly quintuple in size, only to disappear just as quickly.

Rich athletes think that they can get by on a name alone, and maybe they can for a while, but it takes some serious foresight and business sense to hit it big, or even at all, in the world outside of their sport. Great success and financial accomplishment in one field rarely translate to another.

Even if I had gotten well off of wrestling, I knew I'd never do any of that. I always thought about the future, hoping to live a stable life, not a luxurious one. I don't need a mansion or gaudy car to live well. I invested, I managed, I saved my money. When I went to the bank, the tellers didn't say, "Hey, did you win your last match?" They said, "How much do you want to deposit?" Those who win the most matches in a venue of entertainment don't always end up well. I don't have millions of dollars and never have or will, but I think I'm doing better today than many who made more than I did.

Once a wrestler leaves his work behind, it's sometimes tough to figure out what to do next. When you've been in a business like wrestling, one that goes as fast for as long as any, with very little off time in between, the world outside of it can become a different place very quickly.

And that's just for those that leave by choice. When WCW and ECW went down together in 2001, many were still ready, willing, and able to do their jobs, only to suddenly have no place to do them. Even after leaving active competition, many choose to stay in the business in one capacity or another. Training, running a wrestling school, something else. But even most of those were gone.

Once you've spent so much time in one profession, transferring into a whole other field is almost unimaginably difficult for many, especially when you're all but forced to do so. You're stuck back at the starting line, or pretty close to it.

I certainly hoped the wrestling business would find its way back around and get back to the boom of the late 90s, but no one could be too sure. I needed something else to do, and fast. I wasn't quite at the starting line, but I was only a few steps in front of it. I hadn't been near a school in decades, and even then, I hadn't gotten anywhere close to a degree.

So I started chatting with a group of people down in the Tampa area. They knew I was a pro athlete. They had learned that I had, to a minuscule degree, studied sports nutrition back at Florida State.

Most of all, they were impressed by my Jewish-ness. Someone who shared their faith might make a great addition to their health food company.

So they and I decided to go halves on a store just a few minutes from my house, one of about twelve such stores they were running at the time.

I didn't specifically work in sales, but I'd step in there once in a while. I was something of an impromptu health guru. Customers would come in, and I'd do what I could to help them with their health issues, new training techniques, diet nutrition, all of that. I didn't push my opinions on them, and they were aware from the start that I was no doctor, not even the owner of a degree. But I'd been through so many of these issues myself, or around those who had, and many of them were willing to trade my business inexperience for my life's work. I'd tell them to go and get a second or third opinion. Many came back to tell me they had done just fine with only my help, and they kept coming back.

The first year was great, and the second was fine too. Again, I wasn't a salesman, but this was my money getting used, so I kept some very strong track of the place's financial numbers. We were doing very well, enough that I didn't have to think, or *worry*, about getting back into wrestling.

Wrestling Is My Gimmick

Honestly, my involvement with wrestling was down, way down, at that point, but not completely out. I don't need a whole hand to count the number of times I actually wrestled in that period, but I was still doing meet and greets, albeit not as many as when I'd been active.

And I certainly kept up to date on the business. I'd be watching the WWE programs, and, yes, I wished I could have still been there. I think my biggest unrealized dream match would have been a battle with Kurt Angle. I was already awed by his winning an Olympic gold medal with a broken neck, and I'd never seen anyone adapt to the business faster. I think he and I could have put on a half-hour masterpiece without leaving the ring or even either of us climbing the ropes.

And I'd certainly be ready if I got any kind of chance. I got a ton of discounts and freebies from our suppliers. I'd get medication, supplements, fish oil, whatever. We had stuff for the muscles, ligaments, muscles, eyes, even prostate health, and I used it all. I got to attend a ton of nutrition classes for free.

And we kept doing well. Until we didn't.

After five or six years, I started to notice little dark spots and red flags popping up all over the business.

First off, they started having me work more and more at a location about half an hour away. Not too big of an inconvenience, but when they kept doing it, I felt like I was getting sent a message.

Then some guy about young enough to be my kid, with a hell of a lot less experience, got appointed as a manager. He started handing out discounts and sales left and right, without even telling all the employees. I'd be working with a customer who'd say something like, "Hey, that guy told me this was on sale. Why aren't you giving it to me?" Well, because it was news to me too!

Then I started getting other customer complaints. Not for bad service, more out of confusion. The bosses were totally overthinking everything. They'd say that something was on sale, then backtrack and give it less of a discount than advertised. They'd hand out coupons, then tell people that they needed two or three coupons to get the full deal.

By now, you should know that I wasn't the type to stay silent about this sort of thing. I told everyone that a few small changes would make a huge difference. After all, I wasn't just some cashier making minimum wage; I was an investor, and I had as much interest in making this work as anyone.

One day, I got called into the corporate office.

"Such-and-such doesn't want you in his school anymore," the bosses informed me of this clown. They were going to transfer me—much farther away, and permanently.

No, they weren't.

"I'm not moving," I informed them. "You three are the owners, the chummy chum-chums. He manages the store. You tell that motherfucker to chew it up and swallow it and get along with me. You force him to get along with me, and then he'll let his guard down, and then I'll get along with him good, and let bygones be bygones."

I don't know what they expected. They'd been around me long enough that I wasn't going to let them bully me. Not because I was a wrestler, but just because I don't back down from that sort of shit.

In any case, they recommended that I find other employment. Fine, but not empty-handed.

"I'm out of here," I responded. "I'm not dealing with this bullshit. Give me my severance package, and I'm gone. You try and sue me, and I'll own this fucking practice."

And then I walked out, severance in hand. Not long after, the whole company, with over a dozen locations, went down. Even the buildings were torn down. Just as I had with WCW and ECW, I felt bad for the innocent employees who were unemployed, but it's another lesson of what happens when business owners worry more about the few than the many.

Living in a Dark Hole

And hence, the darkest chapter of my life kicked into high gear. I had just walked away from a business, which ultimately was the right thing to do, but I couldn't have known that then. Along with that, I was heading into unstable territory. I knew I wasn't going into full-time wrestling again, and I couldn't be sure if there was a place for me there, solid or otherwise, anyway. My work commitments had caused me to have to decline many one-shot deals and meet-and-greets for years, and if a wrestler keeps saying no, promoters eventually stop calling. Even if I were to grab some work there, the fans might, just might, have forgotten me enough not to come see me.

But all of that was nothing compared to what happened around the same time. Because that was when my daughter died.

I was questioning everything. Along with all the sad frustration I'd go through with her death, of course I spent time here and there trying to figure out if I should have just put up with the crap from the health food store a little longer. Maybe just given myself enough time to see if I still had an option with wrestling. Had I jumped too quickly to a conclusion?

I think I was just trying to find *some* direction. Some people will follow any path, anything that moves, just to have somewhere to go. That had never been my mindset before, but I certainly considered it here. Someone, something who would offer me any kind of guidance or comfort.

Well, my wife certainly did her best with that, and she did pretty well. But this was more about getting out of bed and out of the house. She did great comforting me there at home, but there was a world outdoors that had hit me way too hard over the past few months. How could I get back into it? Was there something out there worth trying to get out and see and do?

For a long time, I didn't even try to answer the question. Just laid around all day, trying not to think about anything at all. But I did get going again, literally one step at a time. Like filling in a five-gallon bucket one drop at a time.

A new doctor, a new gym, and, eventually, a new outlook. I started training again, and I was surprised, this time in a good way, about how fast things came back to me. Right off the bat, my trainers were telling me that punches and forearms were spot-on, that they wouldn't have guessed I'd been out if they didn't know already.

Living in a Dark Hole

Dropkicks, leapfrogs, anything causing me to leave both my feet was more and more difficult, but that was due to age as much as time off.

Yes, the phone calls and e-mails had tapered off, but not disappeared. And once I got myself back into the public, they sped up again. I was all over the place, doing podcasts, interviews, everything. I was once again surprised at how many and how much people wanted Barry Horowitz back.

A year later, a period that I'd spent doing conventions like crazy and the occasional wrestling appearance, I calculated my earnings. It turned out that I'd made more from wrestling than I had in the same time at the food store.

Conventions are the greatest, for a few reasons. I did some near my place, and others in states like Mississippi and Georgia, but the main market for them was, and still is, the northeast. Fans in Philadelphia, Boston, New Jersey, and, of course, New York, go crazy for men and women of the mat, even those that haven't been between the ropes for some time.

It used to be the fan belief that (a) if you were in the main event, you were a great wrestler, and (b) that us enhancers weren't worth much of their time and trouble. After all, if we're hardly ever on TV, and even then we usually lose, we can't be too important to the company, right?

That mindset has changed. Almost. You still get the occasional fans who see your name and photo and scoff, walking away to meet a bigger (usually not better) name. But I'd say nine out of every ten people I meet and greet definitely see what an important role people like me play in wrestling, and how difficult it is. These are the people that go out of their way to say thanks and congratulations, even though we didn't win much. Many veterans will angrily tell you that it's that sort of thing that killed kayfabe in wrestling, something I myself am not thrilled with, but fans like this are awesome.

That, and you get taken care of very well at these events. Promotors fly you out to where you need to go, pay you, give you a hotel room, feed you, everything. Along with your flat appearance fee, you make some more taking pictures and signing autographs. There's nothing out of your pocket but a little time, and even that's not too big a deal. I've never had to stay at such an event for more than a few days, and sometimes I'll fly in early, get to the event, do what needs doing there, then get right back on a plane and be home by the evening.

I've heard many of my colleagues say that wrestling fans have short memories. I used to believe that myself. But being at one of these events, having people come up and recall every detail of something I did decades ago, sometimes that I don't remember, changed my mind there in a major way.

The Bio That Wasn't

To be honest, this story was supposed to come out three or four years ago. Not in this form here on the page, but actually seen.

In late 2020 or early 2021, my phone rang. The Caller ID claimed that nowhere other than Titan Towers was on the line.

I almost didn't pick up. I figured someone was trying to pull a fast one on old Barry.

But, hey, why not? I answered.

Well, it wasn't a joke. A director from the WWE was calling about his next projects—as in, a set of shows about those of us that have spent years helping other talent move up in the companies. Like Steve Lombardi, me, and some others.

Yes, I'd be interested. Very much so.

"How fast could you be ready for an interview?" he asked.

"I'm ready," I responded. "Right now." He laughed, and told me I could have a few weeks to get ready.

One morning soon after, I walked into a Marriott in Tampa. I'd left early, all spruced up, ready to help others see my biography.

And no one was there. Not him, no cameras, nothing but a couple of clerks downing huge mugs of coffee between yawns. Maybe it had been a joke after all. Perhaps someone was commandeering a phone at Titan and pretending they were someone else.

I turned around. Then he walked in. I suddenly felt about forty pounds lighter.

He and the crew had purchased out the entire second floor, and the few of us sat down in a ballroom-sized area.

We talked about everything. So much so. The only real instructions I got were to use WWE, not WWF. He asked me quite a bit about working with Goldberg. He said I could say whatever I wanted; if I went over anything problematic, they'd just edit it out.

We chatted for about six hours that felt like one or two. We went over just about everything I'd done by then, in and out of the ring. Soon, they filmed me at a meet-and-greet. I had a bunch of photos to sign and give away, then found out that I had to replace most of them because they had the old WWF logo imprinted.

Yes, I drew one heck of a crowd that day, and I'm *totally* sure it had *nothing* to do with people finding out they might have a chance to show up in a documentary or anything! Several wrestlers much more popular than myself saw their lines dwindle when fans saw me and those cameras. I'm sure some of them wondered why the cameras were all on me, instead of some of them.

Here was my chance to shine. It was going to re-boost my career on the indy circuit. I'd be getting more meet-and-greet invitations, more interviews on podcasts and everywhere else. People would want me to do more seminars for their students. Maybe it was a feeler for the WWE to bring me back in as a trainer, a backstage personality, whatever.

So you might be wondering right now, "Heck, Barry, that sounds cool! I'd like to see that! How come it's not on the WWE Network or any of the other big cable channels?" Hey, I hope that's what you're thinking!

There's a sad answer. It was never released.

And to this day, I've never been told why. I sat around for months waiting for a call, an e-mail, anything. But nothing came in. I called the guy about a year ago and left messages. Still nothing, not even a message like, "Sorry, we decided not to do it." I'm not even sure if he still works there.

It could have been something very special. Not just to me, but to the WWE, wrestling fans of today and yesterday, everyone. But again, much ado about nothing.

Wrestling Is My Gimmick

Well, at least it wasn't a total loss and waste. I'd made it quite clear before the camera rolled that I wasn't working for free, and I got my money from the company. And I'm telling my story with this piece, although it certainly took *significantly* longer than the filming.

I think one of the main messages that the series would have conveyed is one that's pretty simple, but doesn't really get acknowledged all that much. Again, telling not just my story, but the others who have made a long career out of enhancing, would have shown just how much respect we get from the fans, and how many of them appreciate the work we do.

Look, not everyone comes to a show for the main event, or at least not just for that. If they did, a show would only be one match long. People are there for the entire performance. They want to see every part of the puzzle as it comes together. Sometimes they might show for their favorites, but end up finding new reasons to watch. Especially today, when there's so many fans out there that are so analytical about the business, looking over every tier in the show.

Sometimes people tell me they'd rather watch me and my colleagues than those in the main events. I'm sure much of the enhancing community has heard similar sentiments.

Conclusion

> "I think Barry Horowitz should be in the Hall of Fame.... Barry Horowitz was a really good wrestler. Never hurt anybody, ever, was always a pro in there every night. That's a guy that should be in the Hall of Fame. Barry was a really good wrestler, he really was, especially for beginners and stuff. He was a guy that could go in there and get you through a match."
> —WWE Hall-of-Famer Bret Hart, April 2022

I sum up my career today the way I always have: I'm not famous, but I'm known.

I got what I wanted from wrestling, and even more. I was on the second-biggest show at *Summerslam*. I was one of the last few in a *Royal Rumble*. I won pay-per-view matches. I was a part of the biggest wrestling company ever for years, and people today still remember me from it. Aside from that, I won titles in Florida, did great in Memphis, worked in just about every indy federation of the time. I proved that you don't have to be in the main event to make a difference in wrestling.

People may wonder, and quite often ask, to my face and behind my back, why? Why did I stay in the business so long if everyone knew I was going to lose about every match even before the show began? Only in wrestling could a competitor lose so much and still be playing around the big boys.

Well, they might be looking at it from the wrong perspective. Wrestling's not like other mainstream sports, where those without success in the game usually quit soon, or at least get benched in favor of a new first-stringer. Obviously, a quarterback who led his team to one win per season, a batter who was hitting .050, a goalkeeper who allowed eight goals a game, none of them would be playing for long.

It's not like that. It's how we distinguish between wrestling and

Conclusion

It's almost time for me to stop patting myself on the back in the ring, but fans will always remember me doing so, and I will never forget them.

other mainstream sports. Promoters don't sit around at the end of the year, saying, "Well, he only won two matches last year, so let's get rid of him for good." When the outcome's known well before the game even starts, the standards for success are very different. Putting on a good show that people want to see and keep seeing is what counts.

My career could have gone elsewhere. Barry Horowitz could have opened the show. Maybe gotten close enough to tap on the upper level's glass ceiling. Heck, I know I could have handled the main event. But there's just too many variables in that equation. At the end of the day, the bookers hold the pencils to your career, and pencils have erasers at the top. They can change their minds and knock you down or out of the picture overnight. I've been there more than a few times. But it's about getting back up when (not if) it happens. It's about realizing that, at least for the time being, you're not going to move up here, and having the guts to try something new, maybe in a different location.

Wrestling was my career, one of them. My job, if you will, or one of them. My life? Maybe, but not to the extent that it is for some people. I had a college degree. I had other things I wanted to pursue. I've had other things I have pursued, especially since I stopped wrestling full time in the early 2000s and quit altogether in 2006 and stayed out for about a decade.

Conclusion

I made my money, saved my money, and managed my money. I wasn't one of the guys who quit, spent everything, and then went crawling back because it was all I had. The wrestling bug had me for over twenty years, and the itch is still there today. But not like it is for so many others. There have been other things in my life since before I started my career, and I never went so far into the business that it was hard to climb out and walk away.

Not to say I have, not all the way. I was out of the business for a decade when I came back and wrestled a couple of times in early 2022.

Later that year, I showed up in All Elite Wrestling.

"Take it from a top guy like me!" I asserted, the all-too-accurate Legendary Jewish Wrestler label below me on the screen. "(Current AEW talent) Shawn Dean … is a jobber!" We were spoofing the wrestling tabloid show *Dark Side of the Ring* at the time, but I don't think that show has ever had such an earth-shattering revelation!

Then in January 2023, I was at a meet-and-greet in North Carolina. Suddenly, up walked Scott D'Amore. A fellow WWF enhancer next to me a few decades before, he'd moved to vice president of Impact Wrestling (he'd eventually be president). His company often did shows near my homeland, and he asked if I'd mind showing up to do a bit of business.

Right around then, my colleague Johnny Swinger was on a roll in Impact. Actually, he was trying to get on one. The company higher-ups had finally made him a deal: he'd get a title shot … once he won *fifty* matches!

And whom better from which to snare his first?

"I've found somebody whose record is *way* worse than ours!" Swinger's second Zicky Dice bellowed at the crowd at TV taping that same month. "There's absolutely no way you can lose this one!" My music hit, and I came strolling out.

With me hampered by a leg that was already killing me, Johnny tore me up for a while. Then he went roaring towards me on the turnbuckle. I stepped out of the way.

"Now," I informed in the audience, "it's time to go to school!"

They erupted. And as I started whaling on Johnny, I heard something unexpectedly wonderful.

Conclusion

"You've still got it!" they let me know. "You've still got it!"

That was pretty special. These people, who had no clue I was even in the building just a few moments before, all got together to chant something like that. It really showed that I'd made my own impact on them, and that it was still around.

Johnny came back, and it looked like I'd be his first win. But then his old enemy the Kiss Demon strolled up (one hell of an inside joke, considering that, like Swinger had with me, he and the Demon had battled decades before in WCW), giving me just enough of a distraction to lock him in an abdominal stretch, then roll back for a pin. Trendsetting lady ref Allison Leigh slapped the mat three times, and I slapped my own back in victory.

But, hey, why quit then? Later that night, I just happened to catch a meeting with federation matchmaker Santino Marella to inquire about my own potential title shot.

He said sure ... if I could just beat Rhino.

Rhino? As in, a guy who was over a decade younger than me, and had speared his way through ECW, the WWE, and even Impact in a previous stint?

Yeah, no thanks. I'd just as soon end my Impact career undefeated.

Johnny Swinger: That match was out of the blue. I think the idea came about to bring in somebody from the old school, and Barry fit that to a T, and I also had a history with him. We had hoped that more would come of that, but that's up to (Impact) to do more with that, and they just didn't. For a one-night shot, though, it was pretty darn good, and it worked as a surprise, too. If people don't know that someone's gonna be there, it adds to the show too. To the people, the reaction is much bigger if they're not expecting somebody, and then somebody just shows up, so they got a shock value out of that too. We really could have stretched that out longer, but they ended up getting rid of (Dice), and I think that changed the plans. It's not a movie, where you script it all out in advance. Our thing changes as it goes, and then you can look at it in retrospect and say, "That wasn't the right thing to do." What we were doing was working, and you usually keep going with that, but they didn't. Watching that match, people

Conclusion

were probably like, "Hey, there's going to be a tag team match, with Johnny and Dice against Barry and the Demon," but there wasn't. That would have drawn viewership if they'd advertised for the next week, but they didn't, and I don't know why.

Like I've been saying since the cover of this book, wrestling was a job. Just that. Rather, only that. A job that you work at for as long as you want, as long as you can, do the right things along the way, and then get out because you want to. It's the same as police officers, teachers, doctors, cashiers, everyone else. If you do the right things in and out of the workplace, you might have a little more freedom as to what that workplace is if you're looking for a change. You save your money, make it work for you, and you can pick and choose a little. I always had my drive and determination, and I always had gas in my tank. If there had even been a time during my runs in the 1980s and 1990s that I couldn't work as hard as I should have or done my job to the best of my abilities, I would have quit.

In wrestling, it's about respect. The respect you show to your employers and your co-workers, and them to you. You stay out of dressing room issues, you stay clean outside of the ring, you show that you're willing to do what you're told with a smile on your face and come back for more, at least at first.

Not long ago, I was sitting in catering at an AEW show. A guy who happened to be sitting nearby decided to give me a little advice.

"When you're in your own spot," he pontificated, "they'll believe you a little bit more."

Wow! Earth-splitting wisdom! Just one problem; I'd been in the business since before this guy's parents were even talking about having him. I'd actually been in his tryout match for the WWF a few years before.

Not that he probably remembered or cared. Just a guy who thought that moving up in a company meant he was qualified to advise people with thrice his experience. That's the opposite of the respect issue I just mentioned.

Once you've been around long enough to establish yourself, promoters might be a little more accommodating to your complaints, or at least your questions. There's no one individual secret to making

Conclusion

it in the business, but there's steps one can keep taking all the way through a career, to even *have* a long career.

And then there's the respect that fans show you as well. They'll watch and they'll cheer and they'll boo you as a character, but eventually, they'll be able to tell the difference between someone who's working for the company and someone who's just out for himself. Many wrestlers who had the tools inside and out to be major stars in the business have seen their careers end, or at least stagnate, because they made it more about themselves than about the team they were playing for. That's what every successful federation, regardless of size, truly is: a team.

People might think that just because a character is alone in the ring, the person must be as well. Some might believe that once you get big, once you start winning, once you get a big push, once you get a title, then it can be all about you, and you don't have to worry about anyone else.

Sorry, that's not how it is in wrestling. Anyone can disappear, or at least see a push end and a title taken away, at a moment's notice. Promotors might give you some leeway if you sell tickets, but no one lasts forever. People don't usually last more than a few years in the business, let alone at the top. And if you push people out of the way or ignore them when you get there, they'll remember. Promoters don't like putting their money in your pocket if it's being used to swell your head. Even the biggest stars are sometimes forced to hand the spotlight over to someone else once in a while, to let someone beat them because that's just part of wrestling's job.

And as for people like me, who are, a bit condescendingly, known as "jobbers," we do it to make a living. Because I guarantee you something about wrestling. While I was out of the business before the WWE became the only game in town with WCW's and ECW's demise shrinking the job pool like crazy in 2001, this has been the case for a *long* time in wrestling.

At every level, if you don't want to do a job, it'll take any promoter about a quarter second to find someone who will. Anyone's replaceable, and saying no to anything in wrestling will cause the higher-ups to quit asking. If I hadn't taken the losses and the paychecks that came with them, someone else would have, albeit

Conclusion

maybe not to the same skill level! Better to lose and get paid than be poor.

Buff Bagwell: To me, Barry should have been one of the top guys. He always had all of the pieces to be one of the best. Barry was a great ring general. He always had a great body. He had the hair, he had the look. It's a tricky area, but I always thought Barry was a top-talent guy, and got the raw end of the deal a little bit more than some guys.

But getting back to the fans, they'll stand by you if you show your devotion to the business. I may not sell as many tickets or merchandise as those who held the top titles in WCW or WWE, but there have been an unspectacular, yet steady stream of people coming to see me. You'll never hear me brag about my accomplishments, but I think I probably hold the unofficial record for balancing the worst win-loss record with the highest popularity and recognition. That shows that I'm still earning respect from the fans today, even those who have to go on the Internet to see my biggest victories.

When I show up for autograph signings, people are there to say thanks, and there to mimic my back-patting motion. When I came back to the ring in the 2020s, people still remembered. The AEW trusted that the community would still know me when they brought me in, and they did. Who knows? I'm in my early sixties now and pretty comfortable where I am, so I'm not heading back on the road again, but don't be surprised if Barry Horowitz makes a quick appearance here and there.

At this point, people don't expect me to get in there and tear things up for ten or fifteen minutes. I don't know if I could, at least not on a regular basis. But they remember me up to a degree. They want to see me get in there, do a few moves, and head out. I get pinned or I don't. By now, it hardly matters—as long, of course, that I do my trademark back-patting at some point! I'm just semi-retired, not retired all the way. I don't think any wrestler ever is, until the coffin's literally in the ground.

But I know I'm about done. I've been able to see the finish line for a few years now, and it gets closer every day. My left leg's always

Conclusion

going to hurt, and I've had sciatica up and down my right side for over a decade now. Ironically enough, as painful as that side is to use in the gym, it actually hurts worse if I don't work out, because inactivity screws up the blood flow to that area. More and more of my matches have been as a member of a team, with my partner(s) doing more and more of the work.

Fans don't seem to notice, or are nice enough not to mention anything. I'll be at a meet-and-greet, and people will walk up and say, "Wow, you still look like you did back when you were Jack Hart, or back when you were fighting Skip!" I'm thankful that these people don't have to see me get up and walk around much.

So when the day comes when I have to step out of the ring for the last time, assuming it hasn't already, I'll still be around. The same fans that relive the best moments of my career all over the Internet won't soon forget me. I'll still be all over social media, doing the same podcasts and interviews that I used to revive my career after my layoff. I'll do what I can to stay relevant. If those training or agent positions I still hope for pop up in the WWE or AEW, that will help me even more.

Finally, I've been asked a few times if I consider myself underrated. Probably so, in a couple of ways. I think many would agree with that very nice quote from Bret Hart at the start of this chapter. Wrestling-wise, I think I'm ahead of several guys who already are in the Hall. You never know—maybe I'll get that call someday, like my fellow enhancer Koko B. Ware did in 2009, and jobbing colleague S.D. Jones a decade later. Wrestling gave me a comfortable life for me, my family, and my future. To them, to the fans, to the business, I say thank you.

For years of heel work, I could get the fans upset in about two seconds by patting myself on the back. Now there's generations of wrestling fans and fellow men of the mat to do it for me.

Index

Abdullah the Butcher 157
Ace, Johnny 156, 157
Adams, Chris 110–1
All Elite Wrestling (AEW) 6, 174, 180, 189, 211, 213, 215, 216
American Wrestling Association (AWA) 90, 91, 94, 154
Anderson, Arn 85, 177
André the Giant 30, 63, 72, 112
Angle, Kurt 5, 202
Argentino, Nancy 33, 35–6
Armstrong, Brad 69, 182
Arquette, David 187
Austin, Steve (Stone Cold) 3, 91, 110, 161–4, 186–7, 188

Backlund, Bob 29, 33, 68
Bagwell, Marcus Alexander (Buff) 92–4, 113–4, 116, 181, 215
Barr, Art 86–9
Barr, Jessie 60, 87
Benoit, Chris 36–40, 176–7, 190
Benoit, Nancy 37, 39–40
Bischoff, Eric 170–1, 180, 185, 186, 187
Bogan, Lee 128
Bonsall, Joe 63–4
Boone, Brady 73, 112–3
Bradley, Bob 30, 32, 33–4
Brisco, Jack 14, 43, 46, 57
Brisco, Jerry 144
British Bulldogs 31, 66
Brody, Bruiser 52, 54
Brooks, Garth 126
Burns, Keith 128
Bushwhackers 120, 133

Cabana, Colt 174
Candido, Chris (Skip) 8–10, 117, 134, 135, 138, 139–146, 147, 149–154, 159, 161, 164, 183, 189, 190, 216
Colon, Carlos 27–8, 43
Combs, Ray 124
Cornette, Jim 117, 137, 138
Crockett, Jim 32, 41, 58
Cyrus, Miley 126–7

Demolition 68, 71, 92, 132
Dibiase, Ted 36, 155, 163
Diffie, Joe 128–9
Dillon, J.J. 118–9, 182
Disco Inferno 168–9
Doink the Clown (Matt Borne/Steve Lombardi) 73, 78, 131, 134, 136, 155
Donovan, Chick 61–2, 65
Duggan, Jim 66
Dundee, Bill 61, 65
Dynamite Kid (Tom Billington) 25, 40, 75

Earthquake (John Tenta) 79–81
Eaton, Bobby 51–2, 181, 182
Extreme Championship Wrestling (ECW) 6, 64, 151, 152, 188–90, 191, 200, 203, 212, 214

Flair, Charlotte 176
Flair, David 175–7
Flair, Reid 176
Flair, Ric 3, 32, 41, 43–4, 58–59, 60, 85, 120, 175–7
Florida State University 17–8, 201
Florida wrestling 4, 14, 16, 20, 23, 36, 37, 44–6, 50, 52, 53, 54–7, 58–60, 61, 64, 66, 87, 89, 94, 112, 170, 209
Funk, Allan (Kwee Wee) 183–5
Funk, Dory 14, 33, 133
Funk, Terry 14, 42, 60, 87, 123, 133, 183

Gaylord, Jeff 108–9, 123, 124–5
Gilbert, Doug 97–8, 108–9, 116
Gilbert, Eddie 90–1, 94, 108–10, 123
Global Wrestling Federation 4, 37, 89–98, 99, 108, 110, 113–6, 117, 118, 123, 131, 155, 161, 167, 181, 194
Godwinn, Henry 158, 159
Goldberg, Bill 148, 171–4, 175, 207
Goldust 159, 164, 165
Gordy, Terry 156, 165
Gotch, Karl 21, 22
Graham, Superstar Billy 14, 54, 72
Graham, Bob (Florida governor) 40–1
Graham, Eddie 14, 29, 45, 49

Index

Graham, Mike 14, 16–7, 45, 55–7, 60, 153
Guerrero, Chavo 41
Guerrero, Eddie 37, 69–70, 89, 133, 190
Guerrero, Hector 46, 50, 54, 55

Hakushi 146–7, 149, 150, 151, 154
Hall, Scott (Razor Ramon) 73, 133, 134, 136, 138, 151, 164
Hansen, Stan 58, 155–7
Hardy family 5
Hart, Bret 33, 34, 65–6, 69, 75–6, 78, 112, 116, 120, 121–5, 127, 133, 139, 144, 147, 158, 164, 168, 179, 209, 216
Hart, Gary 33
Hart, Jimmy 65
Hart, Owen 69, 76–7, 78, 111, 112, 120, 121, 122, 123, 124–5, 133, 139, 146–7, 153, 159, 163–4, 166, 178–180, 187
Hart, Stu 28
Hart family 5, 66, 72, 75–81, 116, 124, 125
Hart Foundation 66, 72, 75–6, 116
Hayes, Michael 33, 46, 158
Haynes, Billy Jack 55, 112
Headshrinkers 125
Hebner, Dave 77, 135, 142
Heenan, Bobby 73
Helmsley, Hunter Hearst (Triple H) 139, 143, 149, 159, 163, 164, 165
Hennig, Curt 7, 9, 32, 60, 69, 79, 133, 139, 164–6, 170, 179
Hernandez, Hercules 54
Heyman, Paul (Paul E. Dangerously) 64–65, 189
Hogan, Hulk 14, 35, 63, 65, 66, 70, 71, 74, 79, 81, 82, 111, 120–1, 127, 176
Holly, Hardcore (Bob) 125, 149, 151
Horner, Tim 85–7, 94, 117, 166–7
Horowitz, Barry: alcohol, drugs avoidance 67, 132, 150; conventions 36–7, 157, 181, 205; daughter 100–5; depression 105–107, 203–4; football interest 11–2; Hart, Barry 29–31; Hart, Jack 1, 46, 48–50, 57, 59, 61, 216; independent work 4, 90, 107, 117, 128, 129–30, 153, 174, 183, 188, 189, 191–4, 196–9, 207, 209; injuries 50–1, 74–5, 76, 196–7; Jewish faith 13, 19, 100, 147–9, 173–5, 189, 194, 201, 211; marriages 4, 48, 49, 50, 68, 99, 100, 101–4, 107, 204; music tastes 4, 62–4, 125–30, 193; ribbing 24–7, 78–9; son/stepson 1–2, 49–50, 99–100, 105, 107; title wins 52, 54–7, 59, 60, 61–2, 94–6, 183, 191; training work 21–2, 194–5, 207
Horowitz, Diane 49–50, 99–100, 104, 127
Horowitz, Josh 1–2, 100
Humperdink, Oliver 60, 64, 128–9
Hyatt, Missy 93

Impact Wrestling 6, 211, 212
In Your House December 1995 154
In Your House October 1996: Buried Alive 164–6
In Your House September 1997: Ground Zero 116
Iron Sheik 32, 65

Jannetty, Marty 122, 125, 151, 152, 182
Jarrett, Jeff 61, 108, 110, 130, 136, 138, 139, 159, 179
Jarrett, Jerry 61, 127
Jericho, Chris 82
Johnson, Rocky 61
Jordan, Ben 89–90, 91–2, 94, 96, 131

Kane (Isaac Yankem/Glenn Jacobs) 154, 163, 164, 173
Kanyon, Chris 113
Kawada, Toshiaki 156–7
Keith, Toby 130
King of the Ring 1995 159
King of the Ring 1996 82, 162

Lane, Lenny 134–6, 170
Lanza, Blackjack 81–2, 140, 141
Lawler, Jerry 61, 63, 65, 78, 121–2, 124, 136, 159
Lombardi, Steve 73, 125, 206
Luger, Lex 68, 84, 131, 134
Lynn, Jerry 94, 96

Mabel 136, 150
Malenko, Boris 20, 21, 78
Malenko, Dean 21, 37, 174, 181, 190
Malenko, Joe 18–9, 22, 23, 57, 181
Mankind (Cactus Jack, Mick Foley) 82, 116, 160, 164–5
Marella, Joey 111–2, 113
McDaniel, Wahoo 54–5
McMahon, Vince, Jr. 10, 31, 32, 35, 66, 71, 123, 133, 137, 140, 141, 144, 146, 150, 151, 164, 167, 168, 170, 185, 186–7, 188
McMahon, Vince, Sr. 31, 167
Michaels, Shawn 9, 122–4, 136, 139, 143, 146, 159, 163, 164, 179
Miss Elizabeth 37, 68
Monsoon, Gorilla 28, 29, 75, 112, 141–2
Mosca, Angelo 29–30, 43
Mulligan, Blackjack 48
Muraco, Don 14, 31, 36, 72

Nash, Kevin (Diesel) 9, 84, 133, 141, 150–1, 163, 164, 173, 181
Neidhart, Jim 66, 75, 77

Okerlund, Gene 70
Orndorff, Paul 14, 74, 117–8

Index

Orton family 5
Ottman, Fred (Tuboat/Typhoon) 140
Over the Edge 1999 178
Owen, Don 27, 31–2

Page, Diamond Dallas 183
Patterson, Pat 9–10, 14, 66, 123, 141, 144
Pillman, Brian 85
Piper, Roddy 32, 41, 43–4
Poffo, Lanny 73, 120, 183
Powers, Jim 146
Pride, Tyree 52–4
Pringle, Percy (William Moody, Paul Bearer) 47–8, 55, 57, 59–60, 65, 165
Pritchard, Tom 152
Pro Wrestling Illustrated 159–63

Race, Harley 43, 44, 58
Raven (Scott Levy) 91, 114, 115
Rea, Johnny 139, 151, 152
Reynolds, R.D. 5, 140–1, 167
Rhodes, Dusty 14, 43, 44, 45, 57
Riggins, Reno 125, 194–5
Rikishi 162, 163
Ring of Honor 189
Road Warriors (Legion of Doom) 58, 120
Roberts, Buddy 60
Roberts, Jake "The Snake" 66–7, 68, 73, 86, 165
The Rock (Dwayne Johnson) 61, 82, 153
Roma, Paul 82
Rose, Buddy 30–1
Ross, Jim 141–2, 150
Rotundo, Mike 32, 60
Royal Rumble 1989 146
Royal Rumble 1996 119, 162, 163, 209
Royal Rumble 2020 176
Rude, Rick 41, 47, 55, 86
Russo, Vince 185, 186, 187–8

Sammartino, Bruno 72
Sammartino, David 72
Santana, Tito 72, 96, 120
Saturday Night's Main Event 72, 120
Savage, Randy 37, 66, 68, 72, 73, 174
Sawyer, Buzz 16–7, 82
Schwarzenegger, Arnold 155
Shamrock, Ken (Vince Torelli) 82
Sharkey, Eddie 134–5
Slammy Awards 159
Slaughter, Sgt. 120
Smith, Davey Boy 31, 136, 164
Smith, Grizzly 86
Smokin' Gunns 133, 154
Smoky Mountain Wrestling 117–8, 137
Snuka, Jimmy 31, 33, 34–6, 55
Solie, Gordon 15, 47
Starrcade 1983 40–4, 45

Starrcade 1990 85
Steamboat, Ricky 32, 45, 58, 66
Sting 85, 160, 179–80
Strongbow, Chief Jay 76
Sullivan, Kevin 37, 65
Summerslam 1988 71
Summerslam 1989 36
Summerslam 1993 7, 78, 121, 183
Summerslam 1994 125, 146
Summerslam 1995 146, 149–50, 209
Sunny (Tammy Sytch) 8, 10, 37, 138–9, 140, 141, 142, 150, 151
Survivor Series 1992 122
Survivor Series 1993 7, 121
Survivor Series 1994 125
Survivor Series 1995 146, 147, 151–2, 209
Survivor Series 1997 168
Swinger, Johnny 182, 211–3

Total Nonstop Action (TNA) 130, 153, 189

Ultimate Warrior (Jim Hellwig/Dingo Warrior) 68, 73–4, 81–4, 155, 159
Undertaker 7, 9, 60, 69, 133, 139, 164–6, 179
Universal Wrestling Federation (UWF) 108, 144, 145–6

Valentine, Greg 43, 123
Valiant, Jimmy 32, 58
Van Dam, Rob 113, 190
Vicious, Sid 64, 84, 85, 152, 154
Virgil 61, 131, 182
Von Erich, Kerry 120
Von Erich family 23

Waltman, Sean (1–2–3 Kid/X-Pac) 94, 116, 125, 133, 149, 151–2
Wanz, Otto 154–5
Ware, Koko B. 68–9, 70–2, 74, 77, 96, 216
Watts, Bill 143–6
WCW Nitro 179, 180, 183, 188
WCW Saturday Night 172, 180, 181, 183, 184
WCW Thunder 172, 176, 183
WCW Worldwide 175
Whatley, Pez 48, 85
Wilkes, Del (Patriot) 37, 90–1, 94, 108, 114, 116, 157
Williams, Steve 133, 156
Windham, Barry 48, 54, 57
Windham, Kendall 59, 60
Wippleman, Harvey 112
World Championship Wrestling (WCW) 3–4, 20, 23, 38, 51, 64, 69, 84, 85–9, 90, 91, 92, 93, 110, 113–4, 115, 116, 118, 119–20, 133, 134, 148, 152, 153, 164, 167–71, 172, 175, 179, 180–8, 189, 191, 196, 198, 200, 203, 212, 214, 215

Index

World War 3 1998 119
World Wrestling Federation/Entertainment (WWF/E) 6, 14, 39, 64, 90–1, 94, 99, 110, 111–2, 115, 116, 117, 118–125, 130, 131–155, 157, 158–167, 170, 173, 175, 176, 179, 180–2, 186–7, 188, 191, 194–5, 196, 198, 202, 206–8, 209, 211, 212, 213–216
Wrestlemania 6, 9, 36, 58, 70, 149
Wrestlemania III 112
Wrestlemania IV 55, 59
Wrestlemania VI 79, 82–3
Wrestlemania X 125
Wrestlemania XI 164
Wrestlemania XII 152, 158, 164, 179
Wrestlemania XIV 161–2

Wrestlemania 35 176
Wrestlemania 37 22
Wright, Charles (Godfather) 116, 163
WWF Superstars 140–1
WWF/E Hall of Fame 14, 47, 58, 116, 160, 162, 163, 173, 209
WWF/E Raw 8, 9, 39, 90, 130, 133–4, 136–8, 147, 188
WWF/E Smackdown 188
WWF/E Wrestling Challenge 9
Wynette, Tammy 127

Yamamoto, Tojo 62
Yokozuna 9, 133, 153
Youngblood, Jay 43, 45, 58–60

Milton Keynes UK
Ingram Content Group UK Ltd.
UKHW041924301024
450490UK00015B/124